Legal Research, Writing & Analysis

BY PETER JAN HONIGSBERG
University of San Francisco

EDITH HO
University of San Francisco

Eleventh Edition

EDITORIAL OFFICES: 1 North Dearborn St., Suite 650, Chicago, IL 60602
REGIONAL OFFICES: Chicago, Dallas, Los Angeles, New York, Washington, D.C.

PROJECT EDITOR
Karlyn R. Meyer, B.B.A., J.D.
Attorney At Law

SERIES EDITOR
Elizabeth L. Snyder, B.A., J.D.
Attorney At Law

QUALITY CONTROL EDITOR
Sanetta M. Hister

Summary of Contents

Capsule Summary

Capsule Summary

I. DEFINITIONS

A. LANGUAGE OF THE LAW

1. In General §1

Legal research necessitates the understanding of specialized words and phrases customarily used by the law profession. For terms not defined in this text, reference to one of several law dictionaries would be helpful.

2. Statutory Language §2

Unfamiliar words are frequently defined in the first part of the statute.

B. SOME SPECIAL DEFINITIONS

1. Civil and Criminal §3

Civil law covers actions between private parties. Criminal actions are brought by the state and generally include the possibility of jail or imprisonment. Statutes defining crimes and penalties constitute the criminal or penal code.

2. Substance and Procedure §4

All civil and criminal cases include ***both*** procedural and substantive law. ***Substantive law*** defines the rights and duties of people. ***Procedural law*** is the set of rules and procedures to be followed in bringing suit.

3. Facts and Law §5

In civil and criminal trials, after the evidence is presented, the jury (or judge in a nonjury trial) determines the facts of the case. The judge applies the appropriate law throughout the trial and then instructs the jury on the applicable law in ***jury instructions. Appeals*** may be taken only on ***questions of law***.

4. Common Law §6

Common law includes English law prior to 1776, which was incorporated into American law. The term is also used to identify the collection of prior court decisions, in contrast to statutory law.

5. Equity §7

Equity courts were originally the courts of fairness or justness, created to provide remedies not available in courts of law (*e.g.*, specific performance, injunction). Today, American courts of law and equity have merged and can grant both legal and equitable remedies.

II. UNDERSTANDING OUR LEGAL SYSTEM

A. COURT SYSTEMS

1. In General §8

State and federal court systems generally have a trial court, an appellate court, and a supreme or high court.

a. Original jurisdiction §9

The first court to hear a case (usually the trial court) has original jurisdiction. An appellate court or supreme court may also have some original jurisdiction (*e.g.,* two disputing states may file a claim first before the United States Supreme Court).

b. Trial courts §10

The trial court determines the facts of the case.

c. Appellate courts §11

The losing party in the trial court may appeal the case only on questions of law, not fact. The appellate court must then decide whether the trial judge applied the proper legal principles. Everyone has the right to request one appeal (except, perhaps, in small claims court).

d. Supreme or high court §12

This is a higher appellate court which reviews the intermediate appellate court decision. Generally, the high court can limit which cases it will hear.

2. Federal Court System

a. Federal district court §13

This is the federal trial court. There is at least one district court in each state and one in Puerto Rico. More than one judge may sit on a district court.

b. Federal court of appeals §14

This is the federal appellate court. There are 13 circuits, which cover several states each, except for the District of Columbia Circuit, which takes cases only from the Washington, D.C. district court, and the Federal Circuit, where most of the government's cases are brought. A court of appeals has from six to 28 judges; if the entire court or a substantial portion of it sits on a case, the case is heard "en banc." A court of appeals decision is ***precedent***—*i.e.,* binding on all district courts in that circuit.

c. United States Supreme Court §15

This is the highest court in the land and has nine justices. The Court must take certain kinds of cases (*e.g.*, disputes between states), but generally chooses which cases it will hear. Usually, these are cases involving new principles of law, especially if the Constitution is involved, or cases involving conflicting decisions made by the federal courts. A Supreme Court decision on federal law is binding on all federal courts; a constitutional decision is binding on all courts—state and federal.

d. **Special federal courts** §16

There are separate trial courts established to deal with special areas of the law (*e.g.*, Court of Federal Claims, Tax Court).

3. **State Court System** §17

Most states mirror the federal system in having trial, appellate, and supreme or high courts. However, each state has its own name for its courts.

a. **Small claims court** §19

These courts, sometimes called "people's" or "pro se" courts, handle cases dealing with small amounts of money damages. Procedure is much less formal than in ordinary trial courts.

b. **Reminder** §22

Since the importance and binding effect of a court opinion depends on which court issues it, it is necessary to determine which level of court is involved, despite the variety of court names.

B. PRECEDENT—PERSUASIVE AUTHORITY

1. **Stare Decisis** §23

Anglo-American courts follow the principle of stare decisis, which means that courts should adhere to precedents set in earlier decisions. Binding authority comes from higher courts ***in the same jurisdiction.*** However, all federal courts must follow United States Supreme Court decisions. All courts must follow a United States Supreme Court decision if it involved interpretation of the federal Constitution, and all courts are bound by their own earlier decisions unless reversed by a higher court, or themselves, later.

2. **Persuasive Authority** §24

Authority from courts on the same level or from other jurisdictions is merely ***persuasive***, not binding.

C. THINGS TO KEEP IN MIND FOR LEGAL RESEARCH

1. **In General** §25

Legal researchers should be guided by two concepts: (i) the division that exists between federal and state governments; and (ii) the separation of state or federal government into executive, legislative, and judicial branches. Note that, for purposes of clarity, this text includes municipal and county actions as part of the state law.

2. **State and/or Federal Law?** §26

Some actions may be brought only in state court or only in federal court, but others may be brought in either. Thus, it is sometimes necessary to search ***both*** state and federal sources to find the correct law.

3. **Which Branch(es) of Government?** §27

All three branches of government can be "lawmakers." Therefore, it is sometimes necessary to research statutes (legislative), court decisions (judicial), and administrative regulations (executive) to be certain of the applicable law.

III. CASES

A. THE REPORTING SYSTEM

1. In General §28

After a federal or state appellate court or supreme court decides a case, it usually issues a written opinion. These written opinions are used by judges and lawyers to determine the precedents in a given area of law.

2. Official and Unofficial Reports §29

Official reports are published or authorized by a government. Unofficial reports are published by private commercial companies.

3. National Reporter System §30

West publishes most of the opinions of the federal and state courts. Many of its federal, regional, and state reporters comprise the National Reporter System.

4. Citations §31

All reporters, official and unofficial, have accepted abbreviations, called citations.

B. REPORTERS OF FEDERAL CASES

1. Supreme Court Decisions §32

Official reports are in *United States Reports*. Unofficial reports are *Supreme Court Reporter* (West), *United States Supreme Court Reports, Lawyers' Edition* (the LexisNexis Group), and *United States Law Week* (BNA), and can be found on computerized databases such as Westlaw and LexisNexis.

a. Advance sheets §38

Every few weeks, the reporters issue advance sheets in pamphlet form prior to the cases' publication in the bound volumes. The other federal reporters, many state reporters, and West's National Reporter System also issue advance sheets for their cases.

2. Federal Appellate Court Decisions §39

There is no official reporter for the federal courts. The courts of appeals decisions appear only in West's *Federal Reporter* (prior to 1880, cases are in *Federal Cases*) and on Westlaw, LexisNexis, and other commercial websites. *United States Law Week,* "Case Alert" may contain important recent cases. Additionally, West's *Federal Appendix* publishes unpublished decisions from some circuits.

3. Federal District Court Decisions §42

These are selectively published in West's *Federal Supplement* (and in the *Federal Reporter* prior to 1933).

4. Specialty Court Decisions §44

Specialty courts, such as the Tax Court, publish official reporters, but opinions of some specialty courts are also available in commercial looseleaf services. West's *U.S. Federal Claims Reporter* contains decisions of the United States Court of Federal Claims and the Court of Appeals for the Federal Circuit.

5. **Bankruptcy Decisions** §45

West publishes the *Bankruptcy Law Reporter,* which includes cases from the United States Bankruptcy Courts and certain cases in the federal court system. Collier *Bankruptcy Cases* (Matthew Bender & Co., Inc.) and *Bankruptcy Law Reports* (CCH) also publish bankruptcy decisions.

6. **Federal Rules** §46

Federal Rules Decisions (West) contains district court cases interpreting federal procedural rules. *Federal Rules Service* also reports these cases.

7. **Other Special Subject Reporters** §47

West and others also publish federal decisions in special subject areas (*e.g.*, *Military Justice Reporter*).

C. REPORTERS OF STATE CASES

1. **West Regional and State Reporters** §48

West publishes seven regional reporters: *Atlantic, North Eastern, North Western, Pacific, South Eastern, South Western*, and *Southern*. It also publishes two state reporters, *California Reporter* and *New York Supplement*.

2. **Official Reports** §49

Although approximately one-half of the states issue official reports, many researchers prefer to use West reporters because of familiarity and the West Key Number System.

3. **Advance Sheets** §50

West and most of the states publish advance sheets to their publications.

D. HEADNOTES AND SUMMARIES §51

Preceding all cases published by West is a summary of the decision followed by "headnotes" setting forth the principles of law stated in the case. The key number from a headnote can refer you to the same key number in a West digest, to find other cases that cover the same point of law. Note that these headnotes include principles of law not directly involved in reaching the decision and thus may be only ***dicta*** and not precedent. You must ***read the case*** to distinguish dicta from holdings.

E. OTHER CASE REPORTS—SPECIALIZED EDITIONS OF CASES §53

Several companies publish cases in select areas of the law (*e.g.*, taxation, labor law), grouping their cases and material by subject matter. These are generally known as ***looseleaf materials***, even though some cases may be in bound volumes. In addition to case law, these reports often include statutory materials and administrative agency decisions and regulations.

F. CITATIONS AND CASE FINDING

1. **Using Citations to Find a Case** §54

A citation or "cite" is a shorthand guide to the location of legal materials. A cite includes the volume number, page number, name of the reporter in which the case appears, and the year in which the case was decided, and is always placed next to the case name (*e.g.*, *Bush v. Gore*, 531 U.S. 98 (2000)). *A Uniform System of Citation* (the Bluebook) and the *ALWD Citation Manual* provide the accepted abbreviations for each reporter, and otherwise are the standard authorities for methods of citation.

2. **Parallel Citations** §55

Where a case is reported in both an official and unofficial reporter, it is customary to include all the citations, although the official citation should be the first. Parallel cites may be found by using Shepard's *Citations*, West's *National Reporter Blue Book*, or LexisNexis or Westlaw.

3. **Finding a Case Without a Citation** §56

The best way to find a case when you do not have the cite is to search in LexisNexis, Westlaw, or other Internet sources. Otherwise, you can use digests and reporters. If you know the ***name*** of a case and the jurisdiction, refer to the ***table of cases*** of a ***digest*** for that jurisdiction. If only the defendant's name is known, check the digest's ***defendant-plaintiff table.*** If the case is recent, check the tables of cases in the ***pocket parts*** or supplement used to keep the digest current. For important federal and state court decisions, refer to *United States Law Week*, "Case Alert" or "Supreme Court Today," and also check daily law journals. If the jurisdiction is unknown, refer to *Shepard's Acts and Cases by Popular Name, Federal and State* or to the various Decennial and General digests of the *American Digest System*.

IV. STATUTES, CONSTITUTIONS, LEGISLATIVE HISTORY, AND TREATIES

A. IN GENERAL §58

Researchers frequently begin their research by looking for a statute on point. The question then becomes one of ***interpretation*** of the statute. ***Annotated*** statutes provide short abstracts of cases that have interpreted the statute. Judges often consider legislative intent when interpreting statutes. ***Legislative histories*** are an aid in determining intent.

B. STATUTES

1. **In General** §59

Bills are introduced into the federal or state legislature and are given a number, which remains with the bill during that legislative session. ("S" or "H" precedes the number, depending on whether the bill was introduced in the Senate or House of Representatives.) The bill becomes law when passed by the legislature and signed by the appropriate authority (President or governor); otherwise, the bill dies and must be introduced again in the next legislative session.

2. **Statutes and Codes** §60

Statutes are published in chronological order (*see, e.g.*, *Statutes at Large,* which contains federal laws in chronological order). Codes group together the laws under specific titles (*e.g.*, probate laws), which makes research much easier.

3. **Federal Codes—Annotated and Unannotated** §61

Federal laws are codified in *United States Code*, which is unannotated. Most researchers use the commercially annotated editions, of which there are two, *United States Code Annotated* ("U.S.C.A.") by West and *United States Code Service* ("U.S.C.S.") by Matthew Bender & Company, Inc. The annotated editions include statutory history, cross-references to related statutes and constitutional provisions, and administrative regulations issued under the authority of the relevant statute.

4. **Supplementing the Federal Codes** §64
Each of the United States Code publications has an annual update service. United States *Statutes at Large* issues ***slip laws*** as soon as the law is passed. LexisNexis, Westlaw, and several commercial publications provide the text of recently enacted statutes.

5. **Federal Rules and Court Guidelines** §73
Federal rules of civil, appellate, and criminal procedure are published in U.S.C.A. and U.S.C.S. *Federal Local Court Rules* (West) publishes current local court rules of individual appellate and district courts. *Federal Court Guidelines* (Aspen Publishers) publishes the rules of practice and policies of district court judges and their biographical information. LexisNexis, Westlaw, and other online services also have the rules.

6. **Researching the Federal Codes** §74
You can search codes through LexisNexis, Westlaw, or other Internet sources. Each of the annotated code publications has a descriptive word ***index.*** You may also refer to the specific chapter of the code (***topic***); however, this method may cause you to overlook other related areas and statutes. If the law is known by a ***popular name,*** it may be looked up in indexes or various publications such as *Shepard's Acts and Cases by Popular Names.* One last method is to check the cross-references contained in the code to related statutes.

7. **State Codes** §80
Each state has its own code with differing formats. Many states issue multi-volume sets similar to the federal publications. Each state also has a set of statutes chronologically arranged, which are called session laws. There are always publications of parallel tables between the state's code and session laws.

8. **Researching the State Codes** §81
Some states have broad indexes to their codes similar to the federal system; others are more limited. Thus, use caution and search under a variety of synonymous terms when consulting indexes of different state codes.

9. **Municipal Ordinances** §82
Ordinances are codified but generally are not annotated. For cases interpreting ordinances, check state digests or West's *Ordinance Law Annotations*, or try searching Internet sources.

10. **Both Federal and State Law May Apply to Your Problem** §83
When jurisdiction is not exclusive, be certain to check both state and federal sources for any law applicable to your subject.

11. **Citing a Statute** §84
Federal statutes are cited to volume and section number of the United States Code (*e.g.*, 42 U.S.C. §3601). Sometimes the source and year are added (*e.g.,* 42 U.S.C.A. §3601 (West 2000)). State statutes are usually similarly cited. For proper citation forms, see *A Uniform System of Citation* (the Bluebook) or the *ALWD Citation Manual.*

C. CONSTITUTIONS

1. In General §86

A constitution sets out the general powers of government and the basic rights and duties of the people. A constitution takes precedence over a statute.

2. Researching the Federal Constitution §87

Annotated editions of the federal codes (U.S.C.A. and U.S.C.S.) include volumes covering the Constitution. Additionally, digests accompanying the commercial Supreme Court and federal court reporters are also helpful in locating cases interpreting constitutional provisions.

3. Researching State Constitutions §89

State constitutions and appropriate annotations are found in their respective state code editions. State or regional digests, local law reviews, and state encyclopedias are also helpful.

D. LEGISLATIVE INTENT—LEGISLATIVE HISTORY

1. In General §90

In interpreting statutes, judges sometimes use the "plain meaning rule," but they are more often concerned with legislative intent in enacting the law. Legislative histories help you discover legislative intent. Among the items included in legislative history are changes and amendments made on the original bill, legislative committee reports, legislative hearings, and comments made about the bill in debate on the legislature's floor.

2. Sources of Federal Legislative History §91

The Internet is a good place to start. Otherwise, try one of the compiled legislative histories available for relatively few pieces of legislation or an index. The *Congressional Index* (by CCH) provides the most up-to-date report on a bill's status. The *Congressional Information Service* (by ProQuest) provides an index of legislation, abstracts of committee hearings and debates, and legislative histories. The *Congressional Record* covers debates on the floor of Congress and daily legislative activity. Other publications provide some assistance in determining the status of legislation.

3. Tracking Down the Material §98

Once you have found the bill number and checked the status tables, you must locate the actual source materials (unless you depend on CIS abstracts). You might check the Library of Congress's THOMAS website or ask your law librarian.

4. Sources of State Legislative History §99

State legislative histories generally lack the more sophisticated bibliographic control that is provided for federal legislation. The best source is usually the state legislature's website or the legislator who sponsored the bill.

E. TREATIES §100

Treaties prior to 1950 are in United States *Statutes at Large*, and subsequently in *United States Treaties and Other International Agreements. Treaties in Force* indexes treaties still in force by subject and country and is available on the State Department's website.

V. SECONDARY SOURCES

A. IN GENERAL §101

Secondary sources are useful when a researcher cannot find a pertinent statute or needs some general information about the relevant area of law.

B. SPECIFIC SECONDARY SOURCES

1. Treatises §102

Treatises offer a thorough, in-depth analysis of one area of the law. The important cases and authorities are cited and discussed with usually expert commentary.

a. Hornbooks §104

These are treatises combined into one volume, and usually prepared for law students.

b. Gilbert Law Summaries §105

These are designed as study aids for law students, but they provide concise discussion on numerous areas of law. They are arranged in an outline format.

2. Legal Encyclopedias §106

Whereas treatises cover one area of the law in detail, legal encyclopedias provide a general outline of the law. There are two American law encyclopedias, *Corpus Juris Secundum* ("C.J.S.") and *American Jurisprudence 2d* ("Am. Jur. 2d"), both by West. Both volumes have pocket supplements, and Am. Jur. 2d has an updating looseleaf service. Many states also have encyclopedias with yearly supplements.

a. *Martindale-Hubbell Law Digest* §110

The United States law digest volumes are similar to an encyclopedia. The *Digest* also publishes summaries (in English) of many foreign countries' laws.

3. *American Law Reports* ("A.L.R.") §111

A.L.R. (West) provides editorial discussion on particular topics of law and also reports leading cases and summarizes other important cases in the area. The *Index to Annotations* includes a Table of Laws, Rules and Regulations, and an Annotation History Table.

4. Law Reviews and Periodicals §112

Law reviews (usually published by law schools) and other legal periodicals are particularly useful for keeping abreast of recent developments and changing areas of the law. Recent articles may be available in LexisNexis or Westlaw. *Index to Legal Periodicals* covers most legal periodicals; however, *LegalTrac and Legal Resource Index* and the paper edition, *Current Law Index*, are broader in scope with more complete subject headings. Other publications also index articles on specialized and related law areas.

5. **Sources of Recent Scholarship** §116

The Internet provides many alternative channels for publishing legal scholarship and discussion. The Social Science Research Network, electronic law journals, and legal blogs can provide extremely recent, accessible commentary on emerging issues.

6. **Daily Law Journals** §120

Usually published in metropolitan areas, these legal newspapers may be a good source for important federal, state, and local court decisions.

7. **Digests** §121

These are collections of principles of law derived from cases. They are often used to find cases to support particular points of law. West publications use the same Key Number System for classifying points of law in its headnotes, digests, and C.J.S. There are state digests, regional digests, federal digests, and Supreme Court digests. The *American Digest* (the one national digest) is in noncumulative 10-year editions (Decennials) and is supplemented with a *General Digest*.

8. **Looseleaf Materials** §122

Looseleaf services bring together statutes, regulations, cases, and commentary on specified subjects in a well-organized text.

9. **Continuing Legal Education Materials** §123

State bar association continuing legal education programs often publish useful works on local law and practice.

10. **Practice and Procedure Books** §124

These books deal with federal and state procedural codes. They usually include the text of the statute and an explanation of the law.

11. **Form Books** §125

Form books supplement practice and procedure materials. They provide samples of the proper forms to be filed in court, as well as sample forms for such things as leases, contracts, and wills.

12. **Attorney General Opinions** §126

The United States Attorney General and state attorneys general write opinions interpreting statutes, usually by request. Although such opinions are only persuasive, courts often follow them. Annotated codes refer to these opinions, and the federal government and most states publish them. Both LexisNexis and Westlaw have federal and state attorney general opinions.

13. **Restatements** §127

Restatements are written by expert lawyers and law professors setting forth what the law is or should be in a particular field. They provide a source that many courts find persuasive since they are an attempt to codify law in common law areas. Restatements are published by the American Law Institute.

14. **Uniform State Laws** §128

The National Conference of Commissioners on Uniform State Laws ("NCCUSL") promotes uniform laws. Uniform laws are not in effect until actually adopted by a state legislature. West's *Uniform Laws Annotated* provides an annotated set of uniform laws and lists the states that have adopted particular laws and notes any change in the model law made by the adopting states. The NCCUSL website also is a useful source.

VI. ADMINISTRATIVE AGENCIES—LOOSELEAF MATERIALS

A. INTRODUCTION §129

Administrative agencies are frequently given the power to issue rules and regulations and to perform adjudicative functions in their areas of expertise. Agency actions and decisions are usually reviewable in court. Agency action is largely informal. However, rulemaking and adjudication are the two main formal functions and are publicly recorded.

B. AGENCY ACTION

1. Regulations §132

Agencies draft regulations to carry out legislative intent. These regulations have the full force of law.

2. Adjudication §133

Agencies also decide disputes. An agency decision can be appealed, first through several agency levels, and then—but only after "exhausting administrative remedies"—to the courts. Administrative adjudicative hearings are less formal than in court.

C. RESEARCHING AGENCIES AND ADMINISTRATIVE LAW

1. Introduction §134

Federal agency resource materials are more available and more completely indexed than state materials. Administrative researchers should check an agency's rules and decisions, orders and opinions, and internal procedures and files.

2. Federal Materials §135

The *Code of Federal Regulations* ("C.F.R.") codifies regulations and also publishes presidential executive orders. The *Federal Register* publishes all federal regulations in chronological order and also publishes proposed agency rules and regulations. Both publications are available on LexisNexis, Westlaw, and at http://www.gpo.gov/fdsys. Other publications are not as up to date.

a. Federal agency decisions §137

The government publishes federal agency decisions, but most researchers prefer to use commercial looseleaf services, as they are published sooner and are better indexed.

b. Looseleaf services and materials §138

In a number of areas of law (*e.g.*, taxation, labor, trade regulation), there are looseleaf services that bring together statutes, case law, agency decisions, and administrative regulations and arrange them by subject. The three major publishers of looseleaf materials are CCH, BNA, and West. State editions are published for certain areas, the largest being tax. In the use of any looseleaf material, careful reading of the instructions is necessary.

c. **Other sources of administrative agency information and law** §145

Agency publications, the *United States Government Manual*, and the *Federal* and *Congressional Yellow Books* are other sources. Secondary sources and *Shepard's United States Administrative Citations* may also help.

d. **Presidential documents** §150

Presidential Proclamations and Executive Orders are found in the *Federal Register*, title 3 of the *Code of Federal Regulations,* and several other publications.

3. **State Materials** §151

Many states publish their own regulations. Looseleaf services are sometimes available, especially in the area of taxation. A state agency should have a library of past decisions which are public documents.

4. **County and Municipal Agencies** §154

Since an agency should have a copy of its own rules and regulations, a researcher should go directly to the local agency and ask to see them or check the agency's website if it has one. Larger cities may have their own administrative codes.

VII. KEEPING UP TO DATE—USING SHEPARD'S AND KEYCITE

A. INTRODUCTION §155

The law is constantly changing and even the slightest change has impact. Accordingly, a researcher must keep abreast of current law. After you find a precedent, ***always*** verify that it is still good law. Often the quickest way to update materials is to use Shepard's on LexisNexis or KeyCite on Westlaw, or to manually update by using Shepard's in print form ("Shepardize").

B. UPDATING ONLINE—SHEPARD'S AND KEYCITE §157

LexisNexis's Shepard's and Westlaw's KeyCite cite to the subsequent and prior history of your case and refer to cases criticizing your case. These services tell you whether your case is still good law and update daily—sometimes within 30 minutes. Shepard's and KeyCite also cite to secondary materials that mention the case, and KeyCite is integrated with West's Key Number System. LexisNexis also offers LEXCITE, which finds sources that reference a particular citation.

C. SHEPARD'S CITATIONS—USING THE BOOKS

1. **Shepard's Case Citations** §161

There are Shepard's Citations for all reported judicial decisions, official and unofficial. The charts in Shepard's indicate every time a particular case has been cited in later cases, and note whether the case was affirmed, reversed, or modified.

a. **Using Shepard's Citations for research** §164

Shepard's should only be used to determine the history of a case and its later treatment by other cases. Digests, treatises, law reviews, and encyclopedias should be used when one is looking for cases on a specific point of law.

2. **Shepard's Statute Citations** §165

The Shepard's Citations for federal and state law include codified and uncodified statutes, constitutions, and court rules. Additionally, the history of an act and the legislative actions that affect the act are indicated by letter abbreviations, which are explained in the front of each volume.

3. **Other Shepard's Citations** §166

Other Shepard's editions cover administrative actions, law review articles, and specialized areas of law (*e.g., Shepard's Bankruptcy Citations*). Shepard's also publishes popular name tables for well-known federal and state acts.

4. **Updating Shepard's** §171

Shepard's issues various supplements which must always be checked for recent developments. Note, also, that the red bound volumes are not cumulative and ***each must be checked*** from the date of your case forward to the most current supplement. You can also check LexisNexis to update Shepard's.

D. OTHER SOURCES AND METHODS §172

West's *National Reporter Blue Book* provides parallel cites to state and national reporters. Its Blue and White Books cross-refer official and unofficial reports, similar to Shepard's parallel citations. Consulting looseleaf services, checking with appellate courts, using PACER, and looking for state updating services are other methods of updating statutes.

VIII. ONLINE LEGAL RESEARCH

A. INTRODUCTION §176

Computer research can speed up legal research if the operator knows the proper keywords—just as in traditional research. The two major systems are LexisNexis and Westlaw, and both are updated daily. Many governmental institutions now provide online information as well.

B. LEXISNEXIS

1. **Contents** §178

LexisNexis is organized into databases called "sources." Sources consist of materials from specific jurisdictions or particular fields of law including: a federal source containing the United States Code, Supreme Court decisions, federal courts of appeals and district court cases, the *Federal Register,* and federal court rules; state sources containing state case law and statutes (including those of the District of Columbia); international sources; and secondary and other resource sources containing law reviews, news services, reference books, etc.

2. **Other Databases** §185

In addition to statutes, cases, and administrative regulations, both LexisNexis and Westlaw cover bills and committee reports as well as newspapers, magazines, medical reports, and wire services.

C. WESTLAW AND WESTLAWNEXT §186

Westlaw is tied into the West Digest and Key Number System and provides cases and statutes from all states and the District of Columbia, as well as federal cases and statutes. It also contains databases of special interest such as securities, labor, antitrust, etc. WestlawNext is a simplified research option intended to provide a more intuitive searching experience.

each issue using the "IRAC" method (*see* below) will make a significant difference in your thinking and writing.

3. **Keep to the Essentials** **§237**
   Make a point once and then move on. To emphasize a point, use it in a heading, start a paragraph with it, or underline it.

4. **Keep Sentences Short** **§238**
   Keep your sentences to one thought. However, do include sentences of different lengths to avoid choppiness.

5. **Highlight Important Points** **§239**
   Break up your writing into issues or sections to emphasize certain points, but don't overdo it.

6. **Keep the Reader in Mind** **§240**
   Writing on the same subject for a law exam, an attorney, or a trial judge requires three different styles of writing. Always remember for whom you are writing.

7. **Write for an Uninformed Reader** **§241**
   If you assume the reader is not familiar with the subject, you will be less likely to skip essential elements. Basic elements cannot be omitted without affecting the coherence of the writing.

8. **Choose Simple, Straightforward Words and the Active Voice** **§242**
   The main purpose of writing is to get a point across with no misunderstanding by the reader. Use legal terms only when necessary. Also, use the active voice.

9. **Be Subtle** **§244**
   Allow the reader to reach your conclusion along with you through a series of logical steps.

10. **Keep to the Topic and Answer the Question** **§245**
    Provide a clear, direct response to the question without discussing unnecessary issues.

B. USING AN "IRAC" APPROACH TO LEGAL ANALYSIS **§246**

Analyze a situation using the "IRAC" approach. Use this approach ***for each issue*** in your problem.

(i) ***I:*** State the ***issue*** in terms of the facts;
(ii) ***R:*** Set out the applicable ***rule*** gleaned from statutes, cases, or other authority;
(iii) ***A:*** ***Apply*** the rule to the facts of your situation; and
(iv) ***C:*** In your ***conclusion***, tie together the points you have made.

XII. ORGANIZING THE FRUITS OF YOUR RESEARCH

A. USING THE HONIGSBERG GRID **§251**

A grid is a helpful aid to organizing the results of your research—cases, statutes, regulations, and other authorities—in a coherent, easy-to-review manner.

XIII. WRITING A MEMORANDUM OF LAW

A. AN OBJECTIVE PIECE

1. Memorandum of Law §252

A memorandum of law should provide a ***neutral or balanced*** approach to the law. It is an analytical document frequently written for a senior attorney in a firm by a junior attorney or law clerk. However, it should not be an entirely "objective" document. One should attempt to present the law in the best light, but with judicious references to negative aspects of the problem.

2. Format §253

The general format used by many law firms states whom the memo is for, whom it is from, the ***topic*** generally covering the area of law, the date, and the ***issues*** (*i.e.*, principles of law involved), and includes a statement of the ***facts***, an ***evaluation*** (*i.e.*, who will prevail), an organized ***discussion*** using research as it relates to the facts, and sometimes a ***conclusion***.

XIV. WRITING A MEMORANDUM OF POINTS AND AUTHORITIES OR BRIEF

A. A PERSUASIVE PIECE

1. Memorandum of Points and Authorities or Brief §254

A memorandum of points and authorities, trial brief, and appellate brief are designed ***to convince*** a judge or hearing officer. Emphasis should be on your strong points, although your approach must be reasonable.

2. Format §255

This writing is more formal than a memorandum of law, but generally includes a table of contents, a table of authorities used, a jurisdiction statement, the questions presented or issues, a statement of the case, a statement of the facts, a summary of the argument, the argument, and a conclusion.

XV. WRITING AN OPINION OR CLIENT LETTER

A. AN OBJECTIVE PIECE

1. Opinion or Client Letter §256

Since the client or opinion letter is written ***to inform or advise*** the client about the case, it must be an objective document. You need to present both sides of the problem so that the client has a realistic view of the case.

2. Format §257

Since this document is generally addressed to a nonlawyer, the tone should be informal and you do not need to cite legal authority. You should state your purpose in writing (*e.g.*, to keep client informed about the case), briefly state the facts of the client's problem, and then discuss the law in relation to the facts of the case. Any conclusions should be objective so that your client can fairly assess the situation. Finally, your closing should be short and friendly.

Introduction and Approach

Times have changed. Until recently, the deans and administrators of law schools generally believed that they did not need to train their students in practical lawyering skills. Law school curricula were designed to teach students the substantive law and "how to think as a lawyer." Students could learn the skills necessary for day-to-day practice outside the classroom.

However, in the past decade, law school administrators have been reevaluating the needs of law students and have begun instituting more practice-oriented programs. The law faculties have come to realize that law schools have an obligation to effectively instruct their students in basic lawyering skills, including: (i) researching and drafting objective writing pieces such as a memorandum of law or client letter; (ii) researching and drafting persuasive writing pieces such as a memorandum of points and authorities, brief in support of a motion, demand or negotiation letter, trial brief, or appellate brief; and (iii) presenting an oral argument before a judge or jury.

In reassessing their law school curricula, many law faculties have upgraded their legal research and legal writing classes by adding more serious writing exercises and offering more oral presentation programs. Many of these courses are now given equal unit weight with such basic building blocks as contracts and torts.

Law schools have also supplemented their basic research, writing, and analysis courses with more advanced practical classes such as those in client preparation and counseling, mediation and negotiation, trial litigation, and appellate advocacy. Clinical courses in family law, criminal law, environmental law, immigrant rights and refugee law, and civil liberties and civil rights are offered in many schools. Many law teachers have also adopted more creative teaching methods utilizing computers and audiovisual tools.

This book was designed in recognition of the growing concern among law schools for teaching legal research, writing, and analysis skills. The first part of the book covers the basic legal research skills. It focuses on how to research primary sources such as cases, statutes, and regulations; on how legal encyclopedias, digests, looseleaf materials, form books, law reviews, treatises, and other secondary sources are used; and on how to Shepardize a case. Then it expands on the use of computers and the Internet in researching both primary and secondary legal sources.

The writing and analysis skills section begins with chapter XI. You will find chapters discussing how to brief a case, how to use legal indexes and tables of contents most efficiently in searching through legal sourcebooks, and how to organize the fruits of your research in a systemized way using the Honigsberg Grid. We have also provided suggestions for writing a clear, well-presented paper—a paper that a grader, lawyer, or judge would appreciate reading. Chapters XIII and XIV present formats for analytical and persuasive writing pieces and provide examples of each.

We trust that you will find this book a useful contribution to your understanding and development of basic legal research and legal writing skills.

Chapter One: Definitions

Outline

CONTENTS

A. Language of the Law

1. In General [§1]

When learning a new discipline, you must familiarize yourself with its particular terms, its jargon. Law is no exception. The profession has created a set of words and phrases which frequently mystify the layperson and the first-year law student. In this chapter we will explain a few of the basic terms with which you must be familiar if you are going to do legal research. Terms applicable to the material in this book will be defined in context. For other legal terms, you can refer to various law dictionaries, such as *Black's Law Dictionary, Gilbert Pocket Size Law Dictionary*, or one of several law dictionaries for laypersons. A multivolume set known as *Words and Phrases* sets forth, more elaborately, various legal terms as defined by the courts.

2. Statutory Language [§2]

If an unfamiliar word appears in a statute, be sure to check the statute itself. Terms are often defined in the first part of a statute.

B. Some Specific Definitions

1. Civil and Criminal [§3]

Cases brought in court are either civil or criminal. If there is a possibility of ***jail or imprisonment***, the action is most likely criminal. (In certain situations, however, people can be civilly jailed for refusing to answer questions directed to them by a court or legislature. This is known as civil contempt.) Criminal actions are brought by the state or the federal government against someone. The set of statutes defining the crimes and penalties is commonly known as the criminal or penal code. (A code is a collection of statutes arranged by subject.)

Civil law covers actions between ***private parties***, such as a suit against the person who caused a car accident, or one corporation suing another for stealing its trade secrets. The government may also be a party to a civil suit. For example, the federal government may bring an antitrust action against a large multinational corporation, or the state government may sue a chemical company for polluting the rivers; a person may sue the federal government for not releasing all the information required under the Freedom of Information Act or sue the state for discharging her illegally from her civil service job.

2. Substance and Procedure [§4]

If a landlord refuses to repair the falling plaster from the ceiling, he is violating the substantive law. So is the doctor who refuses to release a patient who says she wishes to leave the hospital, or the storeowner who "baits" by an advertisement and then "switches" by offering a more expensive item when the customer is in the store. ***Substantive law*** is the law that defines the rights and duties of people. It is "the law" as we usually think of it. When we say someone "broke the law," we are probably thinking of substantive law.

If you want to sue a person, you must follow certain rules; you must bring your suit in a certain court, file certain papers, properly notify the other party, and present your evidence in court following certain standards. In court, you and your opponent may have rights to an attorney and a jury trial. All these rules are ***procedural.*** Procedural law thus includes court procedure and guarantees both plaintiff and defendant their rights to a fair and proper hearing under the Constitution. All civil and criminal cases include both procedural and substantive law.

3. Facts and Law [§5]

A case arises out of facts. Someone trips on a loose step in a building. Another person buys a fax machine that turns out to be a "lemon." A third person is caught robbing a bank.

At trial, whether civil or criminal, both sides present their evidence, and the jury (or judge in a nonjury trial) then determines the facts: what really happened; who is telling the truth; is there enough evidence to substantiate the wrongdoing? In civil cases you need a "preponderance of the evidence" to win. To convict in criminal cases, the government must present evidence "beyond a reasonable doubt"—a higher degree of proof than in civil cases.

The jury decides only the facts of the case. When it reaches its decision (its "verdict"), the jury's job is done. The trial judge supervises the trial. Throughout, she applies the appropriate principles of law to the conduct of the trial, the presentation of the evidence, and the finding of the facts. (Where the parties decide not to have a jury, the trial judge will also determine the facts.)

When all the evidence has been presented, the judge will direct the jury on the law applicable to the case. The judge's directions are known as "jury instructions." For example, the defendant in a murder case may argue that the killing was in self-defense. The judge will explain the law of self-defense and then instruct the jury to decide whether the defendant was so justified under the circumstances. The same procedure follows in a civil case. For example, in a paternity case, the judge will decide what evidence is admissible for the jury to consider in determining whether the defendant is the father.

If one party is dissatisfied with the judgment in the trial court, she can appeal. But the person appeals on "questions of law," not questions of fact. The appellant claims that the judge erred in applying certain points of law during the trial. The appellant does not challenge the findings of the jury; she only asks the appeals court to review the trial judge's application of the law. (There appears to be an exception—although it, too, is actually a question of law. An appeal can be brought on the ground that no jury could have rationally reached the verdict this jury did; that is, there was not enough evidence to support the verdict.)

Occasionally, a judge will not even allow a trial on the plaintiff's case. This will happen when the judge decides that even if the plaintiff proved all the claims he is making, there is no law to give him relief. For example, when a family brought suit against a television station alleging that the violence shown in a television movie caused some youths to attack their daughter in a similar way, the court dismissed the case, saying the family had no "cause of action." In that situation, the plaintiffs appealed the judge's refusal to try the case. If the appellate court had decided that there was law to support the plaintiffs' case, the plaintiffs would then have gone back to the trial court to prove their case.

4. Common Law [§6]

"Common law" has two definitions. One refers to the law—the court decisions and customs—of England at the time of the American Revolution. When we became a nation, we adopted English common law, including its parliamentary acts, and recognized it as part of our own organic law. The other definition of common law is the collection of court decisions—in contrast to statutory law, the acts passed by the legislatures.

5. Equity [§7]

Equity dates back to the old equity courts of England, which provided remedies that were not available in the rigid common law courts. Equity courts were considered the courts of fairness, of justness. In the United States, courts of equity were integrated with the regular law courts. Judges thus can provide remedies of both law and equity. When courts speak of "equitable relief," they are referring to such court remedies as injunctions (stopping someone from doing, or requiring someone to do, some act), equitable rescission of a contract (annulling a contract and returning the parties to their positions before they entered into the contract), and similar means of relief that were not provided by the common law courts in England.

Chapter Two: Understanding Our Legal System

CONTENTS

A. Court Systems

1. In General [§8]

The court system, whether state or federal, follows a general pattern. There is a trial court, an appellate or appeals court, and a supreme or high court. (*See* chart, *infra.*)

a. Original jurisdiction [§9]

Jurisdiction is the authority a court has over a case and the people and property involved. The court that first hears the case has "original" jurisdiction. This is usually the trial court. The courts of appeal and supreme courts have mostly "appellate" jurisdiction. Some states permit certain trial court judges (those with the broadest jurisdiction in each county) to hear appeals from limited jurisdiction trial courts such as municipal or justice courts. These judges then have both original and appellate jurisdiction.

An appellate or supreme court may also have some original jurisdiction. The Supreme Court of the United States, for example, may directly hear cases between states. Thus, two states arguing over a border dispute could go straight to the United States Supreme Court for a decision, rather than filing their claims in the federal trial court. (However, the Supreme Court will probably first send the case to a referee for a finding of fact.)

b. Trial courts [§10]

The trial court determines the facts of the case. In a criminal case this means determining whether the defendant is guilty. In a civil case it means determining what actually happened between the parties. After the facts are found by a jury or by the judge acting alone, the judge applies the law to the facts. Usually the parties decide whether to have a jury trial, although in certain cases the right is not available.

c. Appellate courts [§11]

The losing party in the trial court may appeal to the appellate court. Occasionally, both parties will be dissatisfied with the decision and both will appeal. For example, a jury in northern California awarded a woman a multimillion-dollar verdict against a law firm for sexual harassment. The judge reduced the amount of the verdict. Both parties had the right to appeal: the law firm for losing the case, the woman for having her jury-awarded amount reduced.

Everyone has the right to request one appeal (except perhaps in small claims court; *see infra,* §19). The appeal is only on questions of law, not of fact. The facts have been established in the trial court, and the question for the appellate court is whether the trial judge applied the proper legal principles to the presentation of the evidence or to the facts found. For example, did the trial judge give the proper jury instructions?

d. **Supreme or high court [§12]**
The supreme or high court is a higher appellate court. It reviews the intermediate appellate court decision, again considering whether the trial court applied the proper principles of law to the case. In most instances, the supreme court can decide which cases it wishes to hear. The court will usually limit itself to cases involving important or newly developing principles of law, cases involving the interpretation of the state or federal Constitution, and cases resolving conflicts between different intermediate appellate courts deciding similar issues differently. In some states, the supreme court may take an appeal directly from the trial court, bypassing the intermediate court. This usually occurs when the case is significant, raising an important new question of law.

In this part of the chapter, we will describe the federal court system and then explain some of the variations to be found in the state court systems. You should have no difficulty understanding your own state court system once you understand the basic procedure each system must follow.

2. **Federal Court System**

a. **Federal district court [§13]**
The district court is the trial court in the federal court system. There is at least one district court in each state, several in the more populous states. For example, New York has four district courts: one for the southern district (which covers New York City), and one each for the eastern, northern, and western districts of the state. California also has four district courts, while Vermont and Utah each have only one. Puerto Rico also has a district court.

More than one judge may sit on a federal district court. Nevada has only one district court but has five district court judges. The district court for the Northern District of California has more than 20 judges.

b. **Federal court of appeals [§14]**
The party who loses in the district court may appeal the decision to the federal appellate court, the court of appeals. There are 13 federal courts of appeals. Each is responsible for hearing appeals from the district courts under its jurisdiction. Necessarily, these courts cross state lines (unlike the district courts). Thus, the Court of Appeals for the First Circuit hears appeals from four New England states plus Puerto Rico, while the Second Circuit Court supervises New York, Connecticut, and Vermont. The Court of Appeals for the District of Columbia Circuit takes cases from only one district court—the federal district court in Washington, D.C. Most of the government's cases are brought in the Federal Circuit, also located in Washington, D.C.

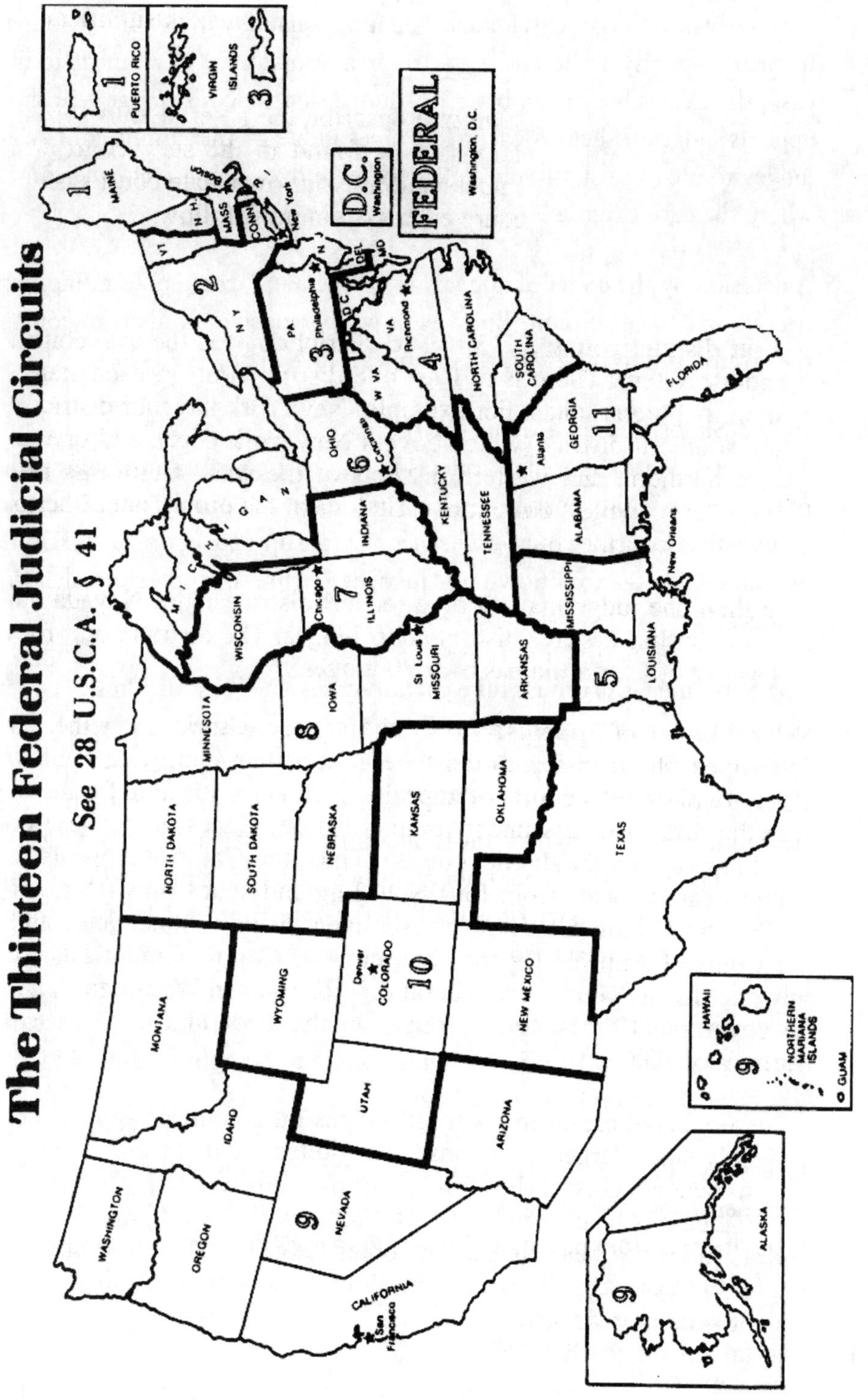
The Thirteen Federal Judicial Circuits
See 28 U.S.C.A. § 41
PUERTO RICO
VIRGIN ISLANDS
D.C.
Washington
FEDERAL
Washington, D.C.
HAWAII
NORTHERN MARIANA ISLANDS
GUAM
ALASKA
WASHINGTON
OREGON
CALIFORNIA
San Francisco
NEVADA
IDAHO
MONTANA
WYOMING
UTAH
ARIZONA
COLORADO
Denver
NEW MEXICO
NORTH DAKOTA
SOUTH DAKOTA
NEBRASKA
KANSAS
OKLAHOMA
TEXAS
MINNESOTA
IOWA
MISSOURI
St Louis
ARKANSAS
LOUISIANA
New Orleans
MISSISSIPPI
WISCONSIN
ILLINOIS
Chicago
INDIANA
MICHIGAN
OHIO
Columbus
KENTUCKY
TENNESSEE
ALABAMA
GEORGIA
Atlanta
FLORIDA
SOUTH CAROLINA
NORTH CAROLINA
VA
Richmond
W VA
MD
DEL
N J
PA
Philadelphia
N Y
New York
CONN
R I
MASS
Boston
VT
N H
MAINE

There are anywhere from six to 28 judges on a court of appeals (some courts obviously have larger caseloads). The judges usually divide into groups of three to hear appeals; if the entire court or a substantial portion of it sits on the case, the case is heard "en banc." Often, a district court judge will sit with two appeals judges to hear a case. The chief judge of the circuit court assigns the judges to a case, usually one of the three judges being from the same state as where the case originated.

A decision by the court of appeals is "precedent," that is, "binding" on all district courts in the circuit. But it is only "persuasive" to district courts outside the circuit and to other courts of appeal. (*See infra,* §§23-24.)

c. United States Supreme Court [§15]

The United States Supreme Court is the highest court in the country, the "court of last resort." Nine justices are on the Court. (In proper judicial circles, those people on a supreme court—whether a state supreme court or the United States Supreme Court—are known as "justices," while members of other courts are "judges.")

The Supreme Court must take certain cases, such as disputes between states, but for the most part, it can pick and choose. Usually, it will limit itself to important cases involving new or developing principles of law—especially those involving the United States Constitution—or to resolving conflicting decisions made by two or more federal courts of appeals acting on similar issues. The Court will also hear important issues raised by cases on appeal from the highest court of a state if the interpretation of the United States Constitution is concerned.

When the Court agrees to hear a case, it grants "certiorari." If it decides not to, it denies certiorari. Four justices must agree to take the case in order for "cert." (the accepted abbreviation) to be granted.

Generally, all nine justices hear each case. A decision by the Supreme Court on federal law is binding on all federal courts. A decision on the United States Constitution affecting the rights and duties of people in a state is precedent in all the states.

d. Special federal courts [§16]

The federal government has set up separate trial and appellate courts to deal more effectively with special areas of the law. These specialty courts include: Court of International Trade, Court of Federal Claims, Court of Veterans Appeals, and Tax Court.

3. State Court System [§17]

Most state court systems are similar to the federal system. There is a trial court, an appellate court, and a supreme or high court (although a dozen states do not have intermediate appellate levels), and each state has its own, often unique name for its courts. Also, most states have added trial courts of limited jurisdiction. It is not necessary to discuss all the state courts here. We will limit ourselves to a general outline and ask that you check for yourself what the court system is in your state. You need only check your state government's website. You may also contact your county clerk, the clerk of your local court, or your local librarian. If you wish, you can look it up in the state constitution under "courts" or "judiciary" and then examine your state statutes for legislation that has created additional courts.

a. Trial courts [§18]

The major trial courts in the states are variously named. For example, they are called "superior courts" in California, "supreme courts" in New York, "district courts" in Texas, and "circuit courts" in Michigan. These courts generally handle civil suits involving large amounts of money and criminal felonies.

Courts of limited jurisdiction—municipal, county, justice, magistrate, and police courts—have been created to handle suits involving small amounts of money and criminal misdemeanors. Your state probably has one or more of these. To understand the difference between major state trial courts and trial courts of limited jurisdiction more clearly, consider California as an example. In California, civil suits worth over $25,000 go to superior court, as do all criminal felonies, juvenile proceedings, and family law cases. Civil suits in amounts equal to or less than $25,000, criminal misdemeanors, and arraignment of felonies are heard in municipal court.

Specialty courts, such as New York's Family Courts, New York City's Civil Court and Criminal Court, and Michigan's Probate Court, have been created in several states.

b. Small claims court [§19]

Small claims courts are sometimes referred to as "people's courts" or "pro se courts," and nearly every state has them. "Small claims" means just that. There are jurisdictional limits on the amount for which a person can sue. It is usually below $5,000. No criminal cases are heard in these courts, just civil. Nor are there jury trials.

The procedure in small claims courts is unique to our court system. Filing fees are low—no more than a few dollars—and no formal papers, complaints, or answers are filed. The plaintiff and defendant just present their own case before a judge. Hearsay and other rules of evidence are not strictly adhered to, since laypersons are often doing the talking. Most states permit lawyers, although a few states, like California, exclude them.

Cases are usually heard within a month of the time of filing the claim, a considerable difference from the wait in city and county courts, which often goes up to six months or more (in the larger cities it can be up to three years).

States vary in the way appeals are handled from small claims courts. Some allow only the defendant to appeal. Others permit both plaintiff and defendant to do so. The appeal may be for an entirely new trial in a regular state court, or it may be limited to an appeal on the law. Several states provide that the defendant, upon receiving notice of the suit, may request that the case be transferred before trial to a regular state court. If the defendant does not make this request, the case is heard in small claims court, and neither party may appeal the decision.

c. Appellate courts [§20]

Appeals from a state's major trial courts go to the state's court of appeals. Names vary here too: Court of Criminal Appeals in Texas, in New York the Appellate Division of the Supreme Court (the Supreme Court being the major ***trial*** court), etc. The appellate court will necessarily hear cases from several trial courts.

Appeals from the trial courts of limited jurisdiction may go directly to a state's court of appeals or to a special appeals division of the state's major trial court. In California, for example, superior court judges in their appellate division hear appeals from small claims courts.

Just as in the federal system, there may be several appellate courts in the state. Each appellate court supervises the trial courts in its jurisdiction, and its decisions are binding on these trial courts.

d. Supreme or high court [§21]

In most states the high court is called the supreme court—although in New York it is called the Court of Appeals, in Massachusetts it is the Supreme Judicial Court, and in Texas the Court of Criminal Appeals is the highest court for criminal matters, while the Texas Supreme Court is for civil matters.

State supreme courts do not have to hear every appeal made to them. Like the United States Supreme Court, they may, in large part, pick and choose. A state supreme court will usually hear cases that have a significant impact or that will resolve conflicting decisions in the lower state courts. Most states have five or seven justices on the high court, although the range is from five in Delaware to nine in Texas. All justices sit on a case. A decision of the state's high court is binding on all courts of the state.

e. Reminder—court names can be confusing [§22]

Because of the variety of state court names, it may not be apparent whether a state's trial court, appellate court, or high court is issuing the opinion. Since the importance and binding effect of the opinion depends upon the court that issues it, be certain to notice which level it is. This leads us into the next part of this chapter—the concept of precedent.

ILLUSTRATION OF COURT SYSTEMS

gilbert

	Trial Court	Court of Appeals	Supreme Court
Federal System:	District Court (including Bankruptcy Court in each district); also specialty courts (*e.g.,* Tax Court)	Court of Appeals (13 circuits for 12 regions and the Federal Circuit)	United States Supreme Court
California:	Superior Court	Court of Appeal (6 districts)	California Supreme Court
New York:	Supreme Court (plus courts of special and limited jurisdiction, such as Family Court, Surrogate's Court, and courts for New York City)	Appellate Division of Supreme Court (4 departments)	New York Court of Appeals

B. Precedent—Persuasive Authority

1. Stare Decisis [§23]

One of the basic principles of Anglo-American law is stare decisis—that courts should adhere to precedents set by earlier decisions. Although our system of judge-made law provides for some flexibility, the stare decisis principle allows for an element of predictability in legal decisions.

a. Illustration

The following simple example serves to illustrate this: One day Molly opens her bottle of soda to find a rat preserved in the liquid. She faints from shock and in falling hits her head on a chair, suffering a concussion. She later brings suit against the soda company for her injuries. No one in her state has filed such a "cause of action" before, and at trial the judge holds that there is no law entitling her to bring the action. Molly appeals to her state's court of appeals, which agrees with the trial court's decision. Undaunted, she takes her appeal to the state supreme court. The high court reverses the appeals court decision, holding that Molly does have the right to sue the company.

The following week, Matthew, who lives in the same state as Molly, finds a rat in his bottle of soda. He faints, hits his head on a chair as he falls and suffers a concussion. Can he now sue for his injuries? According to our legal concept of stare decisis, or adherence to precedent, he can. His situation is identical to Molly's and since they both live in the same state, the trial court that hears Matthew's complaint must follow the rule of law set forth by the state supreme court in Molly's case.

Now what if Matthew had hurt his arm instead of his head in falling? It would have become a different case from Molly's, but would this difference matter? Could the trial court refuse to apply the ruling in Molly's case to Matthew's? What if he fainted but hurt no part of his body in falling? Could he sue for the shock itself?

What if Matthew had found a mouse instead of a rat in his bottle, but still fainted and hit his head—would the case be different then? What if the foreign substance in the bottle was a cockroach, a silverfish, or a human hair, and instead of fainting he got food poisoning? Does the principle established in Molly's case extend to these situations? Or is Molly's case "distinguishable"?

Well, this is what the law is all about. The law is an attempt to forge legal principles that can apply to certain factual situations so that people who later come into these situations will be able to "predict" how the courts will act. But the question remains: Does a person's case fall under one principle of law or another or perhaps a third that has yet to be recognized by the court? (This is why facts are so important to a case. A few changes in the facts can make all the difference in the principle of law that will be applied.)

Judges deal with these problems all the time. Weaving a thread of consistency or even reasonability among similar cases is certainly trying, if not impossible. But our system of law demands that we try.

b. Which court bound by precedent

In understanding precedent, you should also be aware of which courts must follow other courts' decisions on similar sets of facts. Lower courts follow only the rulings of higher courts ***in their jurisdictions.*** That is, the Texas Court of Appeals must follow legal principles laid down by the Texas Supreme Court; the Texas trial courts are bound by what the Texas Court of Appeals, the Texas Court of Criminal Appeals, and the Texas Supreme Court hold. But no Texas court is bound to follow a ruling of the Oregon Supreme Court, another state jurisdiction.

The same is true for the federal courts. The federal district court in Jackson, Mississippi, is bound to follow the rulings of the Court of Appeals for the Fifth Circuit, the court supervising it. But it need not take as precedent the rulings of the Sixth Circuit or any other federal court of appeals. All federal courts, however, whether district or circuit, must abide by the decisions of the United States Supreme Court.

All state supreme courts, or for that matter any state court, must follow a United States Supreme Court decision if the decision involved the interpretation of the federal Constitution as it applies to actions by the states.

Courts on the same judicial level—such as the 13 federal courts of appeals—are ***not*** bound to follow each other's decisions since they are all on equal terms. Using our earlier example, if Molly's case was in the Fifth Circuit and Matthew's in the Sixth Circuit (the cases having similar factual situations), the two courts could decide the cases differently.

All courts are bound by ***their own*** earlier decisions, unless reversed by a higher court or by themselves later on.

2. Persuasive Authority [§24]

Court decisions that are not precedent may be looked upon as "persuasive." Thus, if Molly lived in Louisiana and Matthew in New Mexico, the judges in New Mexico, although not bound by the rulings of the Louisiana Supreme Court, could consider the reasonings of the Louisiana court as persuasive and accordingly reach the same conclusion. Similarly, a decision by the Court of Appeals for the Fifth Circuit would also only be persuasive as to the Sixth Circuit or any other federal court of appeals.

C. Things to Keep in Mind for Legal Research

1. In General [§25]

Whenever you do legal research, keep in mind two things: (i) the division between the federal government and the state governments; and (ii) the separation of either government (state or federal) into its three lawmaking branches (executive, legislative, and judicial). Problems in legal research correspond to these concepts. Is it a state and/or federal law problem? Which branch of government is involved in the problem? Is more than one branch involved? We will conclude this chapter with a discussion of these problems. (At times you will need to consider whether municipal or county law is also involved. But in order to present a clear picture of the state/federal distinction, we have decided to include municipal and county ordinances and administrative acts as part of the state law, and not discuss them separately.)

2. State and/or Federal Law? [§26]

If you are filing for divorce, you go to state court. If you are filing bankruptcy, you go to federal court. If you are filing a discrimination suit, you could go either to federal or to state court. Under the theory of federalism, federal law takes precedence in settling some disputes, state law in others. But in large gray areas, both governments have the authority to legislate and exercise power. For example, many states have stronger consumer protection laws than the federal government provides. Obviously, if the researcher checks only federal law on consumer protection, the research would be incomplete as to those states that have enacted their own, stronger laws and regulations. On the other hand, if she only examines the state law, the researcher might miss a provision of the federal statute not adopted in the state legislation, but nonetheless applicable (besides, she would also not be using the clout of the federal government when attempting to remedy the matter). And, of course, if the researcher checks state law in a state that has minimal legislation in this area and does not think to inquire into federal law, she would wrongly conclude that there is only minimal protection for a citizen of that state.

How, then, does one decide whether the issue is a matter of federal law or state law, or both? Article I of the United States Constitution defines the specific lawmaking powers of Congress, its exclusive domains. But section 8 of that Article gives Congress the power to make all laws "necessary and proper" for carrying out its powers. This Necessary and Proper Clause has provided Congress with great flexibility in preparing and enacting legislation not specifically mentioned in the Constitution. Thus, reading the United States Constitution is usually not enough. The fact is that even lawyers and judges do not always know which areas are exclusively federal concerns, which are exclusively state, and which may be legislated in by both governments. So in doing research, if you want to be certain, you will often have to check through ***both federal and state*** statutes. Overlooking a law can be costly, and often someone's rights or even life may depend on it.

3. Which Branch(es) of Government? [§27]

The legislative branch is generally thought of as the branch that "makes the law." In large measure, this is true. But both the judicial and executive branches can, and in fact do, make law. Your research will not be complete if you inquire only into one branch of government and do not consider whether the others may also be involved. Take an example:

A student wore a black armband to class to protest the Vietnam War. The principal suspended the student from school until he would agree to remove the armband. The student, claiming that his rights to free speech under the First Amendment to the United States Constitution were being violated, brought suit in court. Eventually, it reached the United States Supreme Court which held that "speech" is not limited to words and that the student's wearing of the armband was protected by the First Amendment. [Tinker v. Des Moines Independent Community School District, 393 U.S. 503 (1969)] Here, the Court did not just enforce the law or make a determination of the rights of the parties; it also interpreted a particular provision and applied its interpretation to the case. When a court interprets a statute or constitutional provision—explaining what it "means"—it is making law. Its determination or definition may be used by later courts dealing with similar situations. (For example, in *Texas v. Johnson,* 491 U.S. 397 (1989), the Court followed up on the *Tinker* principle by holding that flag burning was also protected speech.)

Courts make laws in other ways too. They can declare a statute unconstitutional— that is, the statute in question violates part of the state or federal Constitution.

Another way courts make law is by basing a decision on legal principles not found in any statutes, the Constitution, or earlier court decisions. The "right of privacy," for example, is nowhere mentioned in the United States Constitution. Yet the United States Supreme Court, in a case involving the use of contraceptive devices, interpreted the Constitution to include the right of privacy as a constitutional right. [Griswold v. Connecticut, 381 U.S. 479 (1965)]

The executive/administrative branch of government can also make law. The most important instances are when an administrative agency (whether state or federal) issues rules and regulations to implement legislation, and when it adjudicates and resolves disputes concerning parties regulated by the agency. (*See* chapter VI.)

The President and the state governors can also issue executive orders and proclamations which have the effect of lawmaking. Often, when Presidents have sent troops to other countries (*e.g.*, Vietnam, Panama, Kuwait, and Haiti), these decisions were made and acted upon without any laws passed by Congress, yet they greatly affected the lives of people in the United States.

WHAT LAW APPLIES—A CHECKLIST

gilbert

USE THIS TO HELP YOU DETERMINE WHICH LAW APPLIES.

FEDERAL

- ❑ Legislative
- ❑ Judicial
- ❑ Executive/Administrative

STATE

- ❑ Legislative
- ❑ Judicial
- ❑ Executive/Administrative

LOCAL (COUNTY OR MUNICIPAL)

- ❑ Legislative
- ❑ Judicial
- ❑ Executive/Administrative

Executive decisions and administrative agency decisions and regulations are often reviewed by the courts. If the regulations do not conform with the intent of the statute, a person affected may challenge their legality in court.

There are, of course, other lawmaking powers belonging to each branch of government, such as the President's right to enter into treaties with the consent of the Senate and the judiciary's right to issue rules to govern local court practice. But our purpose here is not to give you a detailed lesson on American civics. Rather, it is only to remind you that more than one branch of government may be involved in the making of a law.

When researching, if you are unsure as to whether state and/or federal law applies and which branch or branches are involved, ***check all possible sources.*** It is usually wiser to err in overextending your search than in limiting it too severely.

Chapter Three: Cases

CONTENTS

A. The Reporting System

1. In General [§28]

After a federal or state appellate court or supreme court decides a case, it usually issues a written opinion explaining the decision. (Trial courts may also issue a written opinion, but usually only federal district courts do.) Our system of precedent depends upon these written opinions. In an attempt to maintain the illusion of consistency, judges need to compare their reasonings with those of other courts dealing with similar factual situations. Lawyers, too, in preparing their cases, need to know how other courts have dealt with similar problems.

There are millions of reported cases and the number is climbing steeply (as lawsuits increase). Because of this, many states and the federal government no longer authorize the publication of every appellate decision. California, for example, requires that only appellate cases establishing a new rule of law or modifying an existing rule of law be officially published. However, West and various publishers of looseleaf services publish many of those otherwise unpublished opinions. Also, the online research services LexisNexis and Westlaw include many unpublished decisions in their databases (*see* chapter VIII).

The first half of this chapter will outline the system of reporting court opinions and decisions; the second half will explain how you can actually find a case.

2. Official and Unofficial Reports [§29]

A court opinion may be published by the government and/or by a private commercial company (often West). If the government publishes the opinion or authorizes its publication, it is called an official report; if published by a private company without official authorization, the report is unofficial. In actuality, there is little difference. It is the same opinion, merely appearing in one text or another. Most of the opinions you will be reading will appear in West's National Reporter System.

3. National Reporter System [§30]

West publishes most of the opinions of the federal and state courts. Many of its federal, regional, and state reporters make up the National Reporter System. If you are reading this book in a library, as we suggest you do, you should have no problem locating the various reporters in the West system. They all have the same jackets, differing only in the names of each. (*See* chart, *infra.*) (People sometimes confuse the seven regional reporter districts of West's National Reporter System with the 13 circuits of the federal courts of appeal. There is absolutely no connection between the two. For a map describing the federal circuit courts, *see* the chart on page 7 or the inside of any recent *Federal Reporter.*)

The National Reporter System was started in the last quarter of the 1800s. There are different beginning dates for the various regional reporters. For cases decided prior to the inception of the System, pre-National Reporter System state reports will have to be used.

SUMMARY OF WEST'S NATIONAL REPORTER SYSTEM

Supreme Court Reporter

Federal Reporter

Federal Supplement

Federal Rules Decisions

Atlantic (Conn., Del., D.C., Md., Me., N.H., N.J., Pa., R.I., Vt.)

North Eastern (Ill., Ind., Mass., N.Y., Ohio)

South Eastern (Ga., N.C., S.C., Va., W. Va.)

Southern (Ala., Fla., La., Miss.)

North Western (Iowa, Mich., Minn., Neb. N.D., S.D., Wis.)

South Western (Ark., Ky., Mo., Tenn., Tex.)

Pacific (Alaska, Ariz., Cal., Colo., Haw., Idaho, Kan., Mont., Nev., N.M., Okla., Or., Utah, Wash., Wy.)

New York Supplement

California Reporter

} These state reporters contain precedential decisions not contained in the regional reporters.

Bankruptcy Reporter

Military Justice Reporter

Federal Claims Reporter

(West also publishes several state reporters as part of its National Reporter System and the Education Law Reporter, which is not part of the National Reporter System.)

4. Citations [§31]

Every reporter, whether official or unofficial, has an accepted abbreviation or "citation." The citation guides the researcher to the proper volume. Citations are discussed more fully later in this book (*see infra,* §§54 *et seq.*).

B. Reporters of Federal Cases

1. Supreme Court Decisions [§32]

Decisions of the United States Supreme Court appear in four different reporters. *United States Reports* is the official reporter; the others are unofficial.

a. *United States Reports* [§33]

Until the early 1800s, the official reports of the United States Supreme Court were reported by various people, and the reporter's name was used in place of "U.S." as the volume reference. If you look at these early reports, you will see the names Cranch, Peters, Black, and several others on the spines. Volume one of Cranch is, for example, the same as volume five of *United States Reports.*

b. *Supreme Court Reporter* [§34]

This reporter is part of West's National Reporter System. The *Supreme Court Reporter* began in the late 1800s and does not include early Court decisions.

c. *United States Supreme Court Reports, Lawyers' Edition* [§35]

This bound set of Supreme Court decisions is published by the LexisNexis Group and includes all Supreme Court decisions issued.

d. *United States Law Week* [§36]

Published by the Bureau of National Affairs, Inc. ("BNA"), *United States Law Week* comes in three volumes. One, "Supreme Court Today," contains all the United States Supreme Court decisions as well as other actions taken by the Court, such as agreeing (granting certiorari) or refusing (denying certiorari) to review cases appealed to it. There is also an index and a table of cases appealed to and docketed with the Court. The second volume, "Case Alert," publishes a national survey of current case law, and the third, *Legal News,* describes important developments in the law.

e. Computerized databases [§37]

Westlaw, LexisNexis, and a number of online sites include United States Supreme Court decisions, as well as decisions from other federal courts (*see* chapter VIII).

f. **Advance sheets [§38]**

Since it usually is months before a decision is published in *United States Reports*, *Supreme Court Reporter*, and *United States Supreme Court Reports, Lawyers' Edition*, "advance sheets" of the cases are issued by the reporters every few weeks. Advance sheets are nothing more than the cases issued in pamphlet form prior to their publication in the bound volumes. Most advance sheets follow the same pagination as will appear in the bound volume, although the "slip opinions" issued by *United States Reports* do not. The other federal reporters as well as many state official reporters and West's National Reporter System also issue advance sheets for their cases.

2. Federal Appellate Court Decisions

a. ***Federal Reporter* [§39]**

Published decisions of the 13 federal courts of appeals appear in West's *Federal Reporter.* There is no official reporter published by the federal courts. Advance sheets are issued to the *Federal Reporter.*

b. **Federal Appendix [§40]**

This West reporter publishes unpublished decisions from some circuits.

c. **Other sources [§41]**

Federal appellate court decisions can also be found on Westlaw, LexisNexis, and other commercial, as well as governmental, websites (*see* chapter VIII). You can also check *United States Law Week*, "Case Alert," for digests of important recent cases. Selected appellate court cases decided prior to 1880 are published in *Federal Cases.*

3. Federal District Court Decisions

a. ***Federal Supplement* [§42]**

Federal district court cases are published in one edition: West's *Federal Supplement.* There is no official district court reporter. Prior to 1933, federal district court opinions appeared in the *Federal Reporte*r (and prior to 1880 in *Federal Cases*). Advance sheets to the *Federal Supplement* are issued by West. *Note*: The *Federal Supplement* is a selective, rather than a comprehensive, collection of federal district court cases.

Decisions of the United States Court of International Trade (formerly the U.S. Customs Court) and special panels dealing with railroad reorganization and multidistrict litigation are now also included in the *Federal Supplement.*

b. **Other sources [§43]**

District court decisions may be accessed through various online sources (*see* chapter VIII). Also, check *United States Law Week*, "Case Alert," for summaries of the most important recent cases.

4. Specialty Court Decisions [§44]

The federal specialty courts, such as the Court of Federal Claims, the Tax Court, the Court of International Trade, and the Court of Appeals for the Federal Circuit, each publish their own decisions. West publishes the *Federal Claims Reporter* for cases decided by the United States Court of Federal Claims and the United States Court of Appeals for the Federal Circuit. Several looseleaf publishers such as CCH and BNA publish tax, labor and employment, and other federal appeals and district court cases in select areas of the law. (*See* chapter VI for a description of looseleaf services.)

5. Bankruptcy Decisions [§45]

West publishes the *Bankruptcy Law Reporter.* It includes cases from the United States Bankruptcy Courts and cases in the federal district courts, courts of appeals, and Supreme Court. Bankruptcy decisions are also published in Collier *Bankruptcy Cases* (Matthew Bender & Co., Inc., a member of LexisNexis Group) and in *Bankruptcy Law Reports* (CCH).

6. Federal Rules [§46]

West publishes an edition of district court cases that have interpreted federal procedural rules, both civil and criminal. The series is called *Federal Rules Decisions.* West also publishes, under the brand name Lawyers Cooperative Publishing, the *Federal Rules Service,* which reports opinions relating to the Federal Rules of Civil Procedure.

7. Other Special Subject Reporters [§47]

West and other publishers publish reporters compiling federal decisions in other special subject areas, such as *Military Justice Reporter* (West), *Media Law Reporter* (BNA), and *Labor Law Reporter* (CCH). (*See also* "Specialized Editions of Cases," *infra*, §53.)

C. Reporters of State Cases

1. West Regional and State Reporters [§48]

West has divided the country into seven sections and publishes a regional reporter for each. The reporters are *North Eastern, Atlantic, South Eastern, Southern, South Western, North Western,* and *Pacific.* Although the arrangement of states within these reporters is geographical, it does not follow the pattern we usually think of when sectioning off the country. For example, Kansas and Oklahoma are part of the *Pacific Reporter,* while Kentucky and Tennessee are included in the *South Western Reporter.* (*See* chart, *supra*, for a listing of states in each regional reporter.)

West also publishes some state reporters including *California Reporter* and *New York Supplement.*

2. Official Reports [§49]

About one-half of the states publish their own court opinions in what are known as official reports. Those states that do not publish rely on the appropriate West regional reporter for the reporting of their decisions. Many people tend to use West reporters whether or not their state publishes its own official reports because the reporters are readily available and because they "key into" West digests. (The West Key Number System is discussed *infra,* §51.) Many states also make official decisions available on the Internet (*see* chapter VIII).

3. Advance Sheets [§50]

Advance sheets of the most recent cases are issued by West in paper supplements for its regional and state reporters. Most states also publish advance sheets to their official state reports. (*See also* discussion of parallel citations, *infra*, §55.)

D. Headnotes and Summaries

1. West Headnotes and Key Number System [§51]

At the beginning of a case reported by West, you will find a summary of the facts and the decision followed by "headnotes" setting forth the principles of law stated in the case. These headnotes are written by editors of the company so as to key into the West system of law books. Accompanying each headnote is an illustrative key with a topic name and number. West divides each topic (there are more than 400 major topics) into key numbers, creating more than 800,000 individual units representing specific legal concepts. It then takes every principle of law stated in a case and includes it under one of these topics. Thus, someone who finds a headnote relevant to his research can turn to any West digest, look up the headnote topic and key number, and find a list of cases presumably dealing with the same principles of law. The researcher saves a certain amount of time by not needing to use the indexes in the digests. (*See* chapter V for an illustration of digests and the key number system.)

Unfortunately, people do not always use these headnotes for the purpose designed. They sometimes rely on them for an understanding of the case. Rather than read a decision to determine what a case said, the person will read only the headnotes preceding the case. This can be disastrous. The editors who wrote the headnotes do not discriminate between those principles of law that are directly involved in reaching the decision and so become precedent, and those that are merely advisory or helpful to the judges in analyzing and discussing the case. The first set of principles are ***holdings,*** the second set ***dicta.*** From the headnotes alone, you cannot tell which principles of law are holdings, and which are dicta. You can only do so by reading the case.

Why does West assign a key number to every principle of law stated in the case? Why not just pick out the holdings (for these are really what finally determine the importance of the case) and only key them into the system? One reason is that dicta, although not binding precedent, may be "persuasive." That is, the statement of law may still be helpful to your case. Although not the basis for a decision, dicta are

ILLUSTRATION OF A CASE

(Edited version of case from West's Federal Supplement)

Case Name

PRINCETON UNIVERSITY PRESS, MacMillan, Inc. and St. Martin's Press, Incorporated, Plaintiffs,

v.

MICHIGAN DOCUMENT SERVICES, INC., and James M. Smith, Defendants.

Court Docket Number

No. 92–CV–71029–DT.

Court

United States District Court, E.D. Michigan, Southern Division.

Date of Opinion

June 9, 1994.

Case Syllabus

Publishers of copyrighted works brought copyright infringement action against commercial copying service that prepared and sold unauthorized anthologies to university students without paying royalties or permission fees. On publishers' motion for summary judgment, the District Court, Hackett, J., held that: (1) copying was not fair use, even though anthologies were sold to university students; (2) infringing activity was blatant and willful for which increased statutory damages were warranted; and (3) reasonable attorney fees for publishers were clearly justified.

Decision

Granted.

West Key Number

1. Copyrights and Intellectual Property ⚷56

Headnote

Photocopying of anthologies of copyrighted works by commercial copying service for university students without paying any royalties or permission fees did not qualify as "fair use" of copyrighted materials, where copying was purely for profit even though consumers of material happened to be students, excerpts copied ranged from 5% to 30% of authors' original works, and permission fees represented significant source of revenues for publishers of copyrighted works. 17 U.S.C.A. § 107.

2. Copyrights and Intellectual Property ⚷51

Copyright infringement may be found even in absence of profit for copying. 17 U.S.C.A. §§ 106, 106A.

* * *

Parties' Attorneys

Ronald S. Rauchberg, Herman L. Goldsmith, Law Firm of Proskauer, Rose, New York City, James E. Stewart, J. Michael Huget, Law Firm of Butzel Long, Detroit, MI, Jon A. Baumgarten, Law Firm of Proskauer, Rose, Washington, DC, for plaintiffs.

Susan M. Kornfield, Law Firm of Bodman, Longley, Ann Arbor, MI, for defendants.

ORDER ACCEPTING IN PART AND REJECTING IN PART MAGISTRATE JUDGE'S REPORT AND RECOMMENDATION AND GRANTING PLAINTIFFS' MOTION FOR SUMMARY JUDGMENT AND DENYING DEFENDANTS' MOTIONS FOR SUMMARY JUDGMENT

Court's Opinion

HACKETT, District Judge.

This matter is before the court on cross-motions for summary judgment and/or dismissal. The court has reviewed the file, the record, and the magistrate judge's report and recommendation and accepts in part and rejects in part the magistrate judge's recommendation. Objections to the report have been filed by both parties within the established time period. Responses to the objections have been filed by the opposing parties. All of these have been reviewed and considered by this judge.

The court hereby adopts the magistrate judge's report and recommendation in part as the findings and conclusions of this court. The court differs with the findings and conclusions of the magistrate judge only as they address the matter of willfulness and penalties to be imposed. Plaintiffs' motion for summary judgment is granted. Defendants' motions for summary judgment on infringement and statutory vagueness are denied.

The court adopts the following factual background as stated by the magistrate judge in the report and recommendation:

> This is a copyright infringement case. The facts are not really in dispute. Plaintiffs are publishers of copyrighted works. Princeton Press is a not-for-profit entity; Macmillan and St. Martin's Press are for-profit corporations. Each plaintiff operates a permissions department that passes upon requests for permission to copy ex-

* * *

better than nothing at all. Also, dicta in one case may be a holding in another, and the key system will lead you to those other cases.

Another reason for including every principle of law is to minimize the chance of error by a West editor who, in writing the headnotes, may have erred in understanding the case. It happens. Lawyers often argue over the holding or meaning of a case, one or perhaps both attorneys misunderstanding it. Moreover, it may not even be the editor's fault. Judges themselves at times do not comprehend what they are writing; certainly few, if any, are masters of all the legal matters appearing before them. Nor do judges always make themselves clearly understood.

So if you want to know what a case says, ***read it.*** Do not rely on summaries and headnotes to tell you. Decide for yourself. After all, you are finally responsible for deciding whether the case is important to your problem. Do not underestimate your abilities.

2. Official Reports' Headnotes [§52]

Official reports, state or federal, also publish summaries and headnotes. These are usually written or supervised by judges or clerks of the court but are not keyed into the West system. (Occasionally, an official report will have headnotes linked to a digest published by the same publisher.) More importantly, these headnotes do not try to include every principle of law stated in the case. The writers tend to stick more closely to those that are directly related to the actual facts and decision of the case, but here too the headnotes will include dicta. So with official reports, we also advise you to read the entire decision and take nothing for granted.

E. Other Case Reports

1. Specialized Editions of Cases [§53]

Several companies publish cases in select areas of the law, grouping their cases and material by subject matter (rather than by jurisdiction as West usually does). CCH's *Trade Regulation Reporter* and BNA's *Labor Relations Reporter* are examples. *United States Law Week*, mentioned earlier, is another example. These reporters are part of what is known as "looseleaf materials." They include administrative agency decisions and state and/or federal court decisions as well as legislative acts and agency regulations on the subject.

F. Citations and Case Finding

1. Using Citations to Find a Case [§54]

A citation is a shorthand guide to the location of legal materials. A citation or "cite" to a case would include the volume number, page number, name of the reporter in which the case appears, and the year in which the case was decided. If it is not obvious from the reporter citation what court the case is in, you also need to mention it. Where the case appears in more than one reporter, the case will have more than one cite to it. Citations to cases always perch alongside the name of the case. For example:

Bush v. Gore, 531 U.S. 98, 121 S. Ct. 525, 148 L. Ed. 2d 388 (2000), means that the United States Supreme Court opinion in the case of *Bush v. Gore* appears in volume 531 of *United States Reports* at page 98, in volume 121 of the *Supreme Court Reporter* at page 525, and in volume 148 of the second edition (or series) of *United States Supreme Court Reports, Lawyers' Edition* at page 388. The case was decided in 2000. There is no need to mention the court since we know that these texts only report United States Supreme Court cases.

Gannett Co. v. DePasquale, 43 N.Y.2d 370, 401 N.Y.S.2d 756, 372 N.E.2d 544 (1977), would be found in volume 43 of *New York Reports,* second edition, at page 370; volume 401 of *New York Supplement,* second edition, at page 756; and volume 372 of *North Eastern Reporter,* second edition, at page 544. It is a 1977 decision. Again, no mention of the court is necessary because *New York Reports 2d* (N.Y.2d) only reports cases from the state's highest court—the Court of Appeals.

Blue Cross & Blue Shield v. Sanders, 138 F.3d 1347 (11th Cir. 1998), needs to include in the parenthetical that the case is from the Eleventh Circuit since *Federal Reporter 3d* (F.3d) reports cases from all 13 circuits of the federal courts of appeal.

Similarly, *Princeton University Press v. Michigan Document Services, Inc.,* 855 F. Supp. 905 (E.D. Mich. 1994), needs to include the particular district court since *Federal Supplement* publishes decisions from all the federal district courts in the country. "E.D." refers to the Eastern District.

Each reporter has an accepted abbreviation. There are two proper sources for citing any legal authority, the Association of Legal Writing Directors' *ALWD Citation Manual* and *The Bluebook: A Uniform System of Citation* (commonly known as the Bluebook). Both may be found in any law library. A growing number of jurisdictions have moved into medium- or vendor-neutral citations (*i.e.,* citations by document and paragraph number and not tied to a particular publisher). A few law schools use the *University of Chicago Manual of Legal Citation* (the "Maroon" Book) instead of the *ALWD Citation Manual* or the Bluebook. To avoid confusion and misinterpretation, proper citations should always be used.

Reminder: If the case is recent, you may have to look in the advance sheets of the named reporter. Advance sheets generally follow the same pagination as the bound volumes that will eventually replace them. If the case is too recent for the advance sheets, check online research systems such as LexisNexis and Westlaw, and legal newspapers.

2. Parallel Citations [§55]

Cases that are published in both official and unofficial reports will necessarily have more than one citation. Usually there will be two, an official and an unofficial. But there may be three—as is the situation with United States Supreme Court cases appearing in *United States Reports, Supreme Court Reporter,* and *United States Supreme Court Reports, Lawyers' Edition.* Many New York and California cases also appear in three separate reporters. The official citation always appears first.

Citations to the same case appearing in different reporters are known as "parallel citations." Thus, 17 Cal. 3d 425, 551 P.2d 334, and 131 Cal. Rptr. 14 are parallel citations to the California Supreme Court case of *Tarasoff v. Regents of the University of California,* appearing in *California Reports* (third series), *Pacific Reporter* (second series), and *California Reporter.*

Generally, you should give all the citations to a case—the person reading your material may possibly have access only to one set of reporters. To discover the parallel citation(s), you may use either Shepard's *Citations* or West's *National Reporter Blue Book* (*see* chapter VII), or LexisNexis or Westlaw.

3. Finding a Case Without a Citation [§56]

What if you only know the name of a case and not its citation; can you still locate it? The best way to find cases when you do not have the citation is by conducting a search in LexisNexis, Westlaw, or other Internet sources (*see* chapter VIII). When you do not have access to online sources, you can still find cases using the various digests and reporters described below.

You can locate a case if you know the jurisdiction. Just check the Table of Cases in the digest for that jurisdiction. For example, a United States Supreme Court case would be found by checking in the *United States Supreme Court Digest* (published by West); a federal case would be in West's *Federal Practice Digest* series. If it is a state case, you can search in the state digest or in the regional digest if there is one. Every digest also contains a Defendant-Plaintiff Table, useful when you know only the defendant's name. (Digests are covered in chapter V.)

If the case is recent, you may have to check the table in the "pocket part" or supplement in back of the digest and any supplemental advance sheets. (Pocket parts and supplements keep the material up to date in most secondary sources and in the codes.) If the case is too recent to appear in the supplement, you will have to search the table of cases in the latest issues of the advance sheets to the reporter in which you expect the case to appear. For important federal and state court decisions and for all United States Supreme Court decisions, you can try the two volumes of *United States Law Week,* "Case Alert" or "Supreme Court Today." Daily law newspapers in major metropolitan areas also sometimes publish important cases, either in the daily edition or in a weekly supplement. For example, the *Los Angeles Daily Journal* publishes within a week after issuance the full text of all California Supreme Court and Courts of Appeal cases, and the decisions of the United States Supreme Court, the Bankruptcy Panel, and the Ninth Circuit Court of Appeals. Again, it may be very helpful to check online sources.

When looking for a case, you may often find two or more cases with the same names. These could be the same case having gone through the various stages of appeal—different citations would necessarily be given for each court opinion. Or the names could refer to entirely different cases. Knowing the year may help you figure out which case is the one you are looking for. Otherwise, you will just have to read the case to decide.

If you do not know the jurisdiction of the case, you may have trouble locating it. If it is a well-known case, you can try Shepard's *Acts and Cases by Popular Names, Federal and State* (published by LexisNexis) (*see* chapter VII). Otherwise you will have to check the tables of cases in the various Decennial and General digests of the *American Digest System* (*see* chapter V).

4. Now What? [§57]

Finding a case is generally not that difficult. The real problem is in knowing which case to find. That is, which cases can be useful to you in working out your problem and how do you find them? Chapter V will review this in detail. It will explain how to use secondary legal sources to find cases and statutes and administrative regulations.

When you locate a case, how can you be certain it is important to your problem? What exactly is the case saying? Understanding a case comes largely with experience. Even lawyers and judges often disagree on what a case stands for. In chapter IX, we will analyze a case. We will diagram the different parts, outlining the points you should consider when reading it. Nothing does it like experience, and chapter IX will give you a start.

Chapter Four: Statutes, Constitutions, Legislative History, and Treaties

CONTENTS

A. In General

1. Introduction [§58]

People often begin their research with a check through the statutes. Statutes are the laws enacted by Congress or state legislatures. (Laws are also enacted by municipal and county legislative bodies. These laws are generally known as "ordinances" and are briefly mentioned later in this chapter.)

If you find a statute that specifically deals with your problem, you are well on your way. But a statute may mean one thing to one person and another to a second person. Which interpretation should the judge adopt? Following the recital of the statute are case annotations—short paragraphs (similar to headnotes) on how courts have interpreted and applied the statute. Checking these annotations and reading the cases to which they refer should help you see how the statute might be applied to your situation.

This chapter will begin with a discussion of researching statutes and their annotations, followed by a similar description of state and federal constitutions. We will conclude with legislative intent, that amorphous term that attempts to collect together the thoughts of the representatives who passed the law. Judges often use legislative intent and legislative history in making their determinations on the interpretation of a statute.

B. Statutes

1. In General [§59]

The enactment of a statute, whether state or federal, follows a general pattern. When a bill is introduced into Congress or a state legislature, it is given a number. The number stays with it throughout the legislative session (either one or two years). If the bill is not enacted in the session, it dies. Its sponsor, if still interested, must then reintroduce it in the next session, where it will be assigned a new number. You can follow a bill's movement by keeping tabs on its number. The number of a bill is preceded by "S" or "H," depending upon whether the bill was introduced in the Senate or the House of Representatives. Each state publishes recent bills and congressional activity on the state legislature's website, and federal legislation is available online on THOMAS (*see infra*, §194).

A state bill becomes law when it is passed by the legislature and signed by the governor; a federal bill becomes law when passed by Congress and signed by the President. If the chief executive (governor or President) vetoes the bill, it can still become law if two-thirds of the representatives vote for its passage. If the chief executive neither signs nor vetoes the act, most states and the federal government provide that the bill automatically becomes law 10 days after arriving at the chief executive's desk.

Laws may be public or private. Most laws are public. A private act refers to a specific person or small group, rather than to the general population. For example, a bill granting citizenship to a particular person (who does not qualify for citizenship under the normal procedure) is a private act.

2. Statutes and Codes [§60]

When acts are passed, they are published by the federal or state government in chronological order. Federal laws so published are found in the United States *Statutes at Large*, the official source of all laws enacted by the government. State laws are found in each state's edition of its session laws, also the official source. But chronological order does not make for efficient research. It would be a painstaking process to figure out what the law is on a subject by searching in every year's edition of the *Statutes at Large* or the state's session laws to see what, if any, laws were passed that year concerning your problem. Thus, editions known as codes were developed.

Codes group together or "codify" the laws under specific titles. Thus, the laws on obtaining unemployment insurance would be in one section of the codes, the laws on setting up nonprofit corporations in another section. Of course some laws will apply to more than one subject, so you will need to check in more than one place for a complete survey of the law affecting your problem.

3. Federal Codes—Annotated and Unannotated [§61]

The federal laws are codified in a government-published edition known as *United States Code*. Most people, however, use the commercially annotated editions, *United States Code Annotated* (published by West) and *United States Code Service* (published by Matthew Bender & Company, Inc., a member of the LexisNexis Group). These annotated editions publish citations to cases that have interpreted or applied a particular act. This is important because one cannot always tell just by reading a statute precisely what it means or to whom it applies. One word or phrase can easily conjure up a wealth of possibilities. For example, consider 42 U.S.C. section 1983:

> §1983. Civil action for deprivation of rights. Every person who, under color of any statute, ordinance, regulation, custom, or usage, of any State or Territory or the District of Columbia, subjects, or causes to be subjected, any citizen of the United States or other person within the jurisdiction thereof to the deprivation of any rights, privileges, or immunities secured by the Constitution and laws, shall be liable to the party injured in an action at law, suit in equity, or other proper proceeding for redress. For the purposes of this section, any Act of Congress applicable exclusively to the District of Columbia shall be considered to be a statute of the District of Columbia.

This is a civil rights statute of basically only a few lines. Yet in West's *United States Code Annotated*, this statute—along with annotations explaining, interpreting, and referring to it—fills up more than one whole volume.

By checking to see how a statute has been interpreted through court decisions, you will be able to gauge the actual meaning of the statute and sense how it would apply to your situation.

The annotations are written by editors of the publishing company. They are sentences or short paragraphs similar to (and often the same as) the headnotes to cases. The advice given earlier not to rely on headnotes to tell you what the case held also applies to annotations. The annotations are helpful only in leading you to the cases; they cannot accurately show you how the statute was applied to the factual situation in the case. You must read the case for that.

At times you will find an annotation to an opinion by the (state or federal) attorney general, giving an interpretation of part or all of the law. These opinions are only persuasive; they do not have the force of law that a judge's opinion has. Nevertheless, they are referred to as having some authority on the matter and should be consulted.

You may also find references to law review articles or to other secondary sources that have commented on the statute (*see* chapter V). You may wish to check these too, especially when there are only a few cases in the annotations.

There are two annotated federal codes:

a. ***United States Code Annotated* ("U.S.C.A.") [§62]**
This multivolume West publication is organized by titles. Besides annotations, it includes references to the history of a statute, cross-references to related statutes and constitutional provisions, and references to other West publications like digests and encyclopedias for additional material. (*See* Addenda for sample pages.) It also contains a section called Westlaw Electronic Research that tells you the topic number to use to search for cases. U.S.C.A. provides references to the Code of Federal Regulations ("C.F.R."). Because regulations adopted by a federal agency to implement a statute have the force of law, they need to be examined. (*See* chapter VI on administrative law.) U.S.C.A. is available online through Westlaw and WestlawNext (*see infra*, §186).

b. ***United States Code Service* ("U.S.C.S.") [§63]**
Published by Matthew Bender & Company (a member of the LexisNexis Group), this set, also organized by titles, was designed to replace *Federal Code Annotated* ("F.C.A."). U.S.C.S. provides references to the history of a statute and cross-references to related statutes and constitutional provisions just as *United States Code Annotated* does. U.S.C.S. also is a rapid tool to lead you into the C.F.R. U.S.C.S. serves LexisNexis Group publications in the same way U.S.C.A. serves West publications—namely, to provide references to appropriate sections of their sourcebooks. U.S.C.S. is available online through LexisNexis (*see infra*, §178).

ILLUSTRATION OF A STATUTE

(Edited version of statute from West's U.S.C.A.)

Ch. 53 ILLEGALLY TAKEN FISH AND WILDLIFE 16 § 3372

Title and Statute Number

* * * *

Statute

§ 3372. Prohibited acts

(a) Offenses other than marking offenses

It is unlawful for any person—

(1) to import, export, transport, sell, receive, acquire, or purchase any fish or wildlife or plant taken or possessed in violation of any law, treaty, or regulation of the United States or in violation of any Indian tribal law;

(2) to import, export, transport, sell, receive, acquire, or purchase in interstate or foreign commerce—

(A) any fish or wildlife taken, possessed, transported, or sold in violation of any law or regulation of any State or in violation of any foreign law, or

(B) any plant taken, possessed, transported, or sold in violation of any law or regulation of any State;

(3) within the special maritime and territorial jurisdiction of the United States (as defined in section 7 of Title 18)—

(A) to possess any fish or wildlife taken, possessed, transported, or sold in violation of any law or regulation of any State or in violation of any foreign law or Indian tribal law, or

(B) to possess any plant taken, possessed, transported, or sold in violation of any law or regulation of any State;

(4) having imported, exported, transported, sold, purchased, or received any fish or wildlife or plant imported from any foreign country or transported in interstate or foreign commerce, to make or submit any false record, account, label, or identification thereof; or

(5) to attempt to commit any act described in paragraphs (1) through (4).

(b) Marking offenses

It is unlawful for any person to import, export, or transport in interstate commerce any container or package containing any fish or wildlife unless the container or package has previously been plainly marked, labeled, or tagged in accordance with the regulations issued pursuant to paragraph (2) of section 3376(a) of this title.

Public Law and Statutes at Large References

(Pub.L. 97–79, § 3, Nov. 16, 1981, 95 Stat. 1074.)

16 U.S.C.A. §§ 3101 to End—6 121

Historical Information

Historical Note

Legislative History. For legislative history and purpose of Pub.L. 97–79, see 1981 U.S. Code Cong. and Adm. News, p. 1748.

References to Related Topics

Cross References

Exceptions to applicability of this section, see section 3377 of this title.
Forfeitures, see section 3374 of this title.
Penalties and sanctions, see section 3373 of this title.
Regulations for implementation of this section, see section 3376 of this title.

Code of Federal Regulations

Wind River Reservation Game Code, Bureau of Indian Affairs, see 25 CFR 244.1 et seq.

Annotations to Statute

Notes of Decisions

Birds within section 3
Burden of proof 5
Constitutionality 1
Construction with state laws 2
Indictment or information 4

1. Constitutionality

North Carolina regulation, N.C.G.S. § 113–291, prohibiting the hunting of fox without authorization precisely and unambiguously delineates the elementary notion that dealing in untagged pelts is illegal in North Carolina, so that this chapter is not unconstitutionally vague when prosecution under it is predicated on violation of North Carolina regulation. U.S. v. Bryant, C.A.Tenn. 1983, 716 F.2d 1091, certiorari denied 104 S.Ct. 1006, 79 L.Ed.2d 238.

While this chapter was viewed by Congress as federal tool to aid states in enforcing their own laws concerning wildlife there is nothing in either this chapter or its legislative history which expresses clear intent of Congress that this chapter was meant to insulate state legislation from attack under the commerce clause, U.S.C.A. Const. Art. 1, § 8, cl. 3. U.S. v. Taylor, D.C.Me.1984, 585 F.Supp. 393, reversed on other grounds 752 F.2d 757.

2. Construction with state laws

This chapter does not incorporate all existing state laws regulating possession, transportation or sale of fish. U.S. v. Taylor, D.C. Me.1984, 585 F.Supp. 393, reversed on other grounds 752 F.2d 757.

3. Birds within section

Section 705 of this title was not confined to migratory birds. Bogle v. White, C.C.A.Tex. 1932, 61 F.2d 930, certiorari denied 53 S.Ct. 656, 289 U.S. 737, 77 L.Ed. 1484.

Act May 25, 1900, c. 553, § 4, 31 Stat. 188, incorporated in former section 393 of Title 18, was limited in its application to animals or birds killed in violation of the game laws, and animals or birds killed during the open season and "the export of which is not prohibited by law"; and an indictment would not lie for a failure to mark a package containing game killed during the open season but the export of which was prohibited by the law of the state where the same was killed. U.S. v. Thompson, D.C.N.D.1906, 147 F. 637. See, also, U.S. v. Spear, D.C.N. D.1906, 147 F. 640.

4. Indictment or information

Under a regulation made pursuant to former section 43 of Title 18, an information charging illegal purchases and sales should have negatived possession of a permit by defendant. In re Information Under Migratory Bird Treaty Act, D.C.Mont.1922, 281 F. 546.

Under the Game Law of Oklahoma Territory, Wilson's Rev. & Ann.St.1903, §§ 3069, 3078, which permitted the killing of quail between October 15th and February 1st following but prohibited the shipping of quail from the territory at any time, an indictment charging a violation of former section 392 of Title 18, by knowingly delivering to a carrier for transportation from the territory into another state the dead bodies of quail killed in the territory in violation of its laws, was sufficient where it averred that such quail were killed "with the intent and for the purpose of being shipped and transported out of the territory," and need not have alleged the months in which such quail were killed. Rupert v. U.S., Okl.1910, 181 F. 87, 104 C.C.A. 255.

It was essential to constitute an offense under former sections 391 to 395 of Title 18, that the prohibited game should either have been shipped or delivered to a carrier for

4. Supplementing the Federal Codes [§64]

United States Code Annotated and *United States Code Service* publish yearly pocket parts. The pocket parts revise the statutes that have undergone legislative change during the past year, whether through revision, deletion, or repeal. U.S.C.A. and U.S.C.S. also issue supplemental pamphlets during the year to further update the material. *United States Code* is supplemented by annual hardbound books, but they are not published in a timely fashion.

Yearly supplements are often sufficient for research purposes. Many laws do not take effect until the year following passage. But there will be times when you will need to check on a law that was recently enacted, one that has not yet been included in an annual supplement. How do you find it?

a. Slip laws—United States *Statutes at Large* [§65]

When a law is passed, it is published in its entirety and distributed to various libraries. These slip laws are bound into United States *Statutes at Large* volumes at the end of the congressional session.

b. *United States Code—Congressional and Administrative News* [§66]

Published by West, this prints the text of the new laws soon after they are enacted. Monthly paper supplements with cumulative indexes are first issued, and then they are bound at the end of the year. *United States Code—Congressional and Administrative News* also provides some legislative history of congressional acts.

c. *United States Code Service, Lawyers Edition,* advance sheets [§67]

This Matthew Bender & Company (a member of the LexisNexis Group) publication also prints the text of enacted laws and of regulations, proclamations, and executive orders, with a cumulative index. In addition, Matthew Bender & Company publishes *U.S.C.S. Cumulative Later Case and Statutory Service.* This edition contains later case annotations and references to legislative history.

d. Commerce Clearing House *Congressional Index* [§68]

If you need to know whether a certain bill has become law, this weekly updated index is a current print source. This reporter, published by CCH Incorporated, will tell you the status of the bill—that is, what committees have considered it, and any changes it has gone through.

e. LexisNexis and Westlaw [§69]

Both LexisNexis and Westlaw have online full text of pending federal and state bills. Westlaw's database is called "Bill Tracking"; LexisNexis's database is called "Legislative Histories." They have archival material as well.

f. Internet sources [§70]

Federal and state legislative information is available from various online sources; for example, for federal information, check http://thomas.loc.gov. (*See* chapter VIII.)

ILLUSTRATION OF A POCKET PART

(Edited version of a section from Supplement to West's U.S.C.A.)

CONSERVATION **16 § 3372** } **Title and Statute Number**

§ 3372. Prohibited acts

(a) Offense other than marking offenses

It is unlawful for any person—

(1) to import, export, transport, sell, receive, acquire, or purchase any fish or wildlife or plant taken, possessed, transported, or sold in violation of any law, treaty, or regulation of the United States or in violation of any Indian tribal law;

[See main volume for text of (2) and (3)]

(4) to attempt to commit any act described in paragraphs (1) through (4).

[See main volume for text of (b)]

(c) Sale and purchase of guiding and outfitting services and invalid licenses and permits

(1) Sale

It is deemed to be a sale of fish or wildlife in violation of this chapter for a person for money or other consideration to offer or provide—

(A) guiding, outfitting, or other services; or

(B) a hunting or fishing license or permit;

for the illegal taking, acquiring, receiving, transporting, or possessing of fish or wildlife.

Changes to Original Statute

(2) Purchase

It is deemed to be a purchase of fish or wildlife in violation of this chapter for a person to obtain for money or other consideration—

(A) guiding, outfitting, or other services; or

(B) a hunting or fishing license or permit;

for the illegal taking, acquiring, receiving, transporting, or possessing of fish or wildlife.

(d) False labeling offenses

It is unlawful for any person to make or submit any false record, account, or label for, or any false identification of, any fish, wildlife, or plant which has been, or is intended to be—

(1) imported, exported, transported, sold, purchased, or received from any foreign country; or

(2) transported in interstate or foreign commerce.

(As amended Pub.L. 100–653, Title I, § 101, Nov. 14, 1988, 102 Stat. 3825.)

Historical Information

HISTORICAL AND STATUTORY NOTES

References in Text

This chapter, referred to in subsecs. (c)(1), (2), was in the original "this Act", meaning Pub.L. 97–79, Nov. 16, 1981, 95 Stat. 1073, known as the Lacey Act Amendments of 1981, which enacted this chapter; amended section 1540 of this title and section 42 of Title 18, Crimes and Criminal Procedure; repealed sections 667e and 851 to 856 of this title and sections 43, 44, 3054, and 3112 of Title 18; and enacted provisions set out as notes under sections 1540 and 3371 of this title. For complete classification of this Act to the Code, see Short Title note set out under section 3371 of this title and Tables.

1988 Amendment

Subsec. (a)(1). Pub.L. 100–653, § 101(1), substituted "taken, possessed, transported, or sold" for "taken or possessed".

Subsec. (a)(4). Pub.L. 100–653, § 101(2), struck out par. (4), which made it unlawful for any person having imported, exported, transported, sold, purchased, or received any fish or wildlife or plant imported from any foreign country or transported in interstate or foreign commerce, to make or submit any false record, account, label, or identification thereof and redesignated former par. (5) as (4).

Subsec. (a)(5). Pub.L. 100–653, § 101(2), redesignated former par. (5) as (4).

Subsecs. (d), (c). Pub.L. 100–653, § 101(3), added subsecs. (c) and (d).

Legislative History

For legislative history and purpose of Pub.L. 100–653, see 1988 U.S. Code Cong. and Adm. News, p. 5366.

Law Review References

LAW REVIEW AND JOURNAL COMMENTARIES

Fragmenting the unitary executive: Congressional delegations of administrative authority outside the federal government. Harold J. Krent, 85 Nw.U.L.Rev. 62 (1990).

Noah's farce: Regulation and control of exotic fish and wildlife. 17 U.Puget Sound L.Rev. 191 (1993).

Annotations

NOTES OF DECISIONS

Collateral attacks 12
Construction with Magnuson Act 1a
Construction with Migratory Bird Treaty Act 1b
Construction with tribal laws 2a
Defenses 9
Foreign law 2b
Guides, purchase 14
Harassment 11
Instructions 13
Interstate commerce 7
Necessity of taking 10
Probable cause 8
Purpose ½
Weight and sufficiency of evidence 6

Statute prohibiting any party from importing fish or wildlife into country in violation of any "foreign law" was not void for vagueness, for failing to expressly state that term "foreign law" included regulations as well as statutes. U.S. v. 594,464 Pounds of Salmon, More or Less, W.D.Wash.1987, 687 F.Supp. 525, affirmed 871 F.2d 824.

1a. Construction with Magnuson Act

Prosecution under Lacey Act for allegedly taking fish in violation of Bahamian Fisheries Resources Act, which prohibits foreign fishing without permit in zone extending 200 nautical miles, was not barred by Magnuson Fishery Conservation and Management Act section,

g. Check with your Congressmember [§71]

Often you can obtain copies of a bill from your representative or from the representative who sponsored the legislation. Contact information for the House of Representatives is available at http://www.house.gov, and for the Senate at http://www.senate.gov.

h. United States *Statutes at Large* [§72]

Statutes at Large is not a source for advance copies of bills, but when you have to refer to the actual text of a law no longer in effect or to an earlier edition of a now revised or amended act, these bound volumes are a convenient source. (You could also check the bound volumes of *United States Code—Congressional and Administrative News.*) If you need to find a law that has not been codified—such as, for example, a private law—you will find it in *Statutes at Large. Statutes at Large* publishes all laws in chronological order. Parallel tables of citations between the codes and *Statutes at Large* are published in the annotated codes.

5. Federal Rules and Court Guidelines [§73]

The rules you must follow to bring or defend a federal action can be found in both U.S.C.A. and U.S.C.S. The rules of civil procedure and appellate procedure are in the volumes of title 28 of U.S.C.A. The rules of criminal procedure are in U.S.C.A.'s title 18. U.S.C.S. publishes the rules in its Court Rules volumes at the end of its series. *Federal Local Court Rules* (West) publishes current local court rules of the individual courts of appeal and district courts. *Federal Court Guidelines* (Aspen Publishers, a division of Wolters Kluwer Law & Business, together with the Litigation Section of the American Bar Association) publishes the rules of practice procedures, and policies of district court judges, as well as biographical and contact information for the judges. LexisNexis, Westlaw, and other Internet sources also publish the federal rules online.

6. Researching the Federal Codes [§74]

Researching the annotated codes is similar to researching any legal sourcebook. There is a descriptive word index, the preferred entry into the texts, and a table of contents for people who are familiar with the material and need only check topic headings.

a. Online method [§75]

You can search codes in full text through LexisNexis, Westlaw, and other Internet sources (*see* chapter VIII). Since finding the appropriate statutes online can be difficult without knowing the key search terms, it is often more efficient to begin your search by looking through a hard-copy index where descriptive words overlap and other terms are suggested (*see* below).

b. Index method [§76]

Both U.S.C.A. and U.S.C.S. have multivolumed indexes. They are easy to use, although not always complete. As with any index, there is always the possibility that the descriptive words you have chosen may not be of any help (because the editors did not think of them) or the words may lead you to some legislation but not to the statute most directly on point. Another word or term is needed for that, so check around a bit. Think of a number of different entry words into the material before settling on a statute. The most obvious word may not always lead you to the best statute.

For example, if your problem concerns the right to ride a bicycle on the sidewalk, look up specific words like bicycle, but also check more general terms like vehicles or motor vehicles. If your state has defined a bicycle as a motor vehicle, the laws regulating motor vehicles will apply and just looking up bicycles may be too limiting. Being imaginative will help you to be thorough. Our discussion of the index method of search in chapter X may help you design the key words (people, subject, type of legal action) you need to locate the proper statute.

c. Topic method [§77]

If you know specifically under which subject your problem falls, you can turn directly to the specific chapter of the code dealing with it. Look up the topic in the table of contents and search through the topical outline for precise references to your subject. For example, if your problem concerns kidnappings—a criminal law problem—you could turn to the Penal Code and eye the topical contents for kidnappings.

Most people prefer the index method to the topic method. Using the topic method may limit your search, causing you to overlook other related areas and statutes.

d. Popular name method [§78]

If you are looking for a specific piece of legislation, for example the Federal Equal Credit Opportunity Act, you can find it in the codes. Just check the general index or look for a separate table or index in the index volume. You can also obtain the statutory citation to the act from *Shepard's Acts and Cases by Popular Names*, or in the Federal and State Table of Acts by Popular Names or Short Titles in the state statute editions of Shepard's Citations. (*See* chapter VII.)

e. Cross-references [§79]

Following the recitation of the statute in the codes is a cross-reference section. The cross-references are to related statutes and constitutional provisions. You may want to check these other references before you satisfy yourself that you have found the most appropriate statute.

7. State Codes [§80]

Each state has its own code—its own set of statutes. The format differs in each state. Many states issue multivolume sets similar to *United States Code Annotated*. (West publishes the codes of approximately 25 states in a style similar to U.S.C.A., and LexisNexis Group issues the codes of approximately 35 states and territories.)

Several states have more than one set. For example, California has one published by West, and one by LexisNexis Group, known as *Deering's*.

Each state also has a set of statutes chronologically arranged. These volumes are known as session laws and are similar to the United States *Statutes at Large*. Parallel tables between the state's code and session laws are always available in both sets.

Yearly supplements are published to most state codes. About half the states have commercially published legislative and session law advance sheets for current legislation. A few states publish their own slip laws. Check your state legislature's website or call your local state house or senate representative for information on statute revisions and new legislation. Also, check with your local law library.

8. Researching the State Codes [§81]

The organization of state codes differs in each state. Some have broad indexes similar to those of U.S.C.A. and U.S.C.S.; others have limited indexes. A few independent companies publish indexes not connected with any specific set of codes. *LARMAC* (published by Matthew Bender & Company, a member of the LexisNexis Group) in California is an example of a one-volume index to state annotated codes, and it is easier to use than either West's or *Deering's* code edition indexes.

States deal with similar subjects differently; a key word in one index will lead you nowhere in another. In researching state codes, be extremely cautious. Be certain you have checked all the possibilities and thought of all the key words. Do not rely solely on the first seemingly appropriate statute you find.

State codes are also available, in varying formats, through state legislatures' websites. Links for each state are available at http://thomas.loc.gov.

9. Municipal Ordinances [§82]

Ordinances are laws passed by cities. The legislative body is usually a city council or board of supervisors. Ordinances are codified but unlike the codes are usually not annotated. For cases interpreting an ordinance, you need to check a state digest, the special ordinance section in Shepard's State Citations, or West's *Ordinance Law Annotations*, or try conducting a search using Internet sources (*see* chapter VIII).

A city charter is similar to a constitution (*see infra*, §86)—it sets out the general powers of the city. It is published in the municipal code.

10. Both Federal and State Law May Apply to Your Problem [§83]

Where neither the federal government nor a state has exclusive jurisdiction in an area, both governments may enact laws affecting the same subject. For example, Minnesota and the United States each have an Environmental Policy Act. The acts may overlap in part, but there will be differences. The enforcement powers provided by one act may be stronger than those provided by the other. If when doing research you only refer to one of the statutes, your work will be incomplete and likely misleading, so be careful and take the time to check through the codes of both jurisdictions. (For guidelines on whether the area of law is exclusively state or federal, *see* chapter II.)

11. Citing a Statute

a. Federal statutes [§84]

The Fair Housing Act of the Civil Rights Act of 1968 would be cited as 42 U.S.C. §3601 in the official code. In other words, the Act can be found in title 42 of the *United States Code* at section 3601. If you are using the annotated codes (*United States Code Annotated* or *United States Code Service*), you can cite this statute as 42 U.S.C.A. §3601 or 42 U.S.C.S. §3601. Depending on the type of document in which you are citing the statute, it may be appropriate to add a parenthetical after the code section to indicate the source and year of the reporter; for example, a citation to section 3601 in the 2006 edition of U.S.C.A. would be: 42 U.S.C.A. §3601 (West 2006).

While statutes for the most part are cited to the United States Code editions, occasionally you will see a citation to the *Statutes at Large*. This happens if the statute has recently appeared and has not yet been codified. Thus, 82 Stat. 81 is the citation to the Fair Housing Act as it appears in volume 82 of the *Statutes at Large* at page 81.

You may also see Pub. L. No. 90-284. This citation is to the Act's earliest appearance as a slip law. It is the 284th act to become law in the Ninetieth Congress.

b. State statutes [§85]

State statutes are generally cited in the same manner as federal statutes, depending upon how the code is laid out. In California, for example, a statute in the Civil Code would be cited as Cal. Civ. Code §1942.5. In a document where the full source citation is required, add the text in which the statute appears and the copyright date. Thus, for example, if West's main volume is cited, it would be Cal. Civ. Code §1942.5 (West 1985), or (West Supp. 2010) if the current pocket part is cited. If the citation is to text in both the main volume and the pocket part, the parenthetical should include reference to both, for example, (West 1985 & Supp. 2010).

The session law would be cited as 1970 Cal. Stat. ch. 1280 §5 p. 2316.

For a more detailed description of the citation of statutes and for the proper abbreviations and citations for many states, *see* the *ALWD Citation Manual* or the Bluebook, available at any law library.

C. Constitutions

1. In General [§86]

A constitution sets out the general powers of government and the basic rights and duties of the people. Statutes are enacted pursuant to the framework set out in the constitution. Any federal act that conflicts with the United States Constitution and any state act that conflicts with the state constitution or the United States Constitution is invalid or "unconstitutional." The United States Supreme Court is the final arbiter on matters concerning the United States Constitution; the highest court in each state is the final arbiter on state constitutional interpretation.

Since constitutions write of broad matters in general terms, most of your everyday research will not involve constitutional provisions. But you should always keep the possibility in mind, since a constitution takes precedence over a statute. If, for example, you were interested in the federal law on jury trials in criminal cases, you would check both the federal statutes and the Sixth Amendment to the United States Constitution from which the right originated, as well as the accompanying annotations.

2. Researching the Federal Constitution

a. *United States Code Annotated* and *United States Code Service* [§87]

Both U.S.C.A. and U.S.C.S. have separate indexes to the United States Constitution. The Constitution itself is set off in separate volumes in these codes. Following each provision are annotations of court interpretations, just as you find with the statutes. Many, if not most, of the decisions are from the United States Supreme Court. These are important—be sure to check them.

b. Digests [§88]

The *United States Supreme Court Digest* (West) and the *United States Supreme Court Digest, Lawyers' Edition* (the LexisNexis Group), as well as the *Modern Federal Practice Digest*, the *Federal Practice Digest 2d*, the *Federal Practice Digest 3d*, and the *Federal Practice Digest 4th* (all from West) are helpful in locating cases interpreting federal constitutional provisions. (Digests are covered in chapter V.)

3. Researching State Constitutions [§89]

State constitutions may be found in their respective state code editions, although some editions also publish the constitution in a separate unit. The constitutions are usually separately indexed. Most state constitutions are annotated, providing an important source for state high court decisions interpreting the provisions. State or regional digests, local law reviews, and state encyclopedias are also helpful sources for researching the constitution. State constitutions are also made available through state legislatures' websites (*see supra*, §81).

D. Legislative Intent—Legislative History

1. In General [§90]

Since words are an imperfect medium, and people who draft legislation do not always foresee all the problems the legislation as written might raise, it is not uncommon to find people disagreeing on the interpretation of a statute. For example, assume Congress had passed a law saying that gasoline can contain no more than 0.5 of a gram of lead in each gallon. An oil company executive might interpret this to mean that the level of lead can be as high as 0.549 grams per gallon, for when rounded off to the nearest tenth, it is still 0.5. A consumer advocate concerned with the health of children will, however, argue that the level may not be higher than 0.500. If a case concerning this issue arose in a court, the judge would have to decide what Congress actually had intended when it adopted the law. The judge might draw upon the "plain meaning rule" and interpret 0.5 as it is generally understood. But more likely she would research the legislative history of the Act. The types of questions the judge will want answered will be similar to the following:

- When the bill was first introduced in the House or Senate, how did it read?
- Did the sponsor of the legislation make any comments on the choice of one term of measurement or another?
- When the bill was sent to a House or Senate committee for consideration, did the committee's report on the bill discuss the use of particular terms of measurement?
- Were any committee hearings held on the bill? Did the experts who testified at the hearings comment on this point?
- What revisions, amendments, or deletions did the bill go through? Did any affect this particular wording?
- What was said by the legislators on the floor of either chamber when the bill was discussed?
- Did a joint conference committee of House and Senate members change the wording?
- When he signed the bill, did the President comment on the purpose of the bill as he understood it?

In determining congressional intent, the judge will give more weight to some of these legislative sources than to others. The changes, revisions, amendments, and deletions a bill goes through, whether made by the committees reviewing it or voted upon on the floor of the House or Senate, are helpful because they show the progression of legislative thought on the bill. Committee reports that explain the purpose of the bill and that are issued after the committee has seriously researched and considered the bill are very important sources. Comments made by Congressmembers when the bill is discussed on the floor of the chamber are not as useful. Since each legislator has his own idea of what the bill should do, one cannot really gauge what the entire Congress intended by these individual comments.

Determining legislative intent is often like catching dandelion seeds floating in the wind. It is not possible to assess one rounded voice of agreement from 100 senators and 435 representatives. But by checking the various congressional sources, the researcher gains important insights into the concerns of the legislators as they considered the bill at its several stages and how they compromised and resolved these concerns. These insights are what make up legislative intent, and they are culled from researching the legislative history of the Act.

2. Sources of Federal Legislative History [§91]

The Internet is a good place to start when looking for recent bills, reports, and other legislative documents helpful in finding the legislative intent and history of an Act. If you are unable to find the information online, you should check an index. Unlike the indexes for statutes, digests, treatises, and encyclopedias, which sit right alongside the material, indexes for legislative history may be on microfilm or microfiche and are kept separately from the source materials. The index will give you a bill's number, which stays the same throughout the legislative session. With that number you can follow a bill and its revised versions through committee reports, committee hearings, chamber votes, and House-Senate conference committee compromises to determine the sources you will need to inspect.

a. Commerce Clearing House *Congressional Index* [§92]

This looseleaf service indexes all bills introduced in the House and Senate. It also cross-references companion bills (similar or identical bills introduced in the other house at the same time to speed up congressional consideration). The status of each bill (that is, how far it has progressed) is indexed in the Status Table and in the Current Status Table. Because CCH updates its material weekly, it provides the most up-to-date information on current bills.

b. *Congressional Information Service* ("CIS") [§93]

This multivolume service (by ProQuest) is more than an index. It includes an index, bibliographic data (*e.g.*, Congress and session, title of publication, dates of hearings), a description of the particular document or publication's subject matter and purpose, and an abstract of the contents (*e.g.*, articles, testimony) with reference to pages. These abstracts are excellent in providing information on the various source materials available. Since 1984, CIS has published separate volumes with compiled legislative histories. CIS produces the actual documents from 1970 to the present on microfiche.

The index volume to CIS contains a detailed subject and name index as well as indexes to bills, committee reports, hearings, and other documents. It is updated monthly, with a three-month cumulative index issued each quarter. An annual cumulative index and cumulative abstract volume is also published, with a section containing the legislative histories of public laws passed during the year. CIS also publishes four-year cumulations of the index.

CIS makes all of its indexes, documents, etc., available online through its subscription reference information service, *ProQuest Congressional,* located at http://cisupa.proquest.com.

c. ***Daily Report for Executives* [§94]**

This looseleaf service published by BNA provides coverage of legislative developments that are of interest to the business community. It provides texts of important business-related bills and committee reports. The report is also available on LexisNexis and Westlaw.

d. ***United States Code—Congressional and Administrative News* [§95]**

This text is both a source of recently enacted laws and regulations and an index to legislative histories. It does, however, publish selected House and Senate committee reports and a table of laws actually passed. It is updated monthly with a cumulative index and cross-reference table. Bound volumes are issued each year.

e. ***Congressional Record* [§96]**

A daily record of congressional activity, especially speeches and debates made by the legislators on the floor of the chambers or for insert into the record, is included in the *Congressional Record.* A cumulative bound index is published twice a month. The History of Bills Enacted Into Law is a tabular report included in the annual bound volume of the *Congressional Record.* Note that pagination in the unbound daily digests is different from that in the bound volumes. The *Congressional Record* is also available on LexisNexis and Westlaw, and recent years are available for free at http://thomas.loc.gov and http://www.gpo.gov/fdsys.

f. ***Sources of Compiled Legislative Histories* [§97]**

Occasionally, a publisher such as the Government Printing Office or a commercial publisher, or a private group such as a labor union or women's group, or even a large law firm may compile a legislative history on a major piece of legislation. (Many of these are often incomplete.) If you are researching a major piece of legislation, consult *Sources of Compiled Legislative Histories,* available in HeinOnline's United States Supreme Court Library (*see infra*, §207).

3. Tracking Down the Materials [§98]

Once you have found the bill number and have checked the status tables to determine the bill's progression, you will need to locate the actual source materials (unless you decide to depend upon Congressional Information Service abstracts). The source materials will include:

(i) Each revised version of the bill;

(ii) House/Senate committee reports;

(iii) House/Senate committee hearings;

(iv) Speeches and comments made on the floor of the House/Senate;

(v) House/Senate conference committee reports; and

(vi) Other House/Senate documents and special reports and publications.

Most of these materials are available for recent bills on the Library of Congress's THOMAS website at http://thomas.loc.gov. Additionally, most law libraries store many of these materials. Since each library has its own system of cataloging, you will need to check with the librarian. Many major public libraries also subscribe to federal legislative materials.

Congressional Information Service will provide copies of all materials covered in the CIS index to its subscribers through its microfiche library. Your library may already have copies through this service, or you could request that the library order them from CIS.

4. Sources of State Legislative History [§99]

Most states do not publish anything more than the bills themselves. Your best chance of getting some history of the bill is to check that state legislature's website. A list with each state's website is available on http://thomas.loc.gov. Also, you can find out who sponsored the legislation—your local representative should know—and see if the sponsoring legislator can provide copies of the original bill, revised bills, and any other documents.

Other sources you should check include state law revision commissions, judicial councils, legislative counsels, senate and assembly journals, and the Democratic and Republican caucuses.

Sometimes a new law will be preceded in the supplement by the legislative counsel's comment on what the provision intends to accomplish. Your librarian will know whether there is an organization or company in the state providing legislative information.

E. Treaties

1. Sources of Information [§100]

Treaties and international agreements from 1789 to 1950 can be found in the *Statutes at Large*. For those from 1950 to the present, check *United States Treaties and Other International Agreements*, the *World Treaty Index*, and the *Multilateral Treaties: Index and Current Status*.

The most frequently used index is *Treaties in Force*. Published by the Department of State, it lists the treaties and international agreements still in force by subject and country. *Treaties in Force* is available through the State Department's website at http://www.state.gov.

The text of recent treaties can be accessed through http://thomas.loc.gov and is made available by the Government Printing Office.

For other publications, indexes, and secondary sources interpreting treaties, check the library catalog.

Chapter Five: Secondary Sources

CONTENTS

A. In General

1. Introduction [§101]

If you do not find a statute, or if you would rather begin with some general information on the subject to help you conceptualize the problem, turn to a secondary legal source. These sources not only give you an understanding of the law, but also guide you to cases, statutes, and regulations in the area.

Depending upon what you are looking for, one particular source may be better than another. A treatise on a specific area of state or federal law is an excellent source. A good state encyclopedia may also be helpful. For new and developing areas, law reviews and law journals best survey the field. Practice and procedure books and form books help people draft documents and prepare for legal proceedings. Digests provide lists of cases dealing, whether in holding or dicta, with a particular point of law. Attorney general opinions and the "Restatements" are further expert commentary.

This chapter discusses which source to use and when to use it. These texts are a beginning; they can provide you with a fine understanding of the problems and the law involved in your situation. But unless you are looking only for some general (although expert) discussion of the law, you will still need to follow up by checking into the appropriate cases, statutes, and regulations—the primary sources of the law.

B. Specific Secondary Sources

1. Treatises [§102]

Treatises offer a thorough, in-depth analysis of one area of the law. The important cases and authorities are cited and discussed with usually expert commentary. Whether you want just a quick summary of a point of law or a detailed survey, a treatise—especially if limited to the law of your state—is an excellent source.

Treatises may be one volume, but most often they are multivolumed. They may review a broad tract of law like contracts or torts, or just one aspect of the law like landlord-tenant issues, insurance law, or medical malpractice. They may be written to cover the entire country or just one state. A local treatise will naturally be more precise and complete, being fitted to your state's law. Examples of the various kinds of treatises are included in the Appendix. Also be sure to check the library catalog under the subject you are researching.

a. Updating treatises [§103]

Most treatises are updated with supplements. When supplements are provided, they usually come at regular intervals. Be certain to examine the cases, statutes, and regulations cited as authority in the text; the law may have changed.

b. Hornbooks [§104]

Hornbooks are treatises condensed into one volume. They are generally prepared for law students.

c. Gilbert Law Summaries [§105]

The Gilbert Law Summaries, designed as study aids for law students, provide a concise discussion of a particular area of law. There are Gilbert summaries for most standard courses in law school. Gilbert summaries are arranged in an outline format. (For a complete listing of available Gilbert Law Summaries, check http://www.gilbertlaw.com.)

2. Legal Encyclopedias [§106]

If you cannot find a treatise in your subject area, you may want to turn to an encyclopedia. A legal encyclopedia offers a general outline of the law, whereas a treatise covers one area in detail.

A legal encyclopedia should never be used as the final arbiter of the law (although courts will sometimes cite it). It provides a general introduction to the material, which you can then use to follow up in the appropriate primary authorities: the cases, statutes, and regulations. Search through the indexes to encyclopedias just as you would search through any legal secondary sourcebook.

There are two encyclopedias of American law and about 15 state encyclopedias. If there is one in your state, you would be wise to use it. A national encyclopedia is often too general and is not designed to provide complete citations to authorities in any one particular state. It does contain federal law, but a search through the federal statutes or looseleaf materials would be far more efficient.

a. *Corpus Juris Secundum* ("C.J.S.") [§107]

West publishes this encyclopedia, usually referred to by its initials—C.J.S. It attempts to state the entire body of American law, state and federal. There is a multivolume general index, and each separate volume also has an index. A list defining words and phrases is also included. West issues an annual cumulative pocket supplement. Cross-references are given from C.J.S. to topic and key numbers in West digests. (*See* Addenda for sample pages.)

b. *American Jurisprudence* ("Am. Jur.") *2d* [§108]

Published by West, Am. Jur. 2d is very similar to C.J.S., but in addition to keying to digests, it also keys to *American Law Reports* ("A.L.R."). It too has a multivolume index. The *Am. Jur. 2d New Topic Service Binder* updates the set with a looseleaf service covering new topics and changes. There are also annual pocket supplements. (*See* Addenda for sample pages.)

c. State encyclopedias [§109]

A list of state encyclopedias is included in the Appendix. Since they are published by West or LexisNexis Group, they follow the same general arrangements as the American law texts. They all have yearly supplements.

d. *Martindale-Hubbell Law Digest* [§110]

Part of the LexisNexis Group, Martindale-Hubbell publishes the United States law digest volumes of this directory. The *Digest* provides a summary of the law in each state. It may be a useful source for quick reference into an unfamiliar area, but like any other secondary text, it should not be relied upon exclusively. Use it to lead you to primary sources. The *Digest* also includes summaries (in English) of the laws of 80 countries. The complete *Digest* is available online at http://www.martindale.com.

3. *American Law Reports* ("A.L.R.") [§111]

Published by West, and currently in its sixth series, A.L.R. is different from the usual encyclopedia. It not only provides editorial discussion on the topic of law, but also reports leading cases and summarizes other important cases in the area and adds cross-references to the West Key Number System.

The *Index to Annotations* includes a Table of Laws, Rules and Regulations, and an Annotation History Table.

4. Law Reviews and Periodicals [§112]

If your problem concerns a new area of the law or one going through important change, you may have trouble finding a secondary source that thoroughly examines it. Encyclopedias and treatises take a while to catch up, and digests may bury an important case under an old established topic. For current information, legal periodicals are the place to turn. Law reviews, law journals, and other legal periodicals keep abreast of the most recent developments of the law. They provide background and insight into the problem, along with recent cases, statutes, and other primary authority.

Law reviews and journals are largely published by law schools. The articles and notes are written by professors, attorneys, and students. Private companies and associations may also publish legal journals and periodicals (*e.g.,* some of the American Bar Association sections publish their own topical journals, such as *The Tax Lawyer,* published by the ABA Section of Taxation). Recent articles from many law reviews and journals are available in Westlaw and LexisNexis, making it easier to find articles by using search terms in these services.

a. *LegalTrac, Legal Resource Index* and *Current Law Index* [§113]

Gale (a publishing arm of Cenage Learning) publishes *LegalTrac* and the *Legal Resource Index*. These are index publications with broad coverage, covering articles from legal magazines, legal newspapers, government documents, bar association and specialty journals, as well as law reviews and journals back to 1980.

The *Current Law Index,* published monthly by Gale, is the paper edition of the *Legal Resource Index*. The *Legal Resource Index* is available on LexisNexis and Westlaw. *LegalTrac* (part of Gale's *InfoTrac* database system) is available online by subscription, but many law schools subscribe to the service. Check your school library's website.

b. *Index to Legal Periodicals* [§114]

This separately published index, produced by The H.W. Wilson Company, will lead you into most of the legal periodicals from 1981 to present, and law books published from 1993 to present.

The print version, called the *Index to Legal Periodicals & Books,* is published with monthly index advance sheets and an annual cumulative edition. The *Index to Legal Periodicals Full Text* is available online to subscribers at http://hwwilsonweb.com and on LexisNexis and Westlaw.

c. Other indexes [§115]

You may wish to check the *Current Index to Legal Periodicals*, a subscription service published in 50 weekly print issues by the University of Washington Law Library with the most recent eight weeks available on Westlaw. You might also try the *Index to Periodical Articles Related to Law* (published by Glanville Publishers, Inc.), available through HeinOnline (*see infra*, §207).

5. Sources of Recent Scholarship [§116]

The Internet has many alternative sources of recent scholarship and commentary to aid in your research. However, the ease of Internet publishing is a double-edged sword for the researcher—information is updated more frequently and is often free, but it might not be vetted in the same manner as traditional publications. Still, several quality resources exist to help you begin your research.

a. Social Science Research Network ("SSRN") [§117]

SSRN (http://www.ssrn.com) provides some of the most current research and scholarship that may be available on a particular topic, for free. SSRN's Legal Scholarship Network allows users to upload their legal research, working papers, and law review articles to the SSRN website so they can be shared with other scholars, lawyers, and law students.

b. Online publications [§118]

You should also be aware that some law journals (*see supra*, §112) are published only online. For instance, the Berkeley Electronic Press (http://www.bepress.com) not only hosts articles and working papers like SSRN, but it also publishes electronic law journals on a variety of topics, which can be purchased by subscription.

c. Legal blogs [§119]

Legal blogs may provide the most up-to-date legal commentary available. Thousands of law blogs (often referred to as "blawgs") are online, with many focusing on a specific area of the law or on practice in a particular jurisdiction. They may be produced by law professors or practitioners and can be hosted by a law school or firm, but note that not all are written by experts. The best use of a law blog is to check for recent developments in the field you are researching. To find one, try the *ABA Journal* Blawg Directory at http://www.abajournal.com/blawgs.

6. Daily Law Journals [§120]

Legal newspapers, usually known as daily law journals, are published in major cities. They include the local court docket and calendar for state and federal trials. These journals are also often a very fine source for important federal, state, and local court decisions. Several of these newspapers (like the *Los Angeles Daily Journal*) publish supplements of the recent state and often federal appellate cases.

7. Digests [§121]

There is no discussion of the law in digests. Digests are simply collections of principles of law derived from cases. If all you are looking for is a case to back up your point of law, you may want to use a digest. For a general understanding of the law, use a treatise or encyclopedia; a digest will not help you much.

All digests have descriptive word indexes. You can search through these indexes in the same way you would search through any other legal sourcebook index. You can also locate a digest topic through West's Key Number System.

No doubt you have noticed that above every headnote in a West Group reporter is an illustrated key sandwiched between a topic name and number. It would appear something like this:

> **Libel and Slander** 🔑 48(1)
> There is a qualified privilege of fair
> comment and criticism . . .

If you look up this topic and key number in any West digest (most of the digests are published by West), you will find a column of paragraph notes, each note discussing similar principles of law on qualified privilege of comment and criticism. In designing the digests, the editors have taken all the headnotes to cases reported in the various West reporters and rearranged them under topics and subtopics in the digests. All the paragraph notes you see in a digest are nothing more than the headnotes you see when you read a case in a West reporter.

When you examine the principles of law indexed in the digest, be sure to look up the case from which it is taken. You need to know whether the principle of law is a holding or dicta. (Remember that a holding is the point of law on which the case is decided; dicta are other statements of law made by the court throughout its opinion.) If it is dicta (the most likely possibility since West headnotes are in large part dicta), the case may not be much support to you.

There are state digests (almost every state has one), four regional digests, federal digests, Supreme Court digests, and an American digest. Because of its immense volume of cases, the *American Digest* is published in noncumulative 10-year editions (Decennials) and is supplemented with a *General Digest* to cover the years from the last Decennial to the present. A list of digests is included in the Appendix. Supplements are usually issued every six weeks.

Each digest has a Table of Cases. Most also have a Defendant-Plaintiff Table which indexes cases by the defendant's name. (*See* the Addenda for sample pages.)

8. Looseleaf Materials [§122]

Looseleaf materials are a wonderful source for information in certain areas of the law. They bring together statutes, regulations, cases, and commentary in a well-organized text. Most of the materials cover federal law, but state looseleaf materials, covering a number of subjects, are also collected and arranged in text. (*See* chapter VI for a survey of this material.)

9. Continuing Legal Education Materials [§123]

Most states have programs and/or publications sponsored by the state bar, an institute of continuing legal education, or a law school. These materials, particularly on local law and practice, are especially useful. For example, Continuing Education of the Bar ("CEB") in California (http://ceb.com) is highly respected for its courses and books. Practising Law Institute ("PLI") holds classes and provides materials throughout the country (for a list of PLI programs and materials, check the PLI website at http://www.pli.edu). For more resources, you may want to check the websites of ALI-ABA (a program from the American Law Institute and the American Bar Association) at http://www.ali-aba.org and the Association for Continuing Legal Education at http://www.aclea.org. Also contact your state bar (many state bar associations have websites; for links to several, check online at http://www.americanbar.org) to see whether an institute of continuing legal education or something of similar name exists in your area.

10. Practice and Procedure Books [§124]

Sometimes you need to know procedural law. For example, how do you take your case to court? What rules of court must you follow? What papers do you file when? The federal government and the states have codes of civil and criminal procedure, setting out the rules you must follow to bring or defend an action. Practice and procedure books explain the process. They usually include the text of the statute, and follow it up with an explanation of the law (similar to the discussion you find in a treatise or encyclopedia). Annotations to cases and secondary sources are often included.

See the Appendix for examples of federal practice and procedure books. State bars and private companies often publish these kinds of books for local use. CEB in California is an excellent resource (*see* http://ceb.com). PLI publishes useful material for many subject areas such as intellectual property, real estate, and tax law (*see* http://www.pli.edu).

11. Form Books [§125]

Form books supplement practice and procedure books. They include samples of the various documents you may need to file in court with references to the appropriate procedural statutes and rules. Form books that publish examples of legal forms not filed in court, such as leases, wills, and contracts, are also available. There are form books for federal and state documents. (*See* the Appendix for examples.) CEB in California and other publishers in other states provide excellent examples of forms used in the local courts.

12. Attorney General Opinions [§126]

The attorneys general of the United States and the states write opinions interpreting statutes and giving other legal analysis. Usually, a state official or a legislator has requested the opinion. The opinions are only persuasive, but courts often follow them. You can find references to attorney general opinions in the annotations to the codes. Most of the states and the federal government publish the opinions. Both LexisNexis and Westlaw have databases with federal and state attorney general opinions. Also, for the United States Attorney General opinions and comments check the Department of Justice website (http://www.justice.gov).

13. Restatements [§127]

Expert lawyers and law professors have gotten together to set a standard on what the law is or should be in a particular field. Courts confronted by a problem in a certain area can turn to these "Restatements" of the law for expert opinion, since the Restatements attempt to codify case law in areas where common law, rather than statutory law, predominates. Restatements are only persuasive authority, but they are respected and followed by many courts. Comments by the authors and annotations to cases and other secondary authority are included with each proposed rule of law.

Restatements are published by the American Law Institute ("ALI"). They are not available in every field—you need to check a library's catalog or the ALI website (http://www.ali.org) for your subject. Another ALI publication, *Case Citations to the Restatement of the Law* (formerly *Restatement in the Courts*), indicates where state courts have adopted portions of the Restatements as the substantive law of the state. Restatements are available on LexisNexis and Westlaw.

14. Uniform State Laws [§128]

The National Conference of Commissioners on Uniform State Laws ("NCCUSL," also known as the Uniform Law Commission) promotes uniform legislation to reduce the problems that arise when each state has its own distinct statutory law. The ALI publishes model statutes as well. In some areas, these efforts have been highly successful (*e.g.*, every state has adopted the Uniform Commercial Code). However, sometimes only a few states may adopt a proposed uniform law.

The NCCUSL website (http://www.nccusl.org) is an excellent source for the text of uniform laws, status on the NCCUSL's drafting projects, and information on the states that have adopted the uniform laws. Additionally, West began publishing an annotated set of uniform laws in 1968. It is called *Uniform Laws Annotated.* It includes lists of the states that have adopted particular laws and notes any changes in the model legislation made by the adopting states. The text of uniform acts is also available on LexisNexis and Westlaw. Remember, ***a uniform law is not in effect until it has actually been adopted by the legislature*** of a particular state.

Chapter Six: Administrative Agencies—Looseleaf Materials

CONTENTS

A. Introduction

1. In General [§129]

Law is not only made by the legislative, judicial, and executive branches of government; administrative agencies are playing an increasingly large role. Your life is far more directly affected by federal, state, and local agencies than by the three main branches of government. The food you eat, the transportation you take, the apartment you rent, the house you build, the shop you own, the wages you earn, the utilities you use, the professional licenses you hold, the schools you attend, the bills you pay, the radio and television you listen to and watch, the Internet you log on to, and the compensation you receive when injured or unemployed are all regulated by agencies. Legislation may have empowered these agencies, but it is not the legislators with whom you deal—it is the agencies established by them.

It makes no difference what the agency calls itself—Federal Communications Commission, National Labor Relations Board, Internal Revenue Service, Occupational Safety and Health Administration, Environmental Protection Agency, Office of Consumer Affairs, Division of Public Safety, Metropolitan Transit Authority—federal, state, or local, they are all agencies.

2. Agency Powers [§130]

An administrative agency owes its existence to the legislation that either creates it or provides for the executive to establish it. (Occasionally, a state agency may derive its powers from the state constitution. Such an agency is often more powerful than one created by the legislature. An example is the Public Utilities Commission in California, which regulates not only all the utilities but also public transportation in the state.) The agency is delegated certain powers by the legislature. Not every agency has the same powers, but all do one or more of the following: issue orders, license, draft rules and regulations, hear and decide disputes (adjudication), negotiate settlements, investigate for possible violations of law, and prosecute the violators. Agency actions and decisions are usually reviewable in court (judicial review).

a. Formal functions [§131]

Agency action is largely informal. Rulemaking and adjudication are the two main formal functions of administrative agencies. Formal actions are publicly recorded.

B. Agency Action

1. Regulations [§132]

Agencies draft regulations to carry out the intent of the legislation. As experts in the area, the agency personnel can best establish the procedure to be followed by parties affected by the statute and can be on the alert for violations. Regulations have the full force of law. Violating a regulation is as much a breaking of the law as is violating a statute.

Often before a regulation is issued, especially when the regulation is of important public interest, the agency will hold hearings on the proposed regulation. Interested groups and persons will attend to voice their opinions and concerns. The proposed regulation may then be revised—or not put into effect at all—as a result of the hearing.

2. Adjudication [§133]

Agencies also decide disputes. For example, if you are denied unemployment insurance, you can appeal to an administrative law judge. This person is hired by the agency, but is paid to be impartial. In most states, if you lose you can take your case to the State Unemployment Insurance Board. Only after the Board has heard and ruled on your claim can you file in court. Since many people win at the administrative level, the overburdened court can be spared even further litigation. Besides, the agency is more likely to know the law and mechanics of your problem than a court which hears hundreds of different types of cases.

Adjudicative hearings in administrative agencies are less formal than in court. Lawyers are not always necessary, and in certain areas where lawyers can make no money because the client is poor—as in welfare and unemployment insurance cases—you rarely see them. People here handle cases themselves, or a paralegal or legal assistant who knows the field (and is often paid by legal aid) may represent them. You need not be a lawyer to argue before many administrative agencies.

The rules of evidence are usually relaxed in these hearings. Hearsay (evidence not from the personal knowledge of the witness but from what he has heard another say) is often admissible. There are no jury trials.

Most agencies have two levels of appeal, although several have three. In most instances you must "exhaust your administrative remedies"—that is, maneuver through the various levels of appeal—before you can take your case to court. Judicial review of an administrative case is usually limited to questions of law. The facts are not retried. (Occasionally, when a constitutional or fundamental right is involved, a court will exercise the power of "independent judgment" and conduct its own review of the evidence.) In reviewing the administrative decision, the judge may consider such questions as: Was there substantial evidence to support the administrative law judge's findings, or did the judge abuse her discretion?

C. Researching Agencies and Administrative Law

1. Introduction [§134]

We will begin with an examination of federal agency resource materials, because they are the most available and the most completely indexed. State and local resource materials, which are often much more limited in access, will be discussed afterwards.

When your research involves agencies, remember to check their rules and regulations, administrative decisions, orders and opinions, internal procedures, and files. Much of this information is available online. (Your access to federal government agency records is clearly set out in the Freedom of Information Act [5 U.S.C. §552]. Many states have comparable legislation, sometimes known as a government records act.)

If you are interested in generally knowing more on the law of agencies, look for an administrative law treatise. *Administrative Law* by Davis and Pierce (published by Aspen Law & Business) is the best known, but there are several others.

2. Federal Materials

a. *Code of Federal Regulations* ("C.F.R.") [§135]

This 50-title softcover edition codifies the regulations issued by federal agencies. It is organized by agency and is similar in titles to those of the *United States Code* (which codifies federal statutes). Presidential executive orders appear in title 3 of the C.F.R.

The index and finding-aids volume includes an explanation of how to use these books. The index can be researched in the same manner as any other legal sourcebook index. However, you may want to use the Congressional Information Service ("CIS") Index to the *Code of Federal Regulations.* It is more thorough.

Parallel tables connecting the regulations to the federal statutes that provide the basis for the regulations follow the index. There is also a table of contents (a list of C.F.R. titles, chapters, subchapters, and parts) and an alphabetical list of agencies appearing in C.F.R. Each title of C.F.R. also has its own index.

The C.F.R. is revised yearly, on a staggered basis, with quarterly updates. There is also a monthly *List of C.F.R Sections Affected*, listing changes to the current C.F.R. It is updated quarterly. (For the most recent changes, you will have to look into another publication, the *Federal Register*, *see* below.) The C.F.R. is also available on LexisNexis, Westlaw, and online at http://www.gpo.gov/fdsys.

b. *Federal Register* ("Fed. Reg.") [§136]

This series is to the *Code of Federal Regulations* what the *Statutes at Large* is to the *United States Code.* The *Federal Register* publishes all the federal regulations in chronological order. Though you can find the particular regulations for a particular subject or agency immeasurably faster in C.F.R. than in Fed. Reg., the *Federal Register* serves a very useful purpose. It is published daily and so will include the very latest changes in the regulations. Check its C.F.R. Parts Affected. The list is arranged under the C.F.R. numbering system (by title and section of C.F.R.). The *Federal Register* is also available on LexisNexis, Westlaw, and at http://www.gpo.gov/fdsys.

(1) Reminder

Be sure to check carefully the effective date of the regulations. Regulations are often issued (publication dates) before they are to become law (effective dates). If you are unsure whether the regulations have gone into effect, call the agency.

The supplements to the *United States Code Congressional and Administrative News Service* or the *United States Code Service* also include listings of recently issued regulations, but they are not as up to date as the *Federal Register.*

Besides keeping the *Code of Federal Regulations* up to date, the *Federal Register* publishes proposed agency rules and regulations, giving interested parties and the public a chance to comment before they are put into effect. It also prints presidential documents.

c. Federal agency decisions [§137]

Both the government and several commercial companies publish the decisions of federal agencies. The official government volumes are often inadequately indexed and published late, but the commercial editions are excellent sources. The commercial sets are included in the general term "looseleaf services," discussed next.

d. Looseleaf services and materials [§138]

In most of your research, you have had to examine several sources—statutes, regulations, reporters, treatises, encyclopedias, digests, law reviews—before you could be certain you had found the proper primary material. For much of federal administrative law, this process has been greatly eased. Many publishers have collected statutes, regulations, agency decisions, and court decisions and arranged them by subject. Thus, if you have a question on federal labor law, housing law, or tax law, you may need only to check the appropriate looseleaf edition on that topic.

Looseleaf services are just that—looseleaf binders of materials. They are usually updated weekly or monthly. CCH, BNA, and West together publish over 200 editions of federal (and some state) topics. (*See* the Appendix for some examples.) An excellent source on looseleaf services is *Legal Looseleafs in Print* (Infosources Publishing). It is an annual listing, by title, of looseleaf services, with indexes by publisher and by subject.

(1) In general [§139]

Each looseleaf service has its unique, sometimes idiosyncratic, approach to the material. Be sure to read the instructions carefully.

Also, be sure to read the decisions themselves; the annotations may be misleading since you cannot tell from them whether the principle of law stated is a holding or dictum.

The texts of the decisions are often published by the company in separate bound volumes, with recent cases appearing in looseleaf supplements. The volumes will include both agency decisions and court decisions. (You can always look to West's *Federal Supplement* and *Federal Reporter* for federal court cases. But occasionally looseleaf services will pick up unpublished federal cases and publish them.)

(2) Commerce Clearing House [§140]

Each CCH edition opens with a page or two on how to use this particular set (known as a reporter). As they say, when everything else fails, read the instructions. You will save yourself lots of time if you first check how these particular volumes are organized and how CCH has channelled the material into various sections. *Note*: Most CCH materials are cited to the ***paragraph number*** located at the bottom of the page, rather than to the page number at the top.

(a) Indexes [§141]

Each CCH series has a Topical Index and some have a Rapid Finder Index. The Rapid Finder Index is similar to a table of contents. Unless you know the material well, you should begin with the Topical Index. It is thorough, with lots of subheadings, and can be used in the same way you would use any other legal sourcebook index. The references in the index are to paragraph numbers rather than to page numbers. (The page numbers are there mainly to help the person filing the new material and removing the outdated pages.)

Each set also has a Table of Cases (for use when you have the name of a case) and Finding Devices (to use when you have the number of a statute, regulation, or agency ruling).

(3) Bureau of National Affairs [§142]

Although BNA materials cover the same types of information as CCH, BNA sometimes organizes them differently. Often, separate pamphlets are issued and filed consecutively. There is no removal of earlier outdated material and substitution of new. The older material is eventually stored in special binders leaving only the more current on the shelf. Cumulative tables and indexes are necessarily included with each edition.

All looseleaf services provide additional material where necessary, such as an index to appropriate articles, a legislative status chart, a court docket, definitions, abbreviations, and forms. The smaller companies that publish looseleaf materials do so in a design similar to that of the major services.

(4) Online sources [§143]

Several looseleaf reporters are now published online as well as in text. For example, both CCH and BNA provide online subscription services. Forms with instructions and many examples are also being made available.

(5) State looseleafs [§144]

State looseleafs are published for many areas of law. The organization is often similar to federal looseleafs. Be sure to read the How to Use introductory section to each reporter.

e. Other sources of administrative agency information and law

(1) Agency publications [§145]

Several agencies issue pamphlets describing the agency, its operations, and structure. These are for the public. You might also see if you can obtain internal agency handbooks and memoranda for employees. An agency's pamphlets and other information may be available on the agency's website, so that is often a good place to start.

(2) *United States Government Manual* [§146]

This *Federal Register* publication gives lots of information on each branch of government. Every agency is described—its history, authorizing legislation, personnel, and functions. It is available through http://www.gpo.gov/fdsys.

(3) *Federal Yellow Book; Congressional Yellow Book* [§147]

Leadership Directories, Inc. publishes these two directories of federal departments, agencies, and employees, and members of Congress, their committees, and aides. Both books are kept up to date and are usually more accurate than the government manual.

(4) Secondary sources [§148]

Do not forget to check in the library's catalog for treatises on the law, *LegalTrac* or the *Legal Resource Index* (both carry identical material) and the *Index to Legal Periodicals* for law review articles on new and developing issues, and of course federal digests and encyclopedias. Also, see whether any attorney general opinions may help you in interpreting a statute or regulation.

(5) Shepard's Citations [§149]

Shepard's United States Administrative Citations (published by LexisNexis

Group) for approximately a dozen agencies is discussed in chapter VII. There are also Shepard's for various federal subjects such as labor, tax, and copyright.

f. Presidential documents [§150]

Proclamations and Executive Orders can be found in the *Federal Register*, title 3 of the *Code of Federal Regulations*, the *United States Code Congressional and Administrative News* (West), the *United States Code Service* (Matthew Bender & Company, a member of the LexisNexis Group), and the *Weekly Compilation of Presidential Documents* (*Federal Register*).

3. State Materials

a. Regulations [§151]

Many states publish their own regulations. Check with your librarian. Note that when the states that publish regulations provide an index, it is often inadequate.

The agency itself may be the best source of the regulations. If you have trouble obtaining the regulations from the agency, check to see if your state has a government records act that guarantees public access to most government files. But even where your state does not have such an act, regulations should always be publicly accessible.

States may also publish a state manual, county memoranda on new laws and regulations, and weekly supplements on the latest changes. The library may have some of these or check your state's website. But since much of this is internal matter, your best source is someone who works in the agency and has access to the regulations.

LexisNexis and Westlaw also have many state administrative codes online.

Do not forget to check whether CCH, BNA, West, or some other company has published a state looseleaf edition on the subject.

b. Decisions [§152]

The state agencies should have a library of past decisions, indexed by subject. Ask to see them—they are public documents.

c. State agencies and personnel [§153]

Your state, the bar association, or a continuing education program may publish a directory to state and county agencies and personnel.

4. County and Municipal Agencies [§154]

Probably your best chance of seeing the regulations issued by local agencies is to go directly to the agency and ask to see them. The agency should have a copy of its own rules and regulations. Larger cities may also have their own administrative code. Again, a good place to start is the local agency's website, if it has one.

Chapter Seven: Keeping Up to Date—Using Shepard's and KeyCite

CONTENTS

A. Introduction

1. Changing Body of Law [§155]

Law is always changing. Courts issue opinions establishing new legal principles, legislatures enact new statutes, and administrative agencies adopt new regulations. Of course, the changes usually are not dramatic, nor does everything change at once. Law would certainly lose its continuity and precedent building blocks if it seesawed or swung in wide arcs every day. But even slight movement will have its impact. Imagine basing your legal arguments on a point of law no longer recognized as valid. The embarrassment does not come anywhere near the possible disastrous consequences it may have for your client.

2. Updating Legal Materials [§156]

To keep on top of developments, companies issue advance sheets and supplements to cases, statutes, digests, treatises, and encyclopedias, and new pages for old in looseleaf services. However, the quickest and most effective way to update your material is electronically, either through Shepard's on LexisNexis or KeyCite on Westlaw. (*See* chapter VIII for more discussion on LexisNexis and Westlaw.) Although it is not up to date, you can also manually update using Shepard's Citations in print form (*see* below). Shepard's Citations (published by Shepard's, a member of the LexisNexis Group) are usually thick red volumes often found together in one section of the library, although they may be shelved separately alongside the state statutes or reporters. Shepard's volumes also appear on LexisNexis, but not Westlaw.

B. Updating Online—Shepard's and KeyCite

1. Using Online Citators [§157]

LexisNexis and Westlaw provide electronic citator verification systems. Westlaw (and WestlawNext) offers KeyCite and LexisNexis offers Shepard's. Both LexisNexis and Westlaw cite to the subsequent and prior history of your case. They also refer to cases that make negative reference to your case (*e.g.*, a case that criticizes your case) and whether a case has been superseded by a statute. Essentially, they tell you whether your case is still good law—and they can update daily, sometimes within 30 minutes. In addition, Shepard's and KeyCite provide citations to secondary materials that mention the case. KeyCite is also integrated with the West's Key Number System to track legal issues. LexisNexis also offers LEXCITE, which finds sources that reference a particular citation.

2. Online vs. Print Versions [§158]

Because the time lag on the print version of Shepard's is quite long—usually a month—you should use the online version of Shepard's on LexisNexis and KeyCite on Westlaw whenever possible and take advantage of their relatively short lag time of 24 hours. However, these services can be in error or incomplete; thus it is advisable to check more than one. There may be times when you are unable to get online to use Shepard's or KeyCite. While online citators are the easiest (and most current) ways to check the status of the law, it is important to know how to Shepardize using the books. (*See infra,* §§161 *et seq.*)

3. Using Shepard's on LexisNexis [§159]

When you access a case in LexisNexis, a symbol will likely appear near the case name alerting you to the status of the law of your case (not all cases will have symbols). If a red octagon appears, this stop sign is warning you that there has been negative treatment of your case—for example, your entire case, or a portion of it, may have been overruled or reversed. A yellow triangle indicates possible negative treatment which may impact your case—for example, the decision might be highly criticized by other courts. A green diamond means your case has been treated favorably.

Other signals in LexisNexis may indicate that your case has been cited, but either the citation is neutral, or it is purely an analysis of your case (for example, a law review article may cite or discuss the case). You can click on any of the signals to see a list of the sources citing to your case.

4. Using KeyCite on Westlaw [§160]

Westlaw's citations research service, KeyCite, provides status flags next to the case or statute you are viewing to indicate that there is history available on your case or statute. A red status flag indicates that your case or statute is no longer good law, either in whole or in part. A yellow status flag indicates that your case has received some negative treatment. A blue "H" lets you know that there is some history on your case, but it is not necessarily negative; and a green "C" indicates that your case has been cited.

As in LexisNexis, you can click on the status flags to see the sources citing to your case or statute. The history displayed, and each citing case will have one to four asterisks (which Westlaw calls "depth of treatment stars") next to it indicating the extent to which your case is discussed—one star means that your case is merely mentioned in brief, while four stars means that your case is examined in an extended discussion within the citing case. In the newest version of Westlaw (*see infra*, §189), WestlawNext has replaced the asterisks with green bars that serve a similar purpose in indicating the depth of treatment discussed in the case.

C. Shepard's Citations—Using the Books

1. Shepard's Case Citations [§161]

Because many more cases are decided each week than statutes are enacted or regulations adopted, Shepard's Citations is most frequently used with cases. Is the case you are researching still recognized as good law? Did a higher court reverse or modify the decision? Have courts followed the principles of law established in the case or did they establish new or different principles? Before you can safely cite a case as authority, you need to know how later courts have treated it. Finding out is simple. Just check the appropriate Shepard's volume, look up the case, and run down the notations below its citation.

There are Shepard's Citations for all reported decisions—official and unofficial. *Shepard's United States Citations*, for Supreme Court cases, includes sections for *United States Reports, Supreme Court Reporter*, and *United States Supreme Court Reports, Lawyers' Edition. Shepard's Federal Citations* includes *Federal Reporter, Federal Supplement, Federal Claims* cases, and *Federal Rules Decisions.*

There are also Shepard's Citations for various states (*e.g., Shepard's Minnesota Citations*), and Shepard's Citations for each of the seven regional reporters in West's National Reporter System (*e.g., Shepard's Northwestern Citations*). (*See* Addenda for sample pages.)

SUMMARY OF SHEPARD'S CITATIONS

- Shepard's state Citations (*e.g., Shepard's California Citations*)
- Shepard's regional Citations (*e.g., Shepard's Pacific Reporter Citations*)
- *Shepard's United States Citations*
- *Shepard's Federal Citations*
- *Shepard's Acts and Cases by Popular Names,* Federal and State
- *Shepard's Law Review Citations*
- *Shepard's United States Administrative Citations*
- *Shepard's Labor Law Citations*
- *Shepard's Intellectual Property Law Citations*
- Other specialized citations (*see infra,* §169)

a. Shepardizing a case [§162]

Let's use the case of *Crawford v. Board of Education*, 17 Cal. 3d 280, 130 Cal. Rptr. 724, 551 P.2d 28 (1976), a California Supreme Court case, as an example. We can Shepardize it in any one of three separate series: *Shepard's California Citations, Shepard's California Reporter Citations,* and *Shepard's Pacific Reporter Citations.*

Shepard's California Citations includes separate citation sections for *California Reports* (the official reporter), *California Reporter*, and California cases appearing in *Pacific Reporter. Shepard's California Reporter Citations* Shepardizes only *California Reporter* citations. *Shepard's Pacific Reporter Citations* Shepardizes only *Pacific Reporter* citations (California Supreme Court cases included). This duplication and overlapping of Shepard's volumes is useful since firms that subscribe to only one of these sets can still Shepardize the case.

There are a few differences in using one of these sets or another. *Shepard's California Reporter Citations* and *Shepard's Pacific Reporter Citations* include citations to cases in other states that cite the case you are Shepardizing; *Shepard's California Citations* does not. However, *Shepard's California Citations*, unlike the other two series, includes citations to legal periodicals and opinions of the attorney general.

When you Shepardize, you must check through each bound volume and paper supplement of the series. The volumes are not cumulative. Since *Crawford* was decided in 1976, you need to check the bound volume and the paper supplements. Very recent cases appear only in supplements. Be certain you are using the ***correct*** volume. The cover of the latest paper supplement tells you which volumes the library should have.

We will use 17 Cal. 3d 280, the *California Reports* citation, to Shepardize *Crawford*. If you are reading this book in a library, please follow along. We begin by finding the latest bound volume of *Shepard's California Citations* and turn to *California Supreme Court Reports 3d*, volume 17. (The top of each page gives the name and volume number of the reports you are using.) The dark printed numbers in the text refer to the page of the reporter in which the case begins. We are looking for 280. Under 280 we find a column of citations (*see* below for examples of ***some*** of the citations we will find; we have skipped some of the citations found in Shepard's so we can illustrate different kinds of citations). Each citation refers to a legal authority (usually another case) that has cited *Crawford*. Shepard's calls the main case (*Crawford* is our example) the "cited material," and the citations referring to it the "citing material."

— 280 —
(130CaR724)
(551P2d28)
#s 46CA3d872
s 458US527
* * *
cc 113CA3d633
* * *
17C3d312
f 17C3d[1]314
d 17C3d316
f 17C3d[6]326

j 18C3d[6]74

* * *

24CLA595

Let's examine some of the citing material to *Crawford*. The first two citations are in parentheses. You should recognize them as ***parallel citations*** (*see supra*, §55), the citations to this case in *California Reporter* and *Pacific Reporter.* Parallel citations appear only in the first volume in which the case is Shepardized.

The next two citations have a lowercase "s" beside them. These citations are to the case at various stages of litigation (*i.e.,* the history of the case). The first "s" citation means that this is a citation to the same case in a lower court—the California Court of Appeals—before it came up to the California Supreme Court. The following "s" citation refers to the case's appeal to the United States Supreme Court. Note that the first of these two citations has a "#" symbol before the lowercase "s"—this "#" symbol indicates that the citing case's value as precedent is questionable (for example, because the case is up for review in a higher court, or the court has ordered the case depublished); you should do more research before citing to this particular case as authority.

The next citation in our illustration is preceded by "cc." The "cc" means that this is a connected case; that is, the case is different from the case cited but arises out of the same subject matter or involves the same parties.

Except for the last citation in our illustration, the remaining citing material can be generally explained as citations to cases that have made reference to *Crawford*. A lowercase letter preceding the citation (like an "f," "d," or "j" here) will tell you something more about the reference. For example, "f" would mean that the case is following a principle of law set forth in *Crawford*, while "d" means that the case is distinguishing itself in law or fact from *Crawford*. The letter "j" refers to *Crawford*'s being cited in a dissenting opinion. The citations given here include the page number that has the reference to *Crawford*, rather than the page number on which the case begins.

An Abbreviations-Analysis chart, explaining each letter abbreviation, appears in the front of every Shepard's volume. The chart separates those abbreviations that refer to the history of a cited case (for example, whether it was "r" reversed or "m" modified on appeal to a higher court) and those that refer to the treatment of a cited case (for example, whether other cases "f" follow its principles or "c" criticize them).

The last citation in our illustration is to a law review that mentions *Crawford*, the *U.C.L.A. Law Review.* An Abbreviations-Reports chart explaining the abbreviations used in the citations is also in the front of each Shepard's volume. You would be wise to consult this chart since Shepard's does not always follow the accepted abbreviations for reporters and other sources.

Several of the citations in the citing material to *Crawford* include a small superior number to the left of the page number. For example, the seventh citation in our illustration contains a superior number 1. This number refers to the principle of law stated in headnote 1 to *Crawford*. (In chapter III, we discussed headnotes, indicating that many more principles of law are stated in the headnotes than the court actually rules upon.)

If you are only concerned with a principle of law stated in a certain headnote, whether dicta or holding, you need only check those citations in the citing material that have the same superior number. Shepard's editors will only include the headnote number when the reference made to the principle stated in the headnote is clear. Thus, sometimes the superior number is more helpful as an elimination device of those principles in the case with which you are not concerned, rather than as an exact finding device. Be wary when using superior numbers to narrow your search. Editors who wrote the headnotes may have misread the case, or the judge who cited the case as authority may have erred in understanding the problem. Also, a case may imply more than it says—it may, for example, overrule an earlier case by implication—and an editor needing to keep a conservative interpretation will not be able to provide an appropriate notation to signal this situation. When in doubt, read the citing case to be sure it does or does not concern your problem.

For further help on how to use Shepard's Citations, check the illustrative case in the front of any bound volume.

(1) Supplements [§163]

Remember, your Shepardizing is not complete until you have checked through the yellow, red, and/or blue paper ***supplements*** to bring you up to date. (*See infra*, §171.)

b. Using Shepard's Citations for research [§164]

Shepard's includes in its citing material every case that cites, whether in holding or dicta, the cited case. The company makes no editorial judgment. Since many of the citations will be taken from dicta, many of the citing cases in Shepard's will be only peripherally (if at all) concerned with the principle of law in your case. Thus, it is usually a waste of time to use Shepard's in a search for additional cases dealing with a precise point of law with which you are concerned.

Moreover, since Shepard's only includes citations to cases that refer to the earlier or cited case, if another case similar to the cited case does not mention the cited case in its opinion, you will not find the other case by using Shepard's. For example, if a judge is considering a problem similar to the one in *Crawford* but does not know of the *Crawford* decision, he will not refer to *Crawford* in his opinion. So in Shepardizing *Crawford*, you will not come upon this other case. This is not an unusual situation. Judges often miss an important case because the opposing lawyers did not include the case in their briefs and the judge relied on their work instead of personally researching the problem. Or perhaps the other case moved through the courts at around the same time as your case and so there was no record of the other decision at the time the decision in your case was rendered.

Shepard's is best suited for, and should only be used in, ***determining the history*** of a case and ***its later treatment*** by other cases. Digests, treatises, encyclopedias, looseleaf services, law reviews, and online sources should be used when you are looking for cases and authorities on a particular point of law.

(1) Reminder

After you have Shepardized your own material and determined that it is still recognized as good law, check your opponent's citations. You will be surprised to see how frequently people do not Shepardize their authorities carefully.

2. Shepard's Statute Citations [§165]

Shepard's publishes Citations to state and federal statutes. The history of an act and the congressional or legislative actions that affect the act are indicated by letter abbreviations. An addition or amendment to the law, the repeal of all or part of the law, or a new provision superseding the law are all clearly marked. Court interpretation of a statute, including declaring it constitutional or unconstitutional, is also indicated in the citing material. Complete tables of abbreviations (Abbreviations-Analysis and Abbreviations-Reports) are in front of each of the volumes.

Shepard's Federal Statutes Citations for federal law and separate state citators for state law include not only codified and uncodified statutes, but also constitutions and court rules. *Shepard's Federal Statutes Citations* Shepardizes the United States Constitution, the United States Code, uncodified statutes in United States *Statutes at Large*, treaties, sentencing guidelines, and federal court rules. Shepard's Citations for various states (*e.g.*, *Shepard's California Citations*) include sections for state cases that cite the United States Constitution, the United States Code, and federal court rules, as well as sections for Shepardizing the state constitution, the state codes, the state uncodified session laws, and state court rules. There is also a table of State Acts by Popular Name or Short Titles, and a section Shepardizing city charters and ordinances. (Another helpful series, published by West and entitled Ordinance Law Annotations, organizes the material topically to simplify your search.) In the larger states, Shepard's publishes a separate statute edition; smaller states combine case and statute citations in one volume. (*See* the Addenda for sample pages.) Shepard's Citations, Statute Editions, are on LexisNexis for all state and federal statutes.

3. Other Shepard's Citations

a. *Shepard's United States Administrative Citations* [§166]

This edition of Shepard's Shepardizes board, commission, and court decisions of approximately 20 federal administrative agencies. Included are Treasury Decisions, Federal Communications Commission Reports, Federal Trade Commission

Decisions, Securities and Exchange Commission Decisions and Reports, and Opinions of the Attorneys General.

b. ***Shepard's Code of Federal Regulations Citations* [§167]**
This edition covers C.F.R., Presidential proclamations, executive orders, and reorganization plans.

c. **Law reviews [§168]**
Shepard's Law Review Citations lists most state and federal court decisions, as well as other law reviews that cite the article in the law review being Shepardized. *Shepard's Federal Law Citations in Selected Law Reviews* contains references from selected major law reviews to federal decisions and statutes.

Shepard's Federal Citations and the various Shepard's Citations for various states also include articles from certain law reviews in their citing material.

d. **Specialty editions [§169]**
Shepard's publishes a number of editions for particular areas of the law. Here are some of the specialty editions:

(1) *Shepard's Labor Law Citations;*

(2) *Shepard's Bankruptcy Citations;*

(3) *Shepard's Intellectual Property Law Citations;*

(4) *Shepard's Professional and Judicial Conduct Citations;*

(5) *Shepard's Federal OSHA Citations;*

(6) *Shepard's Criminal Justice Citations;*

(7) *Shepard's Military Justice Citations;*

(8) *Shepard's Restatement of the Law Citations;*

(9) *Shepard's Federal Tax Citations;*

(10) *Shepard's Federal Energy Law Citations;*

(11) *Shepard's Immigration and Naturalization Citations;*

(12) *Shepard's Labor Arbitration Citations;*

(13) *Shepard's Uniform Commercial Code Citations;* and

(14) *Shepard's Federal Circuit Table Citations.*

e. **Popular name tables [§170]**
What if you wanted to read the several federal Watergate cases or the South

Dakota Dance Hall Act, but did not know the names of the cases or the citation to the statute? How would you find them? One way is to look them up in *Shepard's Acts and Cases by Popular Names.* This set covers both state and federal law.

You can also find popular case names in the *Decennial Digest* and in the *United States Supreme Court Digest* (both published by West) and popular named statutes in most of the annotated state and federal statutes and in Shepard's state statute editions, under Table of Acts by Popular Names or Short Titles.

4. Updating Shepard's [§171]

Shepard's Citations supplements its bound volumes with a yellow-covered intermediate paper supplement, quarterly red paper-covered cumulative supplements, and blue-covered advance sheets. (Some Shepard's editions do not issue the blue advance sheets.) You can also check LexisNexis in updating Shepard's. Shepard's online coordinates all of the volumes, providing a list of all citing cases and case names. Because the LexisNexis Group owns Shepard's, Shepard's appears only on LexisNexis.

When researching through Shepard's, be sure to check if there is more than one bound volume in the series you are using. The red bound volumes may not be cumulative; you need to check through each one that includes your cited material. To be certain you have researched through the complete set, check the covers of the yellow, red, and blue supplements. They detail the bound volumes and supplements that make up that particular series.

D. Other Sources and Methods

1. West's Blue and White Books [§172]

West publishes the *National Reporter Blue Book.* It provides parallel cites to state and national reporters. West also publishes "Blue and White Books" for various states (*e.g., California Blue and White Book*) which cross-reference parallel citations in official and unofficial reports. These books are often found alongside the reporters of the jurisdiction.

2. Looseleaf Services [§173]

Since many looseleaf services are revised weekly (*see* chapter VI), they are frequently a useful source for the latest cases, statutes, and regulations. But looseleaf materials are not available in every field, and where they are they may not be as complete as Shepard's in including all citing material (although what the editors leave out is usually not very important).

3. Websites and Phone Calls [§174]

If a case on which you are relying is now on appeal (Westlaw, LexisNexis, and other electronic services tell you whether a case is being appealed), you can call the appellate court or check the court's website and find out whether a decision has been reached. The National Center for State Courts maintains a list of state court websites at http://www.ncsc.org. For federal appellate court information, use the Court Locator at http://www.uscourts.gov.

Also, if you are tracking a federal case through appeal, Public Access to Electronic Records ("PACER"; http://www.pacer.gov) allows you to search federal filings and docket information electronically. Registration is free, but PACER charges per page retrieved in each search. However, fees of less than $10 per quarter are waived, and some law libraries maintain PACER accounts for public use.

4. State Updating Services [§175]

Several states have updating services for their case and statutory materials. You can check in the library's catalog or with your librarian.

Chapter Eight: Online Legal Research

CONTENTS

A. Introduction

1. Where to Start [§176]

Law schools, law firms, and county and bar association libraries research the law online. Computers can speed up your search of the law, but unless you use the proper keywords—as in traditional legal research—they will not be very helpful. Consequently, you should know something about the subject you are researching before you begin using a computer research system. If the subject is unfamiliar to you, begin with an encyclopedia or a treatise to obtain an overview of the area. Many such secondary sources are also available through the online research systems discussed below.

2. Online Research Systems [§177]

The two computerized legal research systems in widest use are LexisNexis and Westlaw. LexisNexis is owned by Reed Elsevier. Westlaw is a product of West, a division of Thomson Reuters. Both systems also provide access to certain nonlegal materials. Many governmental institutions now provide online information and access to official documents, often in PDF ("Portable Document Format," accessible through free software from Adobe.com). Because Westlaw, LexisNexis, and other online sources are updated daily, they often provide a faster retrieval of current material than do many hard copy sources.

B. LexisNexis

1. Contents [§178]

LexisNexis is organized into more than 15,000 databases, called "discrete sources," which consist of materials from specific jurisdictions or particular fields of law.

a. Federal sources [§179]

The federal sources contain the text of the *United States Code* and legislative history and materials, as well as the *Federal Register* and *Code of Federal Regulations.* Federal sources also contain United States Supreme Court briefs and decisions; federal circuit and district court decisions (including unpublished decisions); and federal court rules.

b. State sources [§180]

State sources include case law (including unreported decisions), court rules, state codes and constitutions, and administrative decisions from each state, the District of Columbia, Puerto Rico, and the Virgin Islands.

c. International sources [§181]

International sources include legal materials from Asia/Pacific Rim, Europe, Latin America, Mideast/Africa, etc., as well as sources on International Law and International Trade.

d. **Other sources [§182]**

Secondary and other resource sources include law reviews, news services, CCH materials, and a full range of Matthew Bender reference materials. LexisNexis also organizes materials into "practice areas" including, for example, antitrust, estate planning, corporate mergers and acquisitions, family law, intellectual property, and real estate, allowing you to access numerous tools and information related to that practice area from one location within LexisNexis.

2. **Searching [§183]**

To conduct a LexisNexis search, you can use either their "natural language" (plain English) method or their "terms and connectors" system. In the latter system, you must first select words that you think would appear in your problem. You then connect them with modifiers, like "AND," "OR," and "W/N" ("N" equals any number of words appearing within a certain proximity). For example, if you were interested in finding cases where a labor dispute has occurred, you might use the terms "Labor AND Dispute." LexisNexis would then find all cases in its database containing the keywords. However, such a search would miss cases where a court did not use these terms. On the other end, because these words appear frequently in cases, your search could be too broad. It is thus important in a computer search, as in any legal research search, to try several other terms as well. In our example, we might add words like strike, lockout, employer, and union, and use the modifiers to obtain different combinations.

When a proper search request has been formulated, you then ask the system to display the cases it has found. In the LexisNexis system, the most recent cases appear first. The screen will begin by displaying the segment of the case that contains the words you selected. You may then request that more of the text be shown, or simply request the computer to go on to the next case.

After the search is completed, the screen will indicate the number of cases containing your operative words. If there seems to be too many or too few results, you may decide to reformulate your command by either broadening or narrowing your list of keywords and changing your connecting terms.

LexisNexis may also be used as a citator. It provides access to LEXCITE and Shepard's Citation Service.

LexisNexis is also developing Lexis Advance, its next generation of the search engine interface, to make the research experience an easier one (similar to WestlawNext, *see infra*, §189). Additionally, Lexis Web pulls content from selected Internet sources and is available for free online at http://www.lexisweb.com. (For a detailed discussion, *see infra*, §199).

3. **Keeping Current [§184]**

Once you have conducted and saved a search in LexisNexis, you can use the Alert feature to receive updated results of that search either monthly, biweekly, weekly, or daily. The Alert feature automatically sends the search results to you (*e.g.*, by e-mail) as LexisNexis databases are updated.

4. Other Databases [§185]

LexisNexis and Westlaw provide a wealth of legal ***and*** nonlegal materials online. For example, you can find cases, statutes, administrative regulations, bills, committee reports, citations, and decisions of a particular judge or involving a particular party, as well as newspapers, magazines, medical reports, and wire services. Check the continually revised catalogs of each company to see what they cover in their libraries and databases.

C. Westlaw and WestlawNext

1. Contents [§186]

Westlaw provides full-text coverage of reported cases from the appellate courts of all states plus the District of Columbia. Other available state materials include statutes and administrative material. Westlaw also contains synopses and headnotes from the West Reporter System.

The federal material available from Westlaw includes: full text of the *United States Code*; decisions from the United States Supreme Court (available within 30 minutes after issuance), circuit courts of appeals, and district courts—all cases from each court's inception; as well as United States Tax and Bankruptcy Courts, Military Courts, Court of Claims, and federal administrative decisions. Westlaw also has an International/Worldwide Directory which includes access to legal materials from various regions throughout the world (for example, legislation, case law, and regulations from the European Union).

In addition, Westlaw provides databases containing material of special interest, such as in the areas of securities, labor, bankruptcy, communications, antitrust and business regulation, government contracts, federal tax, and intellectual property. The text of *Black's Law Dictionary* is also included on Westlaw. Also, as with LexisNexis, Westlaw accesses state codes and certain "unreported" state and federal decisions that although issued by the courts are not published in the reporters.

2. Searching [§187]

Requests to Westlaw may be made by using Westlaw's "natural language" (plain English) language system or by using a connector/modifier system similar to LexisNexis, although Westlaw uses "terms and connectors" such as "/p" (words that appear in the same paragraph) or "/s" (words that appear in the same sentence). You may also search Westlaw by key numbers (as found in West digests, headnotes, case reports, and *Corpus Juris Secundum*). Cases are usually displayed on the Westlaw screen in reverse chronology, although they could also be displayed in descending order of probable importance (based upon frequency of appearance of keywords). Westlaw's citator service is KeyCite.

3. Keeping Current [§188]

WestClip allows you to keep updated on specific legal news. You set up the search terms, the database you would like searched, and how often you would like to be updated, and WestClip automatically delivers the information to you (*e.g.*, via e-mail) as Westlaw's news databases are updated. KeyCite Alert enables you to stay abreast of the status of cases, statutes, and administrative materials. When Westlaw's citator service, KeyCite, is updated, the results are automatically forwarded to you.

4. Other Databases

(*See supra,* §185.)

5. WestlawNext [§189]

Westlaw has introduced WestlawNext as a new option for researching. The changes are intended to provide an easier research experience, similar to Google searching, by allowing the user to search without using terms and connectors or isolating databases. Users may still use terms and connectors if they wish. Other enhanced features allow users to create folders to organize their research, highlight language, and make notes. Both WestlawNext and the classic format are available to Westlaw subscribers. In addition to the website, WestlawNext is also available to subscribers as a mobile application.

D. Governmental and Other Free Online Sources

1. In General [§190]

Much of the material found in LexisNexis, Westlaw, and other online subscription services can be found on governmental websites and through free online services. Examples include:

2. Findlaw [§191]

Findlaw (http://www.findlaw.com), an independent division of Thomson Reuters, is a good place to begin. It will direct you to legal subjects, legal blogs, law school information, professional development, legal organizations, law firms, as well as cases, codes, federal and state government materials, foreign resources, and legal practice materials.

3. WashLaw Web [§192]

The Washburn University website also is a good place to start. WashLaw Web (http://www.washlaw.edu) provides numerous links to state and federal reference information available on the Internet, including court and government news, journals, directories, legal research, and general reference.

4. Legal Information Institute [§193]

A product of Cornell Law School, Legal Information Institute (http://www.law.cornell.edu) offers access to the United States Code, the United States Constitution, the Code of Federal Regulations, the Federal Rules of Evidence, Criminal, and Civil Procedure, the Uniform Commercial Code, and United States Supreme Court and federal circuit courts of appeals decisions, as well as recent decisions of courts of special jurisdiction (Armed Forces, Tax Court, etc.). It also offers recent opinions of the New York Court of Appeals and a community-built legal dictionary called Wex.

5. THOMAS [§194]

THOMAS (http://thomas.loc.gov) is a Library of Congress service, offering legislation (bill status and text, and public laws), the *Congressional Record*, and committee information. THOMAS also provides congressional contact information and voting records, as well as links to the websites of other legislative agencies.

6. GPO Federal Digital System [§195]

The U.S. Government Printing Office ("GPO") provides access to official government documents and publications from all three branches of the federal government and regulatory agencies. GPO's Federal Digital System ("FDsys") is online at http://www.gpo.gov/fdsys. FDsys replaced the "GPO Access" system in spring 2011.

7. Guide to Law Online [§196]

The Law Library of Congress and the Global Legal Research Center provide an excellent international legal resource, the Guide to Law Online (http://www.loc.gov/law/guide). It provides access to sources of global information, including constitutions, statutes, and case law from the world's nations, as well as multinational and international sources.

8. NCCUSL [§197]

The National Conference of Commissioners on Uniform State Laws ("NCCUSL") website (http://www.nccusl.org) contains the text of uniform and model state laws drafted by NCCUSL, as well as summaries of the uniform laws and listings of the states that adopt them in whole or in part.

9. Google Scholar [§198]

Google has created a limited free database of court opinions, books, and journals (http://scholar.google.com). The growing database currently contains court opinions for state appellate courts and supreme courts since 1950; federal trial, appellate, tax, and bankruptcy courts since 1923; and the United States Supreme Court since 1791. Google Scholar does not provide all of the same features found in commercial research systems such as LexisNexis and Westlaw. For instance, the database does not contain statutes and some secondary sources. You also cannot check whether the cases are still good law.

10. Lexis Web [§199]

LexisNexis has introduced a free search engine that pulls results from select Internet sources that have been validated by LexisNexis (http://www.lexisweb.com). The web content is augmented with recommended links to subscription LexisNexis content. As with search engines such as Google, terms and connectors are not required.

However, the search scope may be limited by practice area and jurisdiction, and the results may be filtered by source, file type, etc.

11. Public Library of Law [§200]

Fastcase (*see infra,* §209) has created the Public Library of Law ("PLOL"), a legal web portal available at http://www.plol.org. The site hosts recent state and federal case law, which can be searched in plain English or with "terms and connectors" like LexisNexis. Free registration is required to access the full text of recent cases, but the site makes older cases available only through a paid Fastcase subscription. PLOL's portal also links to court rules, statutes, regulations, legal forms, and more.

12. The Fastcase App [§201]

Fastcase (*see infra*, §209) provides its complete case law and statutory libraries for free through a downloadable application for Apple devices such as the iPhone and the iPad (http://www.fastcase.com/ipad). The company plans to expand to more platforms, making the free application available on other smartphones and mobile devices.

13. Explore the Internet [§202]

Throughout this book, we have referred to websites providing alternative sources of legal information. In addition, the Library of Congress website (http://www.loc.gov) provides links to many federal, state, local, and foreign legal resources on the Internet. The links are organized by source and by topic. Also visit the U.S. Government's official web portal at http://www.usa.gov for information and links to government department and agency websites.

E. Other Online Subscription Services

1. In General [§203]

A number of companies have entered the legal field providing online legal materials through their websites—some by paid subscription, some free (as those in §§190-202, *supra*). Examples of subscription or paid services include the following:

2. LexisONE [§204]

An excellent resource for small law firms, this LexisNexis Group service (http://www.lexisone.com) provides a community web portal with free access to selected state and federal case law from the past 10 years, free access to more than 6,000 legal forms, and a free guide with 20,000 links to other law-related Internet sites in 30 categories. Registration is required to access the free material, and enhanced searching and access to additional LexisNexis materials and databases is available for a fee.

3. Loislaw [§205]

Loislaw (http://www.loislaw.com), a Wolters Kluwer company, offers paid access to cases, statutes, constitutions, court rules, etc., for all 50 states and the District of

Columbia, as well as treatises and legal forms. Loislaw also has federal circuit court and district court databases, and a Bankruptcy Court collection.

4. Versus Law [§206]

The Versus Law website (http://www.versuslaw.com), available by subscription, includes court opinions from the United States Supreme Court, all federal circuit courts of appeals, federal district courts, all state appellate courts, and Native American tribal courts. Versus Law also includes the federal code and *Code of Federal Regulations,* and over 20,000 legal forms.

5. HeinOnline [§207]

HeinOnline (http://heinonline.org) contains dozens of libraries, including the Law Journal Library, the Federal Register Library, the Treaties and Agreements Library, and the United States Supreme Court Library. Although it is available only by subscription, many law schools subscribe to it, thus making it available through the school's website. All HeinOnline libraries are image-based and fully searchable, and exact page images are provided.

6. Bloomberg Law [§208]

Bloomberg Law (http://www.bloomberglaw.com) is an online research system available by paid subscription. It integrates legal research with Bloomberg's established database of financial information. Bloomberg Law's services include a proprietary law digest, law reports, and an online citator verification system (*see supra*, §157).

7. Fastcase [§209]

Fastcase (http://www.fastcase.com) is an online research system available to individuals, law schools, and law firms, and offered by several bar associations as a free member benefit. Fastcase's paid subscription database includes cases, statutes, regulations, news, and legal forms, and integrates the PACER system for federal docket searches (*see supra*, §174). Fastcase also provides a free mobile application that allows users to research cases and statutes without a subscription (*see supra*, §201).

Chapter Nine: Reading and Understanding a Case

CONTENTS

A. Introduction to Case Analysis

1. In General [§210]

Finding a case is only the beginning. The real problem and the place where most people find themselves stymied is in reading and understanding the case they have found. What are the highlights of the decision—the most important points? What were the facts, what issues did the court consider, and how did it resolve these issues? In law school, the method of separating the wheat from the chaff of a decision is called "briefing" a case.

2. Briefing Cases [§211]

As the word implies, a brief is a concise outline of the court decision. (This term "brief" should not be confused with a "brief" filed by an attorney in a court. A brief in the latter context is a forceful presentation of the issues and law involved in the client's case. It is designed to persuade the court to decide in the client's favor.) Briefing a case helps you organize your thoughts and determine what the court is actually saying. Because many court opinions are long-winded and often shrouded in legal terms, briefing is a more difficult skill than first imagined. It is not surprising to find that many law students and even lawyers will misread cases and jumble their analysis of the law on the subject under investigation. Without this skill, you will never be very effective in doing legal research and writing.

There are several times when you should brief a case. The first and most important is to help you understand what is going on. It is to this concern that we have written this chapter.

In doing research, a good brief will cut down your time measurably. You will not have to go back to read the case again because you cannot remember what it said and your notes are all jumbled. It will also make it simpler for you to be well organized in preparing your own case in court or at an administrative hearing.

Remember, a brief is just that. It is designed to give the reader an insight into the basic points of the case—no more. If the reader is interested in knowing more, she can always look up the case.

Following our discussion on briefing a case, we reprint an actual decision of the United States Supreme Court. In the hope that you will first try to brief this case yourself, we will conclude the chapter with a brief of the case.

a. Suggested format [§212]

This is the outline we will use in briefing a case:

(1) Name and citation;

(2) Court;

(3) Judicial history;

(4) Facts;

(5) Issue(s);

(6) Holding(s);

(7) Reasoning;

(8) Decision;

(9) Concurring opinion(s); and

(10) Dissenting opinion(s).

To help illustrate the writing of a brief, we will work with a simple set of facts from a fictitious case:

Lafcadio Hearn's landlord, Knut Hamsun, has not repaired the broken toilet in Hearn's apartment. Hearn decides not to pay rent until Hamsun fixes it. Ten days after the rent is due and unpaid, Hamsun sues to evict Hearn in the state's trial court. In court, Hearn argues that he should not have to pay rent when the place is uninhabitable. The trial judge rules in favor of Hamsun, saying that although he may sympathize with Hearn, there is no state statute allowing this kind of rent withholding. Hearn appeals to the state court of appeals, which agrees with the trial court. Hearn now appeals to the state supreme court. (For an actual decision dealing with a similar set of facts and law, *see Green v. Superior Court*, 10 Cal. 3d 616, 517 P.2d 1168, 111 Cal. Rptr. 704 (1974).)

b. Name and citation (including year) [§213]

The name of a case is usually two names separated by the abbreviation "v.," which stands for "versus." The name of our case is *Hamsun v. Hearn.* The case name is either underlined or in italics. First names are not used unless they are part of an organization's full name or title (*e.g., Joe Roth Fund v. San Francisco Gazette*). It is not necessary to add the names of other plaintiffs and defendants involved in the case, nor even to use the Latin phrase *et al.* to indicate their existence. The name of the case is only a means of identification. If someone is interested in the other parties to the case, he can look it up.

Give all the citations—official and unofficial, the official appearing first. (Citations are discussed *supra,* §§54-55.) The year of the decision follows the citations. Be sure to include it; it makes a difference whether the case was decided in 1959 or 2001.

c. **Court [§214]**

Always note the court that rendered the decision. Because there is a hierarchy in our court system, a decision by one court may be more important than a decision by another. To understand the full effect of the decision—that is, its precedential value—it is necessary to know whether the highest court, an appellate court, or a trial court issued it. Be sure to give the precise name of the court to avoid any confusion. In our example, we are in the state supreme court.

d. **Judicial history [§215]**

The judicial history (often referred to as the "procedural posture") of a case is the history prior to where the case is now. It considers questions such as: What was the plaintiff asking for when he first brought the case; that is, what "judicial relief" did he want? (Sometimes, the defendant may not only defend the action but also bring his own lawsuit or claim against the plaintiff in the same action. The defendant's affirmative suit against the plaintiff is called a "counterclaim" or a "cross-complaint," depending on the jurisdiction.) What happened to the case in the lower court(s)—what decision(s) were made on the rights of the parties?

A judicial history of our example would read: Plaintiff-landlord brought action to evict defendant-tenant for nonpayment of rent and to recover the rent due. Trial court ruled in favor of plaintiff, as did court of appeals. Defendant appealed to the state supreme court.

e. **Facts [§216]**

We cannot overemphasize the importance of facts. Everything else is determined by them. Had the facts been different—even slightly—the issues, the holdings, the reasonings, and the decision would likely have been different.

In reading a case, pay close attention to the presentation of the facts: Which facts does the court consider important, and which does the court pass over? The seed of the decision lies in the facts.

Read the case through. Often you cannot tell which facts the court considered essential to the decision until you have read the entire case. Then, in briefing, you will be able to glean the most important points so that you will not find yourself overwriting.

No matter how long and detailed the facts are in a case, you can usually filter them down to a few sentences. People who begin writing briefs usually write too many facts. Remember, a brief is only an outline; someone who is interested in every detail can always go and read the case.

The facts of our case would be: Landlord did not repair a broken toilet in tenant's apartment. The tenant claimed the place was uninhabitable and refused to pay rent until the landlord made the repairs.

As you gain experience in reading cases, you will see how judges play around with a set of facts, manipulating them to reach a desired decision. They will try to make the plaintiff or defendant an object of sympathy, depending on whom they think should win. Often one judge on an appellate court will emphasize one fact while another judge will emphasize another. Basing their decisions "on the facts," the two judges will then reach different conclusions.

Judges also play around with facts when looking at earlier, possibly precedent-setting cases. If a judge agrees with a decision of an earlier case, she will often say that the facts of the earlier case are similar to the facts in the present case, and hence will reach a similar decision. If the judge disagrees with the earlier decision, she may "distinguish" the earlier case "on its facts" and conclude that the earlier decision would not apply in the present case. The judge will then decide her case differently.

The clever attorney will thus present the facts of his case in a way to be as similar as possible to those of an earlier decided case in which the outcome is the same as that which the attorney wishes to reach now.

f. Issue(s) [§217]

The issue is the principle of law the court is considering. It is strictly determined by the facts of the case. If the facts were different, the issue would likely be different.

The issue is presented as a question of law. It may be written in terms of the particular facts of the case, or in general terms. In our example, the issue in specific terms would read: Can the tenant withhold his rent until the landlord repairs the toilet? In general terms it might read: Can a tenant withhold his rent until the landlord brings the place up to a habitable condition?

The problem with writing an issue in general terms is that it may reach too far. For example, in our case what is habitability? Does a broken stove mean the place is uninhabitable? What about a broken shelf or broken drawer? Because cases are interpreted in different ways by different lawyers and judges, a general issue has much more chance of being inaccurate or misleading.

Nevertheless, because law needs to establish precedent, a decision must necessarily yield a principle of law somewhat larger than a statement just to the particular facts of the case. But the question is, how much larger? It differs with each decision—how broad or narrow the judges try to make it—and with how judges in later cases interpret the decision by expanding or constricting it.

You should begin by constructing issues in terms of the specific facts. This will give you a clear understanding of the case. It will be easier later for you to expand the specific issue into a general one, without overextending the principle, once you have grasped the import and direction of the case.

There may be more than one issue in a case. Rarely are there more than two or three. A court can usually make its decision and dispose of the case after deciding one or two points of law raised by the issues. Other issues raised by the parties need not then be considered. In briefing a case, only give the issues that are ***actually decided by the court*** and are necessary to the decision. Remember, as we noted in chapter III, the headnotes to the case refer to many more principles of law than are actually raised by the issues in the case and decided by the court.

g. Holding(s) [§218]

A holding answers the question and settles the principle of law raised by an issue. There is a holding for each issue. Holdings, like issues, may be written in general or specific terms. Here, too, we suggest you begin with a specific holding, one in terms of the particular facts of the case. Then, when you have a good understanding of the decision, you can expand the holding to a more general one, being careful not to overbroaden it. A general holding has more value since it covers more than your specific fact situation. However, later courts, dealing with similar situations, will determine precisely how broad or narrow the range of the holding should be.

The specific holding in our case would be: The tenant can withhold his rent until the landlord repairs the toilet. In general terms it might read: A tenant can raise the defense of "warranty of habitability" and withhold his rent until the landlord makes the necessary repairs to bring the place up to a habitable condition.

Since most courts can decide a case by resolving only one or a few issues, you will rarely find a case with more than two or three necessary holdings. When a court discusses additional incidental points of law, points not necessary to the decision, it is reciting "dicta." A principle of law stated in dicta is not binding precedent on later courts—only a holding is.

If you are having trouble determining the holdings in the case, do not rely on what the headnotes to the case say. Most of the principles in the headnotes are dicta. Instead go back to your issues. Remember, your holdings must answer the questions of law raised by your issues. There are only as many holdings as there are issues, and there are only as many sets of issues and holdings as are needed to dispose of the case.

h. Reasoning [§219]

A judge must give reasons for the holding. She must show that the holding was arrived at thoughtfully and logically and that it is consistent with earlier cases. Our system of law is based on these premises. Even judges who from the first know which way they will decide a case understand that explanations must be given to support their decision.

In our example, the reasonings would include:

(i) The old law requiring tenants to pay rent regardless of the condition of the place dates back to an agricultural era where leases were for land, the house being merely "incidental." The farmer could usually make the necessary repairs. Today, leases are largely for urban dwellings, and the tenant lacks the skills or finances to make the sophisticated repairs.

(ii) In other consumer contracts, the law recognizes implied warranties and the rights of the consumer to enforce them.

(iii) Because of the scarcity of low-rent housing, tenants have little bargaining power to negotiate for proper maintenance and repairs.

Depending on the complexity and the importance of a case, two to four reasons are usually sufficient to support a holding. Remember, you need to give reasons for each holding in your brief.

i. Decision [§220]

The word "decision" is often loosely used interchangeably with "opinion" or "case," *e.g.,* "the decision held that . . . ." But we will give it a narrower, more defined interpretation in our brief outline: The decision disposes of the case. It tells which party prevails. If the case is in a trial court, the judge will grant judgment in favor of the plaintiff or defendant. If the case is in a higher court, the decision will affirm (agree with) the lower court ruling, reverse (disagree), modify (agree in part, disagree in part), vacate (annul), or remand (return) it for further proceedings or a new trial. The precise words are usually found at the very end of the case. Note the difference between a holding, which establishes a principle of law, and a decision, which is concerned with the outcome and the parties.

In our example, the decision would read "reversed and remanded." That is, the supreme court reversed the decision of the court of appeals and remanded the case back to the trial court for a new trial based on the law as established in this case.

j. Concurring opinion(s) [§221]

The court opinion we just briefed is the majority opinion. It is the one with which a clear majority of the judges are in accord. But it is not always the only opinion you will see in a case. Often you will find judges who agree on the outcome of the case—the decision—but who disagree on the principle of law—the holding—that should be applied in reaching that decision. One or two judges may, for example, wish to narrow or broaden the extent of the holding. Or, the judges may agree on the holding but disagree on the reasons for the holding. These judges who disagree with the holdings or reasonings, but agree with the decision, may write concurring opinions explaining their differences.

There will be times when you will find a case with no absolute majority opinion. That is, a majority of the members of the court cannot agree on the same holding. For example, in the United States Supreme Court case of *Regents of the University of California v. Bakke*, 438 U.S. 265, 98 S. Ct. 2733, 57 L. Ed. 2d 750 (1978), four of the members of the Court agreed on one point and four members agreed on another. The ninth member, Justice Powell, voted with one set of four on one issue and with the other group on the other.

Another example would be where a seven-judge court may have four judges who agree on the decision, but only three can agree on a holding, while the fourth would have a narrower holding.

In these kinds of cases, each opinion will be given more concern than a concurring opinion in a case in which there is a clear majority opinion.

The extent of noting a concurring opinion in your brief depends upon its importance in the case. Where there is a clear majority opinion (the usual case), examine the concurring opinion for any additional insight it may give to the problem. If the opinion is written by a learned, well-respected judge, it may merit more attention.

Where there is no absolute majority opinion, each opinion should be considered. (Where more judges join in one opinion than in any other, but there is no "majority" opinion, the lead opinion is called the plurality opinion.) Of course, where a concurring opinion discusses a point of law with which you are particularly concerned, you should note it. Usually, two or three sentences are sufficient to summarize a concurring opinion.

k. Dissenting opinion(s) [§222]

A dissenting opinion is one that disagrees with the decision, and necessarily also with the holding, reached by a majority of the members of the court. For example, the majority decision may be to affirm a lower court ruling, while the dissenting judge(s) would reverse it.

Although the law is determined by majority decisions, minority opinions serve an important purpose. Often they add to the understanding of the problem and expose the holes or weaknesses in the majority's position. In themselves, they may influence future courts or the legislature to change the law. Dissenting opinions may be ahead of their time or may tread behind.

Of course, higher courts will at times reverse lower court decisions; thus a dissenting lower court judge may find herself vindicated later on.

Just as with a concurring opinion, in noting a dissent in your brief, you need only indicate the points of disagreement and any other information that would further your understanding of the case. If the dissent is by a well-respected judge or if you are concerned with the matter (perhaps agreeing with the dissent), you may wish to discuss the opinion in more detail. Usually two or three sentences will do.

3. Reminder—Read Cases Thoroughly [§223]

Before you begin briefing a case, read it all the way through. Get a feel for it. See how the court presents the facts and resolves the issues. If you are unsure as to what is happening, read it again. If, after the second time, you are still uncertain as to what the court is saying, the problem may be with the way the opinion is written rather than with any failing on your part. People often have trouble expressing themselves in print, and judges are no exception. Do not ever simply rely on the headnotes or the summary of a case.

B. Sample Brief

1. Example Case [§224]

On the next several pages, we have reprinted an entire decision of the United States Supreme Court. Read the case through. Then prepare a brief for it using the recommended outline (*see supra,* §§212 *et seq.*). After you have written your brief, compare it to the brief that follows the case.

Remember: There is no magic way to write a brief. People's briefs are as different as people's use of words. As long as your brief is well-organized and covers the main points of the case, you have done well. The following example is only to help you see whether you have gleaned the proper points. Your brief does not have to be precisely the same.

BOUNDS, CORRECTION COMMISSIONER, ET AL. v. SMITH ET AL.

CERTIORARI TO THE UNITED STATES COURT OF APPEALS FOR THE FOURTH CIRCUIT

No. 75-915. Argued November 1, 1976—Decided April 27, 1977

The fundamental constitutional right of access to the courts *held* to require prison authorities to assist inmates in the preparation and filing of meaningful legal papers by providing prisoners with adequate law libraries or adequate assistance from persons trained in the law. *Younger* v. *Gilmore*, 404 U. S. 15. Pp. 821-833.

538 F. 2d 541, affirmed.

MARSHALL, J., delivered the opinion of the Court, in which BRENNAN, WHITE, BLACKMUN, POWELL, and STEVENS, JJ., joined. POWELL, J., filed a concurring opinion, *post*, p. 833. BURGER, C. J., filed a dissenting opinion, *post*, p. 833. STEWART, J., *post*, p. 836, and REHNQUIST, J., *post*, p. 837, filed dissenting opinions, in which BURGER, C. J., joined.

Jacob L. Safron, Special Deputy Attorney General of North Carolina, argued the cause for petitioners. With him on the brief was *Rufus L. Edmisten*, Attorney General.

Barry Nakell, by appointment of the Court, 425 U. S. 968, argued the cause and filed a brief for respondents.*

MR. JUSTICE MARSHALL delivered the opinion of the Court.

The issue in this case is whether States must protect the right of prisoners to access to the courts by providing them with law libraries or alternative sources of legal knowledge. In *Younger* v. *Gilmore*, 404 U. S. 15 (1971), we held *per curiam* that such services are constitutionally mandated. Petitioners, officials of the State of North Carolina, ask us

**Andrew P. Miller*, Attorney General, and *Alan Katz*, Assistant Attorney General, filed a brief for the Commonwealth of Virginia as *amicus curiae* urging reversal.

Opinion of the Court

to overrule that recent case, but for reasons explained below, we decline the invitation and reaffirm our previous decision.

I

Respondents are inmates incarcerated in correctional facilities of the Division of Prisons of the North Carolina Department of Correction. They filed three separate actions under 42 U. S. C. § 1983, all eventually consolidated in the District Court for the Eastern District of North Carolina. Respondents alleged, in pertinent part, that they were denied access to the courts in violation of their Fourteenth Amendment rights by the State's failure to provide legal research facilities.[1]

The District Court granted respondents' motion for summary judgment on this claim,[2] finding that the sole prison library in the State was "severely inadequate" and that there was no other legal assistance available to inmates. It held on the basis of *Younger* v. *Gilmore* that respondents' rights to access to the courts and equal protection of the laws had been violated because there was "no indication of any assistance at the initial stage of preparation of writs and petitions." The court recognized, however, that determining the "appropriate relief to be ordered . . . presents a difficult problem," in view of North Carolina's decentralized prison system.[3] Rather than attempting "to dictate precisely what course the State should follow," the court "charge[d] the Depart-

[1] The complaints also alleged a number of other constitutional violations not relevant to the issue now before us.

[2] The District Court had originally granted summary judgment for the state officials in one of the three consolidated actions. On appeal, the Court of Appeals for the Fourth Circuit appointed counsel and remanded that case with the suggestion that it be consolidated with the other two cases, then still pending in the District Court.

[3] North Carolina's 13,000 inmates are housed in 77 prison units located in 67 counties. Sixty-five of these units hold fewer than 200 inmates. Brief for Petitioners 7 n. 3.

ment of Correction with the task of devising a Constitutionally sound program" to assure inmate access to the courts. It left to the State the choice of what alternative would "most easily and economically" fulfill this duty, suggesting that a program to make available lawyers, law students, or public defenders might serve the purpose at least as well as the provision of law libraries. Supp. App. 12–13.

The State responded by proposing the establishment of seven libraries in institutions located across the State chosen so as to serve best all prison units. In addition, the State planned to set up smaller libraries in the Central Prison segregation unit and the Women's Prison. Under the plan, inmates desiring to use a library would request appointments. They would be given transportation and housing, if necessary, for a full day's library work. In addition to its collection of lawbooks,[4] each library would stock legal forms and writing paper and have typewriters and use of copying machines. The State proposed to train inmates as research assistants and typists to aid fellow prisoners. It was estimated that ultimately some 350 inmates per week could use the libraries, although inmates not facing court deadlines might have to wait three or four weeks for their turn at a library. Respondents protested that the plan was totally inadequate and sought establishment of a library at every prison.[5]

The District Court rejected respondents' objections, finding the State's plan "both economically feasible and practicable," and one that, fairly and efficiently run, would "insure each inmate the time to prepare his petitions."[6] Supp. App. 19. Further briefing was ordered on whether the State was required to provide independent legal advisors for inmates in addition to the library facilities.

In its final decision, the District Court held that petitioners were not constitutionally required to provide legal assistance as well as libraries. It found that the library plan was suf-

[4] The State proposed inclusion of the following law books:
North Carolina General Statutes
North Carolina Reports (1960–present)
North Carolina Court of Appeals Reports
Strong's North Carolina Index
North Carolina Rules of Court
United States Code Annotated:
Title 18
Title 28 §§ 2241–2254
Title 28 Rules of Appellate Procedure
Title 28 Rules of Civil Procedure
Title 42 §§ 1891–2010
Supreme Court Reporter (1960–present)
Federal 2d Reporters (1960–present)
Federal Supplement (1960–present)
Black's Law Dictionary
Sokol: Federal Habeas Corpus
LaFave and Scott: Criminal Law Hornbook (2 copies)
Cohen: Legal Research
Criminal Law Reporter
Palmer: Constitutional Rights of Prisoners

This proposal adheres to a list approved as the minimum collection for prison law libraries by the American Correctional Association (ACA), American Bar Association (ABA), and the American Association of Law Libraries, except for the questionable omission of several treatises, Shepard's Citations, and local rules of court. See ACA, Guidelines for Legal Reference Service in Correctional Institutions: A Tool for Correctional Administrators 5–9 (2d ed. 1975) (hereafter ACA Guidelines); ABA Commission on Correctional Facilities and Services, Bar Association Support to Improve Correctional Services (BASICS), Offender Legal Services 29–30, 70–78 (rev. ed. 1976).

[5] Respondents also contended that the libraries should contain additional legal materials, and they urged creation of a large central circulating library.

[6] The District Court did order two changes in the plan: that extra copies of the U. S. C. A. Habeas Corpus and Civil Rights Act volumes be provided, and that no reporter advance sheets be discarded, so that the libraries would slowly build up duplicate sets. But the court found that most of the prison units were too small to require their own libraries, and that the cost of the additional books proposed by respondents would surpass their usefulness.

ficient to give inmates reasonable access to the courts and that our decision in *Ross* v. *Moffitt*, 417 U. S. 600 (1974), while not directly in point, supported the State's claim that it need not furnish attorneys to bring habeas corpus and civil rights actions for prisoners.

After the District Court approved the library plan, the State submitted an application to the Federal Law Enforcement Assistance Administration (LEAA) for a grant to cover 90% of the cost of setting up the libraries and training a librarian and inmate clerks. The State represented to LEAA that the library project would benefit all inmates in the State by giving them "meaningful and effective access to the court[s]. . . . [T]he ultimate result . . . should be a diminution in the number of groundless petitions and complaints filed . . . . The inmate himself will be able to determine to a greater extent whether or not his rights have been violated" and judicial evaluation of the petitions will be facilitated. Brief for Respondents 3a.

Both sides appealed from those portions of the District Court orders adverse to them. The Court of Appeals for the Fourth Circuit affirmed in all respects save one. It found that the library plan denied women prisoners the same access rights as men to research facilities. Since there was no justification for this discrimination, the Court of Appeals ordered it eliminated. The State petitioned for review and we granted certiorari. 425 U. S. 910 (1976).[7] We affirm.

II

A. It is now established beyond doubt that prisoners have a constitutional right of access to the courts. This Court recognized that right more than 35 years ago when it struck down a regulation prohibiting state prisoners from filing petitions for habeas corpus unless they were found " 'properly drawn' " by the " 'legal investigator' " for the parole board. *Ex parte Hull*, 312 U. S. 546 (1941). We held this violated the principle that "the state and its officers may not abridge or impair petitioner's right to apply to a federal court for a writ of habeas corpus." *Id.*, at 549. See also *Cochran* v. *Kansas*, 316 U. S. 255 (1942).

More recent decisions have struck down restrictions and required remedial measures to insure that inmate access to the courts is adequate, effective, and meaningful. Thus, in order to prevent "effectively foreclosed access," indigent prisoners must be allowed to file appeals and habeas corpus petitions without payment of docket fees. *Burns* v. *Ohio*, 360 U. S. 252, 257 (1959); *Smith* v. *Bennett*, 365 U. S. 708 (1961). Because we recognized that "adequate and effective appellate review" is impossible without a trial transcript or adequate substitute, we held that States must provide trial records to inmates unable to buy them. *Griffin* v. *Illinois*, 351 U. S. 12, 20 (1956).[8] Similarly, counsel must be ap-

[7] Respondents filed no cross-appeal and do not now question the library plan, nor do petitioners challenge the sex discrimination ruling.

[8] See also *Eskridge* v. *Washington Prison Bd.*, 357 U. S. 214 (1958) (provision of trial transcript may not be conditioned on approval of judge); *Draper* v. *Washington*, 372 U. S. 487 (1963) (same); *Lane* v. *Brown*, 372 U. S. 477 (1963) (public defender's approval may not be required to obtain *coram nobis* transcript); *Rinaldi* v. *Yeager*, 384 U. S. 305 (1966) (unconstitutional to require reimbursement for cost of trial transcript only from unsuccessful imprisoned defendants); *Long* v. *District Court of Iowa*, 385 U. S. 192 (1966) (State must provide transcript of post-conviction proceeding); *Roberts* v. *LaVallee*, 389 U. S. 40 (1967) (State must provide preliminary hearing transcript); *Gardner* v. *California*, 393 U. S. 367 (1969) (State must provide habeas corpus transcript); *Williams* v. *Oklahoma City*, 395 U. S. 458 (1969) (State must provide transscript of petty-offense trial); *Mayer* v. *Chicago*, 404 U. S. 189 (1971) (State must provide transcript of nonfelony trial).

The only cases that have rejected indigent defendants' claims to transcripts have done so either because an adequate alternative was available but not used, *Britt* v. *North Carolina*, 404 U. S. 226 (1971), or because the request was plainly frivolous and a prior opportunity to obtain a transcript was waived, *United States* v. *MacCollom*, 426 U. S. 317 (1976).

pointed to give indigent inmates "a meaningful appeal" from their convictions. *Douglas* v. *California*, 372 U. S. 353, 358 (1963).

Essentially the same standards of access were applied in *Johnson* v. *Avery*, 393 U. S. 483 (1969), which struck down a regulation prohibiting prisoners from assisting each other with habeas corpus applications and other legal matters. Since inmates had no alternative form of legal assistance available to them, we reasoned that this ban on jailhouse lawyers effectively prevented prisoners who were "unable themselves, with reasonable adequacy, to prepare their petitions," from challenging the legality of their confinements. *Id.*, at 489. *Johnson* was unanimously extended to cover assistance in civil rights actions in *Wolff* v. *McDonnell*, 418 U. S. 539, 577–580 (1974). And even as it rejected a claim that indigent defendants have a constitutional right to appointed counsel for discretionary appeals, the Court reaffirmed that States must "assure the indigent defendant an adequate opportunity to present his claims fairly." *Ross* v. *Moffitt*, 417 U. S., at 616. "[M]eaningful access" to the courts is the touchstone. See *id.*, at 611, 612, 615.[9]

Petitioners contend, however, that this constitutional duty merely obliges States to allow inmate "writ writers" to function. They argue that under *Johnson* v. *Avery*, *supra*, as long as inmate communications on legal problems are not restricted, there is no further obligation to expend state funds to implement affirmatively the right of access. This argument misreads the cases.

In *Johnson* and *Wolff* v. *McDonnell*, *supra*, the issue was whether the access rights of ignorant and illiterate inmates were violated without adequate justification. Since these inmates were unable to present their own claims in writing to the courts, we held that their "constitutional right to help," *Johnson* v. *Avery*, *supra*, at 502 (WHITE, J., dissenting), required at least allowing assistance from their literate fellows. But in so holding, we did not attempt to set forth the full breadth of the right of access. In *McDonnell*, for example, there was already an adequate law library in the prison.[10] The case was thus decided against a backdrop of availability of legal information to those inmates capable of using it. And in *Johnson*, although the petitioner originally requested lawbooks, see 393 U. S., at 484, the Court did not reach the question, as it invalidated the regulation because of its effect on illiterate inmates. Neither case considered the question we face today and neither is inconsistent with requiring additional measures to assure meaningful access to inmates able to present their own cases.[11]

Moreover, our decisions have consistently required States to shoulder affirmative obligations to assure all prisoners meaningful access to the courts. It is indisputable that indigent inmates must be provided at state expense with paper and pen to draft legal documents, with notarial services to

[9] The same standards were applied in *United States* v. *MacCollom*, *supra*.

[10] The plaintiffs stipulated in the District Court to the general adequacy of the library, see *McDonnell* v. *Wolff*, 342 F. Supp. 616, 618, 629–630 (Neb. 1972), although they contested certain limitations on its use. Those claims were resolved by the lower courts. See *id.*, at 619–622; 483 F. 2d 1059, 1066 (CA8 1973); 418 U. S., at 543 n. 2.

[11] Indeed, our decision is supported by the holding in *Procunier* v. *Martinez*, 416 U. S. 396 (1974), in a related right-of-access context. There the Court invalidated California regulations barring law students and paraprofessionals employed by lawyers representing prisoners from seeing inmate clients. *Id.*, at 419–422. We did so even though California has prison law libraries and permits inmate legal assistance, *Gilmore* v. *Lynch*, 319 F. Supp. 105, 107 n. 1 (ND Cal. 1970), aff'd *sub nom.* *Younger* v. *Gilmore*, 404 U. S. 15 (1971). Even more significantly, the prisoners in question were actually represented by lawyers. Thus, despite the challenged regulation, the inmates were receiving more legal assistance than prisoners aided only by writ writers. Nevertheless, we found that the regulation "impermissibly burdened the right of access." 416 U. S., at 421.

authenticate them, and with stamps to mail them. States must forgo collection of docket fees otherwise payable to the treasury and expend funds for transcripts. State expenditures are necessary to pay lawyers for indigent defendants at trial, *Gideon* v. *Wainwright,* 372 U. S. 335 (1963); *Argersinger* v. *Hamlin,* 407 U. S. 25 (1972), and in appeals as of right, *Douglas* v. *California, supra.*[12] This is not to say that economic factors may not be considered, for example, in choosing the methods used to provide meaningful access. But the cost of protecting a constitutional right cannot justify its total denial. Thus, neither the availability of jailhouse lawyers nor the necessity for affirmative state action is dispositive of respondents' claims. The inquiry is rather whether law libraries or other forms of legal assistance are needed to give prisoners a reasonably adequate opportunity to present claimed violations of fundamental constitutional rights to the courts.

B. Although it is essentially true, as petitioners argue,[13] that a habeas corpus petition or civil rights complaint need only set forth facts giving rise to the cause of action, but see, Fed. Rules Civ. Proc. 8 (a)(1), (3), it hardly follows that a law library or other legal assistance is not essential to frame such documents. It would verge on incompetence for a lawyer to file an initial pleading without researching such issues as jurisdiction, venue, standing, exhaustion of remedies, proper parties plaintiff and defendant, and types of relief available. Most importantly, of course, a lawyer must know what the law is in order to determine whether a colorable claim exists, and if so, what facts are necessary to state a cause of action.

If a lawyer must perform such preliminary research, it is no less vital for a *pro se* prisoner.[14] Indeed, despite the "less stringent standards" by which a *pro se* pleading is judged, *Haines* v. *Kerner,* 404 U. S. 519, 520 (1972), it is often more important that a prisoner complaint set forth a nonfrivolous claim meeting all procedural prerequisites, since the court may pass on the complaint's sufficiency before allowing filing *in forma pauperis* and may dismiss the case if it is deemed frivolous. See 28 U. S. C. § 1915.[15] Moreover, if the State files a response to a *pro se* pleading, it will undoubtedly contain seemingly authoritative citations. Without a library, an inmate will be unable to rebut the State's argument. It is not enough to answer that the court will evaluate the facts pleaded in light of the relevant law. Even the most dedicated trial judges are bound to overlook meritorious cases without the benefit of an adversary presentation. Cf. *Gardner* v. *California,* 393 U. S. 367, 369–370 (1969). In fact, one of the consolidated cases here was initially dismissed by the same judge who later ruled for respondents, possibly because *Younger* v. *Gilmore* was not cited.

We reject the State's claim that inmates are "ill-equipped to use" "the tools of the trade of the legal profession," making libraries useless in assuring meaningful access. Brief for Petitioners 17. In the first place, the claim is inconsistent with the State's representations on its LEAA grant application, *supra,* at 821, and with its argument that access is adequately protected by allowing inmates to help each other with legal problems. More importantly, this Court's experience indicates that *pro se* petitioners are capable of using lawbooks to file cases raising claims that are serious and legitimate even

[12] Cf. *Estelle* v. *Gamble,* 429 U. S. 97 (1976), holding that States must treat prisoners' serious medical needs, a constitutional duty obviously requiring outlays for personnel and facilities.

[13] Brief for Petitioners 16–17; Tr. of Oral Arg. 3–9, 11–12.

[14] A source of current legal information would be particularly important so that prisoners could learn whether they have claims at all, as where new court decisions might apply retroactively to invalidate convictions.

[15] The propriety of these practices is not before us. Courts may also impose additional burdens before appointing counsel for indigents in civil suits. See *Johnson* v. *Avery,* 393 U. S. 483, 487–488 (1969).

if ultimately unsuccessful. Finally, we note that if petitioners had any doubts about the efficacy of libraries, the District Court's initial decision left them free to choose another means of assuring access.

It is also argued that libraries or other forms of legal assistance are unnecessary to assure meaningful access in light of the Court's decision in *Ross* v. *Moffitt*. That case held that the right of prisoners to "an adequate opportunity to present [their] claims fairly," 417 U. S., at 616, did not require appointment of counsel to file petitions for discretionary review in state courts or in this Court. *Moffitt*'s rationale, however, supports the result we reach here. The decision in *Moffitt* noted that a court addressing a discretionary review petition is not primarily concerned with the correctness of the judgment below. Rather, review is generally granted only if a case raises an issue of significant public interest or jurisprudential importance or conflicts with controlling precedent. *Id.*, at 615–617. *Moffitt* held that *pro se* applicants can present their claims adequately for appellate courts to decide whether these criteria are met because they have already had counsel for their initial appeals as of right. They are thus likely to have appellate briefs previously written on their behalf, trial transcripts, and often intermediate appellate court opinions to use in preparing petitions for further review. *Id.*, at 615.

By contrast in this case, we are concerned in large part with original actions seeking new trials, release from confinement, or vindication of fundamental civil rights. Rather than presenting claims that have been passed on by two courts, they frequently raise heretofore unlitigated issues. As this Court has "constantly emphasized," habeas corpus and civil rights actions are of "fundamental importance . . . in our constitutional scheme" because they directly protect our most valued rights. *Johnson* v. *Avery*, 393 U. S., at 485; *Wolff* v. *McDonnell*, 418 U. S., at 579. While applications for

discretionary review need only apprise an appellate court of a case's possible relevance to the development of the law, the prisoner petitions here are the first line of defense against constitutional violations. The need for new legal research or advice to make a meaningful initial presentation to a trial court in such a case is far greater than is required to file an adequate petition for discretionary review.[16]

We hold, therefore, that the fundamental constitutional right of access to the courts requires prison authorities to assist inmates in the preparation and filing of meaningful legal papers by providing prisoners with adequate law libraries or adequate assistance from persons trained in the law.[17]

C. Our holding today is, of course, a reaffirmation of the result reached in *Younger* v. *Gilmore*. While *Gilmore* is not

[16] Nor is *United States* v. *MacCollom*, 426 U. S. 317 (1976), inconsistent with our decision. That case held that in a post-conviction proceeding under 28 U. S. C. § 2255, an applicant was not unconstitutionally deprived of access to the courts by denial of a transcript of his original trial pursuant to 28 U. S. C. § 753 (f), where he had failed to take a direct appeal and thereby secure the transcript, where his newly asserted claim of error was frivolous, and where he demonstrated no need for the transcript. Without a library or legal assistance, however, inmates will not have "a *current* opportunity to present [their] claims fairly." 426 U. S., at 329 (BLACKMUN, J., concurring in judgment), and valid claims will undoubtedly be lost.

[17] Since our main concern here is "protecting the ability of an inmate to prepare a petition or complaint," *Wolff* v. *McDonnell*, 418 U. S., at 576, it is irrelevant that North Carolina authorizes the expenditure of funds for appointment of counsel in some state post-conviction proceedings for prisoners whose claims survive initial review by the courts. See N. C. Gen. Stat. § 7A–451 (Supp. 1975): Brief for Petitioners 3 n. 1, 12 n. 8, 14 n. 9, and accompanying text: but cf. *Ross* v. *Moffitt*, 417 U. S. 600, 614 (1974). Moreover, this statute does not cover appointment of counsel in federal habeas corpus or state or federal civil rights actions, all of which are encompassed by the right of access.

Similarly, the State's creation of an advisory Inmate Grievance Commission, see N. C. Gen. Stat. § 148–101 *et seq.* (Supp. 1975): Brief for Petitioners 14, while certainly a noteworthy innovation, does not answer the constitutional requirement for legal assistance to prisoners.

a necessary element in the preceding analysis, its precedential weight strongly reinforces our decision. The substantive question presented in *Gilmore* was "Does a state have an affirmative federal constitutional duty to furnish prison inmates with extensive law libraries or, alternatively, to provide inmates with professional or quasi-professional legal assistance?" Jurisdictional Statement 5, Brief for Appellants 4, in No. 70-9, O. T. 1971. This Court explicitly decided that question when it affirmed the judgment of the District Court in reliance on *Johnson* v. *Avery*. Cf. this Court's Rule 15 (c). The affirmative answer was given unanimously after full briefing and oral argument. *Gilmore* has been relied upon without question in our subsequent decisions. *Cruz* v. *Hauck*, 404 U. S. 59 (1971) (vacating and remanding for reconsideration in light of *Gilmore* a decision that legal materials need not be furnished to county jail inmates); *Cruz* v. *Beto*, 405 U. S. 319, 321 (1972) (*Gilmore* cited approvingly in support of inmates' right of access to the courts); *Chaffin* v. *Stynchcombe*, 412 U. S. 17, 34 n. 22 (1973) (*Gilmore* cited approvingly as a decision "removing roadblocks and disincentives to appeal"). Most recently, in *Wolff* v. *McDonnell*, despite differences over other issues in the case, the Court unanimously reaffirmed that *Gilmore* requires prison officials "to provide indigent inmates with access to a reasonably adequate law library for preparation of legal actions." 418 U. S., at 578–579.

Experience under the *Gilmore* decision suggests no reason to depart from it. Most States and the Federal Government have made impressive efforts to fulfill *Gilmore's* mandate by establishing law libraries, prison legal-assistance programs, or combinations of both. See Brief for Respondents, Ex. B. Correctional administrators have supported the programs and acknowledged their value.[18] Resources and support including substantial funding from LEAA have come from many national organizations.[19]

It should be noted that while adequate law libraries are one constitutionally acceptable method to assure meaningful access to the courts, our decision here, as in *Gilmore*, does not foreclose alternative means to achieve that goal. Nearly

[18] Nearly 95% of the state corrections commissioners, prison wardens, and treatment directors responding to a national survey supported creation and expansion of prison legal services. Cardarelli & Finkelstein, Correctional Administrators Assess the Adequacy and Impact of Prison Legal Services Programs in the United States, 65 J. Crim. L., C. & P. S. 91, 99 (1974). Almost 85% believed that the programs would not adversely affect discipline or security or increase hostility toward the institution. Rather, over 80% felt legal services provide a safety valve for inmate grievances, reduce inmate power structures and tensions from unresolved legal problems, and contribute to rehabilitation by providing a positive experience with the legal system. *Id.*, at 95–98. See also ACA Guidelines, *supra*, n. 4; National Sheriffs' Assn., Inmates' Legal Rights, Standard 14, pp. 33–34 (1974); Bluth, Legal Services for Inmates: Coopting the Jailhouse Lawyer, 1 Capital U. L. Rev. 59, 61, 67 (1972); Sigler, A New Partnership in Corrections, 52 Neb. L. Rev. 35, 38 (1972).

[19] See, *e. g.*, U. S. Dept. of Justice, LEAA, A Compendium of Selected Criminal Justice Projects, III-201, IV-361-366 (1975); U. S. Dept. of Justice, LEAA, Grant 75 DF-99-0013, Consortium of States to Furnish Legal Counsel to Prisoners, Final Report, and Program Narrative (1975). The ABA BASICS program, see n. 4, *supra*, makes grants to state and local bar associations for prison legal services and libraries and publishes a complete technical assistance manual, Offender Legal Services (rev. ed. 1976). See also ABA Resource Center on Correctional Law and Legal Services, Providing Legal Services to Prisoners, 8 Ga. L. Rev. 363 (1974). The American Correctional Association publishes Guidelines for Legal Reference Service in Correctional Institutions (2d ed. 1975). The American Association of Law Libraries publishes O. Werner, Manual for Prison Law Libraries (1976), and its members offer assistance to prison law library personnel.

See also ABA Joint Committee on the Legal Status of Prisoners, Standards Relating to the Legal Status of Prisoners, Standards 2.1, 2.2, 2.3 and Commentary, 14 Am. Crim. L. Rev. 377, 420–443 (tent. draft 1977); National Conference of Commissioners on Uniform State Laws, Uniform Corrections Code, § 2–601 (tent. draft 1976); National Advisory Commission on Criminal Justice Standards and Goals, Corrections 26–30, Standards 2.2, 2.3 (1973).

half the States and the District of Columbia provide some degree of professional or quasi-professional legal assistance to prisoners. Brief for Respondents, Ex. B. Such programs take many imaginative forms and may have a number of advantages over libraries alone. Among the alternatives are the training of inmates as paralegal assistants to work under lawyers' supervision, the use of paraprofessionals and law students, either as volunteers or in formal clinical programs, the organization of volunteer attorneys through bar associations or other groups, the hiring of lawyers on a part-time consultant basis, and the use of full-time staff attorneys, working either in new prison legal assistance organizations or as part of public defender or legal services offices.[20] Legal services plans not only result in more efficient and skillful handling of prisoner cases, but also avoid the disciplinary problems associated with writ writers, see *Johnson* v. *Avery*, 393 U. S., at 488; *Procunier* v. *Martinez*, 416 U. S. 396, 421–422 (1974). Independent legal advisors can mediate or resolve administratively many prisoner complaints that would otherwise burden the courts, and can convince inmates that other grievances against the prison or the legal system are ill-founded, thereby facilitating rehabilitation by assuring the inmate that he has not been treated unfairly.[21] It has

[20] For example, full-time staff attorneys assisted by law students and a national back-up center were used by the Consortium of States to Furnish Legal Counsel to Prisoners, see n. 19, *supra*. State and local bar associations have established a number of legal services and library programs with support from the ABA BASICS program, see nn. 4 and 19, *supra*. Prisoners' Legal Services of New York plans to use 45 lawyers and legal assistants in seven offices to give comprehensive legal services to all state inmates. Offender Legal Services, *supra*, n. 19, at iv. Other programs are described in Providing Legal Services to Prisoners, *supra*, n. 19, at 399–416.

[21] See Cardarelli & Finkelstein, *supra*, n. 18, at 96–99; LEAA Consortium Reports, *supra*, n. 19; Champagne & Haas, The Impact of Johnson v. Avery on Prison Administration, 43 Tenn. L. Rev. 275, 295–299 (1976). Cf. 42 U. S. C. § 2996 (4) (1970 ed., Supp. V), in which Congress, establishing the Legal Services Corp., declared that "for many of our citizens, the availability of legal services has reaffirmed faith in our government of laws."

Opinion of the Court

been estimated that as few as 500 full-time lawyers would be needed to serve the legal needs of the entire national prison population.[22] Nevertheless, a legal access program need not include any particular element we have discussed, and we encourage local experimentation. Any plan, however, must be evaluated as a whole to ascertain its compliance with constitutional standards.[23]

III

Finally, petitioners urge us to reverse the decision below because federal courts should not "sit as co-administrators of state prisons," Brief for Petitioners 13, and because the District Court "exceeded its powers when it puts [*sic*] itself in the place of the [prison] administrators," *id.*, at 14. While we have recognized that judicial restraint is often appropriate in prisoners' rights cases, we have also repeatedly held that this policy "cannot encompass any failure to take cognizance of valid constitutional claims." *Procunier* v. *Martinez*, *supra*, at 405.

Petitioners' hyperbolic claim is particularly inappropriate in this case, for the courts below scrupulously respected the limits on their role. The District Court initially held only that petitioners had violated the "fundamental constitutional guarantee," *ibid.*, of access to the courts. It did not thereupon thrust itself into prison administration. Rather, it ordered petitioners themselves to devise a remedy for the violation, strongly suggesting that it would prefer a plan

[22] ABA Joint Committee, *supra*, n. 19, at 428–429.

[23] See, *e. g.*, *Stevenson* v. *Reed*, 530 F. 2d 1207 (CA5 1976), aff'g 391 F. Supp. 1375 (ND Miss. 1975); *Bryan* v. *Werner*, 516 F. 2d 233 (CA3 1975); *Gaglie* v. *Ulibarri*, 507 F. 2d 721 (CA9 1974); *Corpus* v. *Estelle*, 409 F. Supp. 1090 (SD Tex. 1975).

providing trained legal advisors. Petitioners chose to establish law libraries, however, and their plan was approved with only minimal changes over the strong objections of respondents. Prison administrators thus exercised wide discretion within the bounds of constitutional requirements in this case.

The judgment is

Affirmed.

MR. JUSTICE POWELL, concurring.

The decision today recognizes that a prison inmate has a constitutional right of access to the courts to assert such procedural and substantive rights as may be available to him under state and federal law. It does not purport to pass on the kinds of claims that the Constitution requires state or federal courts to hear. In *Wolff* v. *McDonnell*, 418 U. S. 539, 577–580 (1974), where we extended the right of access recognized in *Johnson* v. *Avery*, 393 U. S. 483 (1969), to civil rights actions arising under the Civil Rights Act of 1871, we did not suggest that the Constitution required such actions to be heard in federal court. And in *Griffin* v. *Illinois*, 351 U. S. 12 (1956), where the Court required the States to provide trial records for indigents on appeal, the plurality and concurring opinions explicitly recognized that the Constitution does not require any appellate review of state convictions. Similarly, the holding here implies nothing as to the constitutionally required scope of review of prisoners' claims in state or federal court.

With this understanding, I join the opinion of the Court.

MR. CHIEF JUSTICE BURGER, dissenting.

I am in general agreement with MR. JUSTICE STEWART and MR. JUSTICE REHNQUIST, and join in their opinions. I write only to emphasize the theoretical and practical difficulties raised by the Court's holding. The Court leaves us unenlightened as to the source of the "right of access to the courts"

which it perceives or of the requirement that States "foot the bill" for assuring such access for prisoners who want to act as legal researchers and brief writers. The holding, in my view, has far-reaching implications which I doubt have been fully analyzed or their consequences adequately assessed.

It should be noted, first, that the access to the courts which these respondents are seeking is not for the purpose of direct appellate review of their criminal convictions. Abundant access for such purposes has been guaranteed by our prior decisions, *e. g., Douglas* v. *California*, 372 U. S. 353 (1963), and *Griffin* v. *Illinois*, 351 U. S. 12 (1956), and by the States independently. Rather, the underlying substantive right here is that of prisoners to mount collateral attacks on their state convictions. The Court is ordering the State to expend resources in support of the federally created right of collateral review.

This would be understandable if the federal right in question were constitutional in nature. For example, the State may be required by the Eighth Amendment to provide its inmates with food, shelter, and medical care, see *Estelle* v. *Gamble*, 429 U. S. 97, 103–104 (1976); similarly, an indigent defendant's right under the Sixth Amendment places upon the State the affirmative duty to provide him with counsel for trials which may result in deprivation of his liberty, *Argersinger* v. *Hamlin*, 407 U. S. 25 (1972); finally, constitutional principles of due process and equal protection form the basis for the requirement that States expend resources in support of a convicted defendant's right to appeal. See *Douglas* v. *California, supra; Griffin* v. *Illinois, supra.*

However, where the federal right in question is of a statutory rather than a constitutional nature, the duty of the State is merely negative; it may not act in such a manner as to interfere with the individual exercise of such federal rights. *E. g., Ex parte Hull*, 312 U. S. 546 (1941) (State may not interfere with prisoner's access to the federal court by screening petitions directed to the court); *Johnson* v. *Avery*, 393 U. S. 483 (1969) (State may not prohibit prisoners from providing to each other assistance in preparing petitions directed to the federal courts). Prohibiting the State from interfering with federal statutory rights is, however, materially different from requiring it to provide affirmative assistance for their exercise.

It is a novel and doubtful proposition, in my view, that the Federal Government can, by statute, give individuals certain rights and then require the State, as a *constitutional* matter, to fund the means for exercise of those rights. Cf. *National League of Cities* v. *Usery*, 426 U. S. 833 (1976).

As to the substantive right of state prisoners to collaterally attack in federal court their convictions entered by a state court of competent jurisdiction, it is now clear that there is no broad federal *constitutional* right to such collateral attack, see *Stone* v. *Powell*, 428 U. S. 465 (1976); whatever right exists is solely a creation of federal statute, see *Swain* v. *Pressley*, *ante*, p. 384 (BURGER, C. J., concurring); *Schneckloth* v. *Bustamonte*, 412 U. S. 218, 250, 252–256 (1973) (POWELL, J., concurring). But absent a federal constitutional right to attack convictions collaterally—and I discern no such right—I can find no basis on which a federal court may require States to fund costly law libraries for prison inmates.* Proper federal-state relations preclude such intervention in the "complex and intractable" problems of prison administration. *Procunier* v. *Martinez*, 416 U. S. 396 (1974).

I can draw only one of two conclusions from the Court's holding: it may be read as implying that the right of prisoners to collaterally attack their convictions is constitutional, rather than statutory, in nature; alternatively, it may be read as holding that States can be compelled by federal courts to subsidize the exercise of federally created statutory rights. Neither of these novel propositions is sustainable and for the reasons stated I cannot adhere to either view and therefore dissent.

*The record reflects that prison officials in no way interfered with inmates' use of their own resources in filing collateral attacks. Prison regulations permit access to inmate "writ writers" and each prisoner is entitled to store reasonable numbers of lawbooks in his cell.

MR. JUSTICE STEWART, with whom MR. CHIEF JUSTICE BURGER joins, dissenting.

In view of the importance of the writ of habeas corpus in our constitutional scheme, " 'it is fundamental that access of prisoners to the courts for the purpose of presenting their complaints may not be denied or obstructed.' " *Wolff* v. *McDonnell*, 418 U. S. 539, 578, quoting *Johnson* v. *Avery*, 393 U. S. 483, 485. From this basic principle the Court over five years ago made a quantum jump to the conclusion that a State has a constitutional obligation to provide law libraries for prisoners in its custody. *Younger* v. *Gilmore*, 404 U. S. 15.

Today the Court seeks to bridge the gap in analysis that made *Gilmore*'s authority questionable. Despite the Court's valiant efforts, I find its reasoning unpersuasive.

If, as the Court says, there is a constitutional duty upon a State to provide its prisoners with "meaningful access" to the federal courts, that duty is not effectuated by adhering to the unexplained judgment in the *Gilmore* case. More than 20 years of experience with *pro se* habeas corpus petitions as a Member of this Court and as a Circuit Judge have convinced me that "meaningful access" to the federal courts can seldom be realistically advanced by the device of making law libraries available to prison inmates untutored in their use. In the vast majority of cases, access to a law library will, I am convinced, simply result in the filing of pleadings heavily larded with irrelevant legalisms—possessing the veneer but lacking the substance of professional competence.

If, on the other hand, MR. JUSTICE REHNQUIST is correct in his belief that a convict in a state prison pursuant to a final judgment of a court of competent jurisdiction has no constitutional right of "meaningful access" to the federal courts in order to attack his sentence, then a State can be under no constitutional duty to make that access "meaningful." If the extent of the constitutional duty of a State is simply not to deny or obstruct a prisoner's access to the courts, *Johnson* v. *Avery, supra*, then it cannot have, even arguably, any affirmative constitutional obligation to provide law libraries for its prison inmates.

I respectfully dissent.

MR. JUSTICE REHNQUIST, with whom MR. CHIEF JUSTICE BURGER joins, dissenting.

The Court's opinion in this case serves the unusual purpose of supplying as good a line of reasoning as is available to support a two-paragraph *per curiam* opinion almost six years ago in *Younger* v. *Gilmore*, 404 U. S. 15 (1971), which made no pretense of containing any reasoning at all. The Court's reasoning today appears to be that we have long held that prisoners have a "right of access" to the courts in order to file petitions for habeas corpus, and that subsequent decisions have expanded this concept into what the Court today describes as a "meaningful right of access." So, we are told, the right of a convicted prisoner to "meaningful access" extends to requiring the State to furnish such prisoners law libraries to aid them in piecing together complaints to be filed in the courts. This analysis places questions of prisoner access on a "slippery slope," and I would reject it because I believe that the early cases upon which the Court relies have a totally different rationale than underlies the present holding.

There is nothing in the United States Constitution which requires that a convict serving a term of imprisonment pursuant to a final judgment of a court of competent jurisdiction in a state penal institution have a "right of access" to the federal courts in order to attack his sentence. In the first

case upon which the Court's opinion relies, *Ex parte Hull*, 312 U. S. 546 (1941), the Court held invalid a regulation of the Michigan State prison which provided that " '[a]ll legal documents, briefs, petitions, motions, habeas corpus proceedings and appeals' " which prisoners wish to file in court had to be first submitted to the legal investigator of the state parole board. If the documents were, in the opinion of this official, " 'properly drawn,' " they would be directed to the court designated. Hull was advised that his petition addressed to this Court had been "intercepted" and referred to the legal investigator for the reason that it was "deemed to be inadequate." This Court held that such a regulation was invalid, and said very clearly why:

> "Whether a petition for writ of habeas corpus addressed to a federal court is properly drawn and what allegations it must contain are questions for that court alone to determine." *Id.*, at 549.

A number of succeeding cases have expanded on this barebones holding that an incarcerated prisoner has a right to physical access to a federal court in order to petition that court for relief which Congress has authorized it to grant. These cases, most of which are mentioned in the Court's opinion, begin with *Griffin* v. *Illinois*, 351 U. S. 12 (1956), and culminate in *United States* v. *MacCollom*, 426 U. S. 317 (1976), decided last Term. Some, such as *Griffin, supra*, and *Douglas* v. *California*, 372 U. S. 353 (1963), appear to depend upon the principle that indigent convicts must be given a meaningful opportunity to pursue a state-created right to appeal, even though the pursuit of such a remedy requires that the State must provide a transcript or furnish counsel. Others, such as *Johnson* v. *Avery*, 393 U. S. 483 (1969), *Procunier* v. *Martinez*, 416 U. S. 396 (1974), and *Wolff* v. *McDonnell*, 418 U. S. 539 (1974), depend on the principle that the State, having already incarcerated the convict and thereby virtually eliminated his contact with people outside the prison walls, may not further limit contacts which would otherwise be permitted simply because such contacts would aid the incarcerated prisoner in preparation of a petition seeking judicial relief from the conditions or terms of his confinement. Clearly neither of these principles supports the Court's present holding: The prisoners here in question have all pursued all avenues of direct appeal available to them from their judgments of conviction, and North Carolina imposes no invidious regulations which allow visits from all persons except those knowledgeable in the law. All North Carolina has done in this case is to decline to expend public funds to make available law libraries to those who are incarcerated within its penitentiaries.

If respondents' constitutional arguments were grounded on the Equal Protection Clause, and were in effect that rich prisoners could employ attorneys who could in turn consult law libraries and prepare petitions for habeas corpus, whereas indigent prisoners could not, they would have superficial appeal. See *Griffin*, *supra*; *Douglas*, *supra*. I believe that they would nonetheless fail under *Ross* v. *Moffitt*, 417 U. S. 600 (1974). There we held that although our earlier cases had required the State to provide meaningful access to state-created judicial remedies for indigents, the only right on direct appeal was that "indigents have an adequate opportunity to present their claims fairly within the adversary system." *Id.*, at 612.

In any event, the Court's opinion today does not appear to proceed upon the guarantee of equal protection of the laws, a guarantee which at least has the merit of being found in the Fourteenth Amendment to the Constitution. It proceeds instead to enunciate a "fundamental constitutional right of access to the courts," *ante*, at 828, which is found nowhere in the Constitution. But if a prisoner incarcerated pursuant to a final judgment of conviction is not prevented from physical access to the federal courts in order that he may file therein petitions for relief which Congress has authorized those courts

to grant, he has been accorded the only constitutional right of access to the courts that our cases have articulated in a reasoned way. *Ex parte Hull*, *supra*. Respondents here make no additional claims that prison regulations invidiously deny them access to those with knowledge of the law so that such regulations would be inconsistent with *Johnson*, *supra*, *Procunier*, *supra*, and *Wolff*, *supra*. Since none of these reasons is present here, the "fundamental constitutional right of access to the courts" which the Court announces today is created virtually out of whole cloth with little or no reference to the Constitution from which it is supposed to be derived.

Our decisions have recognized on more than one occasion that lawful imprisonment properly results in a "retraction [of rights] justified by the considerations underlying our penal system." *Price* v. *Johnston*, 334 U. S. 266, 285 (1948); *Pell* v. *Procunier*, 417 U. S. 817, 822 (1974). A convicted prisoner who has exhausted his avenues of direct appeal is no longer to be accorded every presumption of innocence, and his former constitutional liberties may be substantially restricted by the exigencies of the incarceration in which he has been placed. See *Meachum* v. *Fano*, 427 U. S. 215 (1976). Where we come to the point where the prisoner is seeking to collaterally attack a final judgment of conviction, the right of physical access to the federal courts is essential because of the congressional provisions for federal habeas review of state convictions. *Ex parte Hull*, *supra*. And the furnishing of a transcript to an indigent who makes a showing of probable cause, in order that he may have any realistic chance of asserting his right to such review, was upheld in *United States* v. *MacCollom*, *supra*. We held in *Ross* v. *Moffitt*, *supra*, that the *Douglas* holding of a right to counsel on a first direct appeal as of right would not be extended to a discretionary second appeal from an intermediate state appellate court to the state court of last resort, or from the state court of last resort to this Court. It would seem, *a fortiori*, to follow from that case that an incarcerated prisoner who has pursued all his avenues of direct review would have no constitutional right whatever to state appointed counsel to represent him in a collateral attack on his conviction, and none of our cases has ever suggested that a prisoner would have such a right. See *Johnson* v. *Avery,* 393 U. S., at 488. Yet this is the logical destination of the Court's reasoning today. If "meaningful access" to the courts is to include law libraries, there is no convincing reason why it should not also include lawyers appointed at the expense of the State. Just as a library may assist some inmates in filing papers which contain more than the bare factual allegations of injustice, appointment of counsel would assure that the legal arguments advanced are made with some degree of sophistication.

I do not believe anything in the Constitution requires this result, although state and federal penal institutions might as a matter of policy think it wise to implement such a program. I conclude by indicating the same respect for *Younger* v. *Gilmore,* 404 U. S. 15 (1971), as has the Court, in relegating it to a final section set apart from the body of the Court's reasoning. *Younger* supports the result reached by the Court of Appeals in this case, but it is a two-paragraph opinion which is most notable for the unbridged distance between its premise and its conclusion. The Court's opinion today at least makes a reasoned defense of the result which it reaches, but I am not persuaded by those reasons. Because of that fact I would not have the slightest reluctance to overrule *Younger* and reverse the judgment of the Court of Appeals in this case.

2. Brief of Example Case [§225]

Bounds v. Smith, 430 U.S. 817, 97 S. Ct. 1491, 52 L. Ed. 2d 72 (1977) [We have included all three reporter citations, although the case we are reporting only provides its own *United States Reports* citation. The other citations can be obtained by using LexisNexis, Westlaw or WestlawNext, or Shepard's Citations.]

Court: United States Supreme Court, opinion by Marshall, J.

Judicial History: North Carolina prison inmates sued in federal district court, claiming that the state's failure to provide them with legal research facilities denied them access to the courts in violation of the Fourteenth Amendment. The district court granted the inmates' motion for summary judgment, ordering the state to set up a legal research assistance program. A library plan was proposed by North Carolina and approved by the court, with the court holding in addition that the state did not also have to provide legal advisors. The court of appeals affirmed in all but one respect (which was not raised here). The state petitioned for review. The Supreme Court granted certiorari.

Facts: At the time the prisoners filed these claims in district court, there was only one severely inadequate state prison library. No other legal assistance was available to these inmates who wished to prepare and file federal habeas corpus and civil rights actions.

Issue: Must states protect the rights of prisoners to have access to the courts by providing them with law libraries or alternative legal assistance?

Holding: States must provide prisoners with an adequate legal assistance program, *i.e.*, law libraries or legally trained persons.

Reasoning: Prisoners have a constitutional right of access to the courts. Access must be adequate, effective, and meaningful to prevent claimed violations of fundamental constitutional rights.

It is crucial that prisoners file proper procedural claims, since the court may pass on the complaint's sufficiency before allowing *in forma pauperis* and may dismiss the case if it considers the complaint frivolous. Moreover, without a library, a prisoner will be unable to rebut the state's arguments.

The right to legal assistance is especially important here, where civil rights and habeas corpus actions based on constitutional violations are concerned. They frequently raise previously unlitigated issues.

Decision: Affirmed.

Concurring Opinion—Powell: The Court's holding makes no implication as to the constitutionally required scope of review of prisoners' claims in state or federal court.

Dissenting Opinion—Burger: Since there is no federal constitutional right to attack state convictions collaterally in federal court, there is no basis on which a federal court may require states to fund prison law libraries.

Dissenting Opinion—Stewart: Meaningful access to courts is seldom advanced by making law libraries available to prisoners.

Dissenting Opinion—Rehnquist: There is no constitutional right of access to federal courts to attack state court convictions. Prisoners have all had direct appeal through the state court system.

Chapter Ten: Searching Through Legal Sources

CONTENTS

A. Introduction

1. Sourcebooks [§226]

Have you ever wondered how an index is written? Probably not. However, a good indexer—one with organization, imagination, and insight—can make the difference between an inadequate index and one that successfully foresees how people will be using it and the keywords they will be considering.

All legal sourcebooks have indexes. They also have tables of contents. Some include a table of cases. But it is the index that in the end determines whether you will be efficient in finding the appropriate material. This chapter will describe ways of searching through legal sourcebooks, whether codes, treatises, encyclopedias, digests, looseleaf materials, or indexes to legal periodicals. We will begin with a search through an index and follow up with an examination of tables of contents and tables of cases.

2. Online Sources [§227]

Online legal sources like LexisNexis and Westlaw (or WestlawNext) do not use indexes. Rather, they contain databases which you can easily search by typing words in the source's search function. LexisNexis or Westlaw will then display the results of the keyword search for you. (*See* chapter VIII.)

B. Methodology

1. Choosing Keywords for Your Index or Online Search

a. Sample problem [§228]

Robyn is a long-distance runner. While she is meditatively running through Michael's fields, Michael's friendly and loveable dog, Drifter, rushes up to greet her. Robyn's trance is broken. In her surprise, she trips over a rock and breaks her leg. Robyn has to pay $1,500 for medical treatment. Can she collect this amount from Michael?

In considering this problem, or any problem, you need to find the words or terms that will lead you to the proper textual material of the sourcebook you are using. To help you do this, you may wish to use the following chart. Note that the topics to the left of the chart need not be the only ones. If you think of another listing that can help you locate material, by all means use it.

(1) People

What kinds of people are involved? Do they fit into a larger named group—like infants, nutritionists, debtors, or tenants?

CHOOSING KEYWORDS FOR INDEX OR ONLINE SEARCH gilbert

Topics	Keywords	
	General	Specific
People:	____________	____________
	____________	____________
	____________	____________
Subject Matter:	____________	____________
	____________	____________
	____________	____________
Legal Theory:	____________	____________
	____________	____________
	____________	____________
Remedy Sought:	____________	____________
	____________	____________
	____________	____________

(2) Subject matter

What things and places are involved? What groups do these things or places fall into? For example: automobile—vehicles, apartment—housing, redwood tree—forest.

(3) Legal theory

What kind of legal action is it and/or what kind of legal defense can be raised? Filling in this box may be a bit difficult at first since you may have to know some law to find an appropriate term. But commonly known terms like breach of contract, negligence, misdemeanor, nuisance, or libel may often be enough to start.

(4) Remedy sought

What does the person bringing the lawsuit want? A wage attachment, an eviction, a divorce, a name change, money damages for an injury, an injunction to halt a nuisance?

As in the "legal theory" topic, you may have some difficulty filling in appropriate words. But you need not worry. Usually, the "people" and "subject" topics will provide you with a sufficient number of keywords to get you started. Your search will uncover additional words and perhaps even some legal terms.

Topics	**Keywords**	
	General	**Specific**
People:	Athletes Property owners Trespassers	Runner/Jogger
Subject Matter:	Sports Property Animal Injury	 Land/Field Pet/Dog Physical injury
Legal Theory:	Negligence Tort Trespassing	Dog bite Natural hazard
Remedy Sought:	Damages for injuries	Medical expenses

b. Some pointers when using an index or conducting an online search [§229]

(1) You probably will not need all the words you enter into your chart. Some words are obviously better than others. But the more words you think of, the more likely it is that you will hit upon those that are best suited to lead you directly to the textual material.

(2) Look up both general and specific terms in the index. General terms in indexes will often be followed with specific subheadings that can help you pinpoint your sources. Similarly, to conduct an online search, use both general and specific terms in various combinations, and note whether the online service requires you to use specific search terms and connectors or supports plain English searches (*see* chapter VIII).

(3) Always check out several of your words—do not stop with the first one just because it leads you somewhere. Appropriate textual material, cases, and statutes can often be indexed in several places, and the first section you find—although helpful—may not be all there is. It may even mislead you.

(4) When you find that the words you are looking up are cross-referencing each other and/or overlapping on references to the material in the text, you know your search through the index has been thorough.

(5) If you are having trouble thinking of words and synonyms for your chart, try using a dictionary or a thesaurus. The dictionary need not be a law dictionary, since many of the words are nonlegal. Online research systems like LexisNexis and Westlaw may suggest similar terms when you search.

(6) Always check through supplementary indexes (those separate pamphlets or inserts in the back of the main texts) to be certain that you have located the most recent material.

2. Using a Table of Contents [§230]

If you are familiar with a subject, you may decide to approach the material through the table of contents. Turn to the broad topic in the table and scan the subtopics to find your area of interest.

The problem with using the table of contents is that you may overlook other important related and developing areas not arranged under the topic. For example, the right to refuse a measles vaccination for your child may be discussed in both the health and safety and the constitutional law sections of the text. Even someone familiar with the area may forget to check one section or the other. A detailed index, with its many cross-references, reduces the chances of this happening.

3. Using a Table of Cases [§231]

Many legal sourcebooks have tables of cases. If you know of a case dealing with the subject matter in which you are interested, you can look it up in the table and be directed to that section of the text that mentions the case. If you only know the defendant's name, you can use the Defendant-Plaintiff Tables that often accompany the tables of cases.

Finding a section does not guarantee that you will be helped. Cases are often cited for several distinct points of law. The table may refer you to a section covering a point other than yours. And where you are directed to an appropriate section of the text, you may be missing other sections that have nothing to do with the case but are equally or more important. So when using a table of cases, take a few minutes to check the index as well. You may be surprised at all the additional references it will provide you.

4. Possible Next Steps for Research [§232]

Your next steps in researching will depend on how much you know about your topic. If you know very little about your topic, you may want to jumpstart your research by first consulting a secondary source (*see* chapter V), such as a legal encyclopedia, treatise, or law review article, to get a general overview of the topic. You can do this either online or by using the books. Many secondary sources are now available online. If you do not find any secondary sources on your topic, you may then have to turn to the statute and case indexes to help you find relevant authorities.

Chapter Eleven: Legal Writing and Analysis—Basic Guidelines

CONTENTS

A. Essentials of Good Legal Writing and Analysis

1. Introduction [§233]

In all professional areas, and perhaps especially in law, people can be so involved with using professional jargon in their writing that they pay more attention to terms than to meaning. A knowledge of terms is certainly helpful, but it is never a substitute for clear and precise writing habits.

This chapter will help you improve your writing and analysis skills. It is not designed to teach you a new way of writing, nor is it designed to show you how to use words properly. If you are worried about your grammar or the proper use of words (*e.g.*, "effect" or "affect"), check Strunk and White, *The Elements of Style*. By being aware of the following basic guidelines, you can make an appreciable difference in the way you communicate on paper.

2. Organization [§234]

The secret to good writing is organization. There are two kinds of organization: organizing your raw material (research) and organizing your ideas into a document. We discuss organizing your research in chapter XII. To organize your thoughts and ideas, try outlining.

3. Outlining [§235]

Good writing is a result of good thinking. Fuzzy writing means fuzzy thinking. Unless you have thought it through ***before*** you begin writing, your writing will likely be more fuzzy than clear.

Many people think as they write. They work on the assumption that they will "revise" their draft afterwards. After all, how difficult will it be to just move a few paragraphs around on the computer? The problem is that people often find themselves revising their draft over and over again. And in many situations, no matter how many drafts you work through, you can never really transform a poorly written document into a well-written one. So finally, with time pressing, you just accept what you have and move on.

If you identify with this experience, you might want to try outlining the problem before you begin writing. No matter how much you hated it in school, outlining is really quite simple, and once you become comfortable with it, you'll be amazed at how easy it is. Just think and outline first; then write. You'll see the difference.

a. Comment

Sometimes people complain that outlining takes too much time. But how long does it take to do draft after draft after draft? Often, if you think it through carefully before you begin, your first draft will be your only draft, with only minor corrections required. You will ultimately save yourself time.

b. Outlining process [§236]

Begin by articulating the overall problem and the relevant issues. Identify the issues in terms of the facts. The more fact specific your issues are, the better. Remember, you are trying to solve someone's problem. If you cannot clearly identify the issues, you cannot competently write about them.

Consider using a separate sheet of paper for each issue. Then, identify any subissues under each issue. ***For each issue and subissue:***

(i) ***Identify the various rules of law*** that speak to each issue and subissue. If the law can be broken down into elements, identify the elements. Using keywords, jot down the applicable rules of law and any elements that must be met.

(ii) ***Identify the important facts*** of the problem that speak to each issue and subissue. Using keywords, jot down these facts beneath the relevant rule of law or element.

(iii) Looking at each issue and subissue, understand how ***the rule of law applies to the facts*** and how the facts will meet (or not meet) any required elements. Keep your focus on the relationship of the law to the facts and on how the integration of law and facts will ultimately solve the problem.

(iv) Jot down keywords that can help you ***distinguish cases*** and other authorities that go against your position.

(v) ***Draw your conclusion*** on each issue and subissue.

Perhaps you have noticed that the above outlining process basically uses an "IRAC" model (*see infra,* §§246-250). There are other approaches to outlining, but using IRAC is a simple process to get you started. Remember, for each issue, create a separate IRAC outline. The more organized you are in your thoughts, the more your writing will flow.

4. Keep to the Essentials [§237]

People sometimes get carried away with what they are trying to say and cannot stop writing. They make their point in three different ways for fear that if it is said any fewer times, the reader will miss it. Yet there are more effective ways to catch a reader's attention. In fact, repetition often creates the opposite effect by insulting the reader's intelligence.

If you are worried that the reader may miss the point, highlight it. Perhaps you can give it a heading or make it a topic sentence to introduce the paragraph. If necessary, underline it. Whatever you do, make the point and go on.

5. Keep Sentences Short [§238]

Although William Faulkner managed to work with long sentences and paragraphs, most writers cannot. People who write long sentences usually do so, not because they are trying to convey images and a sense of time as Faulkner did, but because they do not know how and when to stop.

Keep your sentences to one thought each. It is much easier to read a short sentence with one thought than a long sentence with several thoughts (some of which may not even be connected). Breaking up a long sentence with several semicolons does not substitute for short sentences. Naturally, however, you do want to mix up the size of your sentences so you do not end up with a choppy presentation.

6. Highlight Important Points [§239]

A reader is much more likely to finish reading your paper if you break it up into issues or sections. Use headings to direct the reader to particular parts of a memorandum. But, on the other hand, do not overdo it. Too many short sections and subsections can cause a paper to lose its continuity.

7. Keep the Reader in Mind [§240]

You are writing for a particular reader. You may be taking an exam, writing a memorandum of law for an attorney, or writing a memorandum of points and authorities for a trial judge. The paper may be on the same subject in all three cases, but the writing will be different. Keep in mind the purpose of your writing and your audience.

8. Write for an Uninformed Reader [§241]

Your writing will probably be more intact and logically presented if you assume that the reader is not familiar with the subject. Even if she is, you are less likely to skip over essential elements if you assume otherwise. Also, you never know who else may read your document. Along these lines, often people are so eager to get into the "sophisticated" areas of the law and show how much they know that they miss the foundation from which to develop. Just because the reader may know the elements of a contract does not mean that you should not include them when demonstrating that the client had a contract. If you leave out a fundamental point (or any issue for that matter), the reader can easily conclude (with some justification) that you did not know of it or did not realize its relevance, regardless of how "obvious" the point was.

9. Choose Simple, Straightforward Words [§242]

The main purpose of writing is to get your point across with no misunderstanding on the part of the reader. A simple phrase or term understood by nearly everyone will often be more effective than a sentence filled with legal jargon and six-syllable words. While you will sometimes have to use legal terms, they should be used only when necessary. Unnecessary legal terms and legal mumbo jumbo (such as "hereby" and "heretofore") give your paper the appearance of being pretentious, and cause the reader to wonder whether you really know what you are talking about or are merely hiding behind legal phrasing.

10. Use the Active Voice [§243]

Generally, the active voice uses fewer words and is more effective than the passive voice in keeping the reader's attention. (For example, "The defendant harassed the plaintiff" is preferable to "The plaintiff was harassed by the defendant.") Take a look at your writing. Change passive voice sentences to the active voice. Note the difference.

11. Be Subtle [§244]

Your work will be far more impressive and convincing if you allow the reader to reach your conclusion along with you through a series of logical steps. Give the reader a chance for reflection. Phrases such as "It is obvious that" or "Anyone can see" often insult the reader, especially if she thinks the issue is more complex than you make it appear. Give your reader the ***opportunity*** to agree with you rather than forcing her to agree.

12. Keep to the Topic and Answer the Question [§245]

Examination questions and legal memoranda usually call for a discussion of particular legal issues. For example, if you are dealing with a question on the kinds of damages that are legally available, discuss the legal aspect of each kind separately, and do not bring in a lot of interesting but uncalled-for information on evidence necessary to support the various damages (unless also asked).

Too often, people talk around a question because they cannot really answer it. As often, they do know the answer but are so proud of how much else they know that they go on and on and on. In either case, you are not providing a clear, direct response to the question. If you write an outline or use a chart or grid before you begin, you probably will have a clearer idea of what is being asked and what information is necessary to answer it.

B. Using an "IRAC" Approach to Legal Analysis

1. "IRAC" [§246]

If you are just learning legal analysis or are having trouble understanding the process, you may want to consider using an "IRAC" approach. Since the law is important only as it applies to a particular factual situation, good legal analysis requires that you show how the law interweaves with the facts of your problem. An "IRAC" approach will help you analyze a situation in terms of the facts.

a. Issue ("I")

Begin by laying out the issue. This lets the reader see what the problem is. The issue should be stated in terms of the facts of the situation.

b. Rule ("R")

After laying out the issue, set out the rule that applies to the issue. Rules can come from statutes, cases, or any other appropriate authority. If there is a statute on point, begin with it. If you take a rule from a case, be sure to also give a few facts of the case so that the reader can see the case's direct relevance to your situation. You should also include the reasoning behind the rule. This will help you in applying the rule later on (*see* "Application" below) because you can show whether the reasoning will hold up when applied to your fact situation.

c. Application or analysis ("A")

This is the ***crucial part of your legal analysis***. After you have set out the rule, you need to show the reader how the rule applies to your situation. If the rule comes from a statute, discuss whether your facts meet the elements of the statute or otherwise fit within the statute. If the rule comes from a case, you need to ***compare and contrast the facts*** of the case with your facts and see whether the reasoning behind the rule in the case is appropriate here in your situation. If you need to distinguish any cases from your position, distinguish them on their facts or their reasoning, or use public policy to argue that the court should not follow them.

Applying the law to the facts may seem very easy to do; it may even seem "obvious." Yet people often have trouble making the connections between the law and the facts of a particular situation. People tend to leave out essential facts by assuming that the reader can see where the writer is going. Yet good legal analysis requires that you discuss all specific facts and interweave them with the rule and reasoning you are applying. Only then can the reader truly see how the law fits into your situation. Do not assume that the reader can figure it out.

If you find that you do not have all the facts you need to complete your analysis, point this out. Then discuss what the analysis would be if the facts were one way or the other. Consider all possibilities.

d. Conclusion ("C")

In your conclusion, tie your points together. Show the reader where the application of the law to the facts has taken you.

2. IRAC Every Issue [§247]

The IRAC approach should be used for ***each issue in your problem***. Thus, if you were writing a memorandum of law (*see* chapter XIII) that involved three issues, you would follow the IRAC process in discussing each issue. Each authority in each issue would be applied in an IRAC-type approach (including authorities that you distinguish as inapplicable).

Note that the IRAC approach is useful in exam writing and in writing all kinds of legal analysis documents like memoranda, points and authorities, and briefs. The approach is the same: IRAC all issues.

3. Modification of IRAC Approach [§248]

Legal writers use many variations to the IRAC approach. For example, some people add an extra "R" to IRAC (they use "IRRAC") to remind them to include the reasoning (after the rule) of any case in their analysis. As you do more legal writing, you will probably find yourself modifying your approach as well. But the IRAC process is a firm foundation on which to build.

4. Using IRAC to Outline [§249]

If you are one of those people who resists outlining or who finds it difficult to outline, try using an IRAC format to structure your outline. You can then write your document right from your outline.

5. Example of Legal Analysis Using the IRAC Approach [§250]

Consider the following example of the IRAC approach. *Note:* In writing your analysis, you do not need to use the words "Issue," "Rule," "Application," and "Conclusion." These words are used here to show you how the process works.

(Issue:) Can two gay men who live together enter into an enforceable agreement where one man shares his income and the other man does the domestic chores?

(Rule:) In *Marvin v. Marvin*, 18 Cal. 3d 660, 557 P.2d 106, 134 Cal. Rptr. 815 (1976), a woman who had lived with a man for seven years claimed that they had entered into a contract whereby he would support her and give her half of all his earnings if she would be his homemaker and do the domestic chores around the house. They were not married. 18 Cal. 3d at 666.

After the man split up with the woman, he refused to pay her any part of the income that he had earned while they had lived together. He claimed that even if there had been a contract, it was illegal because it was meretricious (*i.e.*, the contract was for sexual services). *Id.* at 668.

The court held that a contract to share earnings in exchange for domestic services was not illegal. *Id.* at 670. It reasoned that people who live together and engage in sex are just as capable of contracting as any other people. *Id.* at 674. This was not just a contract for sexual services. The court also felt that with so many people living together today, it would be unreasonable to void these kinds of contracts. *Id.* at 683.

(Application:) Although our fact situation is different in that it involves two gay men as compared to a heterosexual couple, the reasoning behind *Marvin* would also seem to apply here. Since homosexuality is legal, the two men should be able to contract to share their earnings in exchange for doing domestic chores just as the couple in *Marvin* did. Here too, it is not just a contract for sexual services.

However, it could be argued that our situation is distinguishable from that in *Marvin* because the *Marvin* court was interested in promoting heterosexual relationships, and that gay relationships may not be entitled to the same consideration. The breadth of the *Marvin* opinion, however, seems to encompass all kinds of relationships and does not draw a distinction between heterosexual and other relationships.

(Conclusion:) Thus, it seems likely that the two men would be able to enter into an enforceable agreement just as the couple in *Marvin* did.

Chapter Twelve: Organizing the Fruits of Your Research

CONTENTS

A. Using the Honigsberg Grid

1. The Honigsberg Grid [§251]

Finding all the appropriate authorities relevant to your case is not all there is to effective legal research. You need to organize the fruits of your research—the cases, statutes, regulations, and other authorities—in a coherent, easy-to-review manner. The more efficiently you organize, the sooner you will be able to begin writing.

One method found to be very helpful in organizing legal material is the Honigsberg Grid. This grid provides you with an immediate guide to, and comparison of, the cases and other authorities you have found. It will help you quickly see how each case deals with a particular issue and principle of law and allow you to make immediate comparisons among the several cases you have researched.

2. Sample Grid

FACTS & ISSUES

AUTHORITIES—CASES	**Facts** (of each case)	***Issue #1** (e.g., defamation)	***Issue #2** (if necessary) (e.g., right of privacy)	***Issue #3** (if necessary)	***Issue #4** (if necessary)
Sakai v. Mikulak					
Ho v. Jacobson					
Devito v. Choy					
Koenig v. Alexander					
Sanchez v. Vu					

*Identify ***by name*** at the top of your grid each issue you intend to include.

Inside each square indicate how the case or other authority treats the particular issue. Think in terms of ***keywords*** and use abbreviations. Also, include the page number of the case where the subject is discussed. For example, if the *Sanchez* case discusses your Issue #1 on page 830 of the reporter, you would write in the appropriate box a few keywords reflecting what *Sanchez* says about Issue #1, along with page number 830.

After you have filled in the squares, you will be able to see at a glance which issues are discussed in which cases and how the cases size up with each other. You can then write your memorandum or brief working right off the grid.

Chapter Thirteen: Writing a Memorandum of Law

CONTENTS

A. An Objective Piece

1. Memorandum of Law [§252]

A memorandum of law is designed to provide a "neutral" or "balanced" approach to the law. It is an analytical document often written for a partner, senior associate, or single practitioner by an associate or law clerk. The attorney receiving the memo then uses it in preparing a case. The memo may be written in preparation for a meeting with the client, for negotiating with a party, or for a settlement conference. Thus, the writer needs to provide a clear presentation of the ***strengths and weaknesses of both sides.*** With all the information, the attorney can then plan a proper approach and strategy.

A memorandum of law is not, however, an entirely "objective" document. The writer should not concede victory, even if "objectively" the law appears bleak. Remember that you have a client whom you are trying to help. Nor should the writer mislead the reader into thinking that victory is at hand. You can never be certain how a court will rule. The favored approach is to present the law in the best light with judicious references to pitfalls and other concerns.

2. Format [§253]

The following outline is a general format used by many law firms.

To:

From:

Re: (Includes the name of the client and a short phrase reflecting the subject.)

Date:

Questions Presented or Issues: Issues or questions of law should be stated in terms of the essential facts. Review the discussion of issues (*supra*, §217) if you are unsure as to how to draft an issue.

Statement of Facts: If you are assigned a memorandum of law by someone in your office, you probably will be given the client's file. Inside will be an interview sheet detailing what the client told the interviewer (or perhaps you were the interviewer) about the legal problem of the client. The client's view of the situation is basically your set of facts, although perhaps some witnesses also have been interviewed, and some relevant documents may have been obtained. The opposing party will probably disagree on what happened, but that information will not come out until later, as the case moves along. For now, all you can do is use what you feel are the ***legally significant*** facts (the facts on which the issues should turn), ***background*** facts, and any ***emotional*** facts that may be of use later when writing a memorandum or brief to a judge (*see* chapter XIV). Base your memorandum upon them. You would be wise, though, to comment in your discussion on how the law may vary in its application should certain facts be found to be otherwise.

Brief Answer or Evaluation: An evaluation is somewhat like a holding. It responds to the issue. But evaluations are opinions determined by you, whereas holdings are principles of law determined by the court. A brief answer allows the person reading your memorandum to obtain an immediate picture of the problem involved and how you propose to solve it. The reader can then read your discussion to see if you have approached the problem reasonably and researched the material thoroughly.

Since there are usually two sides to a legal problem, your evaluation will probably not be written in absolute, certain terms. Rather, it will be an educated judgment of the issue(s) involved and the resolution of the issue(s). If you think the opposing party has a stronger case than you do, say so, but indicate his weaknesses and your strengths. The discussion will examine how you might deal with this imbalance.

Discussion: Your discussion should be a well thought out, organized presentation on how you reached your evaluation(s). Examine each issue separately. What law supports your side, and what law supports the other party? Where the law seems unclear, point out the inconsistencies. Remember, this is not an advocacy piece. A memorandum of law is an analytical examination of the subject. The reader cannot intelligently decide how to handle the case unless she is given a complete, panoramic view of the law.

Discuss the important cases, statutes, and regulations. ***Show how they apply to the facts of the problem.*** Thus, when you state an important rule from a case, give a few pertinent facts of the case and compare the facts to your situation. Then discuss the reasoning behind the rule to show its applicability to your facts. (*See* chapter XI on using the "IRAC" approach.) Only quote or paraphrase pertinent parts from statutes, cases, and other authorities—be careful about overdoing it.

Be sure to distinguish cases and other authorities that go against your position. You can distinguish a case on its facts, its reasoning, or its policy.

Support any statement you make with legal authority. Do not just give your opinion. Whenever possible, cite to a primary authority—a case, statute, or regulation—rather than to a secondary source. Treatises, law reviews, encyclopedias, and other commentary should be cited as supplemental to the primary authority and should be cited alone only when no primary authority is available. Of course, you can (and should) always discuss secondary sources when they contribute further insight into the problem. Also, make sure that you have thoroughly read each case and other authority you cite. Do not rely on annotations and notes without reading the sources from which they came.

Do not forget to update your cases through a citator such as Shepard's or KeyCite (*see* chapter VII), and check the latest supplements to the codes.

Conclusion: (This is optional; it is similar to your evaluation, although possibly more detailed.)

Signature.

CHECKLIST FOR MEMORANDUM OF LAW **gilbert**

1. **Questions Presented (Issues)**
   - ☑ Have you stated the issues using the key (*i.e.,* legally significant) facts to help frame and focus the issues?
   - ☑ Are the questions written in a neutral tone?
2. **Statement of Facts**
   - ☑ Have you included the key facts so that the reader will fully understand the analysis in the Discussion section?
   - ☑ Have you included both the favorable and the unfavorable facts that may be pertinent to the analysis?
3. **Brief Answers**
   - ☑ Have you stated your conclusions to the issues set out in your Questions Presented?
   - ☑ Have you framed your conclusions using the key facts?
4. **Discussion**
   - ☑ Within each major issue, have you provided the relevant rules, analyzed the relevant facts as they apply to the rules, and given a conclusion if one is possible?
   - ☑ Have you used headings to help guide the reader?
   - ☑ Does your Discussion section reflect the issues in the order you set them out in your Questions Presented and Brief Answers sections?
   - ☑ Did you address the opposing argument and/or authorities for those issues which are in contention?

B. Sample Memorandum of Law

(This memorandum of law was written and edited by members of the Legal Research, Writing and Analysis Program at the University of San Francisco School of Law. Special thanks to Stuart Sutton, Cristina Morris, Ellyn Moscowitz, Rochelle Wirshup, and Jean Allen.)

MEMORANDUM OF LAW

TO: Senior Partner
FROM: Research Associate
RE: General and Limited Jurisdiction: *Clark v. Continental Southern*
DATE: October 25, 2001

QUESTIONS PRESENTED

I. Can California assert ***general jurisdiction*** over Continental Southern when its sole contact with the forum is its membership in Continental Trailways, a national transportation association?

II. Under a three-pronged test, can California assert ***limited jurisdiction*** over Continental Southern when its sole contact with the forum is its membership in Continental Trailways, and plaintiff's injuries occurred in an out-of-state bus accident?

A. Do Continental Trailways's California ticket sales and advertisements constitute sufficient forum-related activity?

B. Does plaintiff's personal injury cause of action have a substantial connection to Continental Trailways's ticket sales and advertising in California, when the ticket sales and advertising are Continental Southern's sole contacts in the forum?

C. Does California's interest in assuming jurisdiction over Continental Southern outweigh the inconvenience of the parties in litigating in the forum?

STATEMENT OF FACTS

Plaintiff Thora Clark ("Clark") is suing Continental Southern ("Southern") in California for personal injuries she sustained in a bus accident in Louisiana on December 27, 2000. Southern is a licensed common carrier and a Mississippi corporation with its principal offices in Jackson, Mississippi. Southern is one of approximately 50 members of Continental Trailways ("Trailways"), an association whose members receive the benefits of national advertising under the banner "Trailways" and the coordination of advertising, ticket sales, and scheduling nationwide, including in California. Southern has no direct contacts with California except through its association with Trailways. Southern has no offices, employees, or designated agent for service of process in California.

Trailways coordinates the use of Southern's equipment by other association members throughout the United States. Southern's service area is in Mississippi and Louisiana. When Southern's equipment passes outside of its service area, control of the equipment passes to the association member using it. Southern's buses occasionally enter California under the control of other association members.

Plaintiff Clark, an 80-year-old California resident, purchased a Trailways bus ticket on December 24, 2000, in San Francisco from Western Trailways ("Western"), a California corporation and Trailways member, for passage from San Francisco to Florida. On December 26, 2000, in San Francisco, Clark boarded a bus owned by Southern but controlled by Western for her trip to Florida. Clark claims to have heard grinding noises in the front of the bus while still in California, and she reported the sounds to various drivers. In Louisiana, the left front wheel of the bus malfunctioned. The bus left the road and rolled onto its side. At that time, one of Southern's drivers was driving the bus. Clark was injured and taken to a local hospital. All of the evidence relating to the accident, including the bus, its driver, eyewitnesses, emergency personnel, and maintenance and medical records, are in Louisiana and Mississippi.

BRIEF ANSWERS

I. A court may exercise general jurisdiction over a defendant corporation when defendant's contacts with the forum are sufficiently substantial, continuous, and systematic. California cannot assert general jurisdiction over Southern because Southern's sole contact with the forum is its membership in Trailways, a national transportation association present in the forum. This contact is not sufficiently substantial for the purposes of exercising general jurisdiction.

II. California courts use a three-pronged test to determine whether California can exercise limited jurisdiction over a defendant corporation. Although California might be a convenient forum for the 80-year-old plaintiff, Southern does not engage in sufficient forum-related activity, and there is an inadequate nexus between plaintiff's cause of action and Southern's contacts with California.

   A. The first prong of the limited jurisdiction test is the character of defendant's activity in the forum. Southern's only forum-related contact is through its membership in Trailways, which provides ticket sales and advertising in California for its members. Such contact is too indirect to justify limited jurisdiction.

   B. The second prong of the limited jurisdiction test is the presence of a substantial connection between plaintiff's cause of action and defendant's contacts with the forum. Plaintiff's personal injury cause of action, arising out of an accident on a Southern bus in Louisiana, has no connection to Southern's contacts with California through its membership in Trailways.

   C. Under the third prong of the limited jurisdiction test, the court balances the convenience of the parties in litigating in California against the interest of the state in assuming jurisdiction. Although plaintiff resides in California, her injuries arose outside of the state. In addition, all evidence and witnesses are outside of the state. Although California may have a minimal interest in hearing plaintiff's action, the inconvenience of the parties in litigating in California outweighs that interest and weighs against the exercise of limited jurisdiction.

DISCUSSION

I. The Exercise of General Jurisdiction over Southern

The exercise of general jurisdiction over a defendant is the most sweeping exercise of jurisdiction under the law. California's broadly framed jurisdiction statute states: "A court of this state may exercise jurisdiction on any basis not inconsistent with the Constitution of this state or of the United States." Cal. Civ. Proc. Code §410.10 (West 1973). [Cal. Civ. Proc. Code Ann. §410.10 (West 1973).]* In *Cornelison v. Chaney*, 16 Cal. 3d 143, 147, 545 P.2d 264, 266, 127 Cal. Rptr. 352, 354 (1976) (citations omitted), [*Cornelison v. Chaney*, 16 Cal. 3d 143, 147 (1976) (citations omitted)], the California Supreme Court stated that where a defendant's in-state activities are "extensive . . . continuous and systematic," California may assert general jurisdiction over the defendant for any cause of action, even one unrelated to the defendant's in-state activity. Conversely, the occasional presence of a defendant in the forum to conduct business is not necessarily sufficient to establish general jurisdiction over all causes of action, whether or not related to the forum contacts.

In *Cornelison*, the defendant, a Nebraska resident, was a truck driver. He made approximately 20 trips into California each year to deliver and pick up cargo. The cause of action was the result of a collision in Nevada between a vehicle driven by a California resident and the defendant's truck on its way to California with a delivery. *Cornelison*, 16 Cal. 3d at 146–47, 545 P.2d at 265–66, 127 Cal. Rptr. at 353–54. [*Cornelison*, 16 Cal. 3d at 146–47.] The *Cornelison* court found these contacts with California insufficient for the assertion of general jurisdiction. *Id.* at 148, 545 P.2d at 267, 127 Cal. Rptr. at 355. [*Id.* at 148.]

The *Cornelison* court relied in part on *Perkins v. Benguet Mining Co.*, 342 U.S. 437 (1952). In *Perkins*, the president of a Philippine corporation sought refuge in Ohio during World War II. The president had an office in his home in Ohio and several corporate bank accounts in the state. He also held meetings of the board of directors in Ohio. 342 U.S. at 447–48. The *Perkins* court found these activities to be sufficiently substantial, continuous, and systematic to hold the Philippine corporation subject to Ohio jurisdiction in an action unrelated to the corporation's forum-related activities. *Id.* at 447–49. The Court found that the corporation was actually present in Ohio via the president's residence, office, and general business operations. *Id.* at 447–48.

**In this memorandum, the first citation is in proper Bluebook form; the second one (in brackets) is in proper ALWD form. Note that for some citations, there is no difference between the Bluebook and ALWD forms, and thus only one citation is used.*

Southern's contacts fall short of those in *Cornelison*. In *Cornelison,* the court did not permit general jurisdiction even though the defendant, and the equipment under his control, entered California as many as 20 times per year. Southern has never sent any employee to California to conduct business on behalf of the corporation. Southern's facts also fall short of those in *Perkins*. Southern has no office, personnel, or bank accounts in California. Southern's sole contact with California is as a member of Trailways. Southern is therefore not present in California in the *Perkins* sense.

In light of *Cornelison* and *Perkins*, Southern's contacts with California through its membership in Trailways are not sufficiently substantial, continuous, and systematic for the exercise of general jurisdiction over Southern.

II. The Exercise of Limited Jurisdiction over Southern

Where the defendant's in-state activities are less pervasive, a court will not assert general jurisdiction. A court may, however, find limited (or specific) jurisdiction where a cause of action has a direct nexus to defendant's forum-related activities. *Cornelison*, 16 Cal. 3d at 147–48, 545 P.2d at 266–67, 127 Cal. Rptr. at 354. [*Cornelison*, 16 Cal. 3d at 147–48.] The *Cornelison* court established a three-pronged test to determine whether a court may exercise limited jurisdiction: "[A] the character of defendant's activity in the forum, [B] whether the cause of action arises out of or has a substantial connection with that activity, and [C] . . . the convenience of the parties and the interests of the state in assuming jurisdiction." *Id.* at 148, 545 P.2d at 267, 127 Cal. Rptr. at 354–55. [*Id.* at 148.]

A. Defendant's Forum-Related Activity

Southern's only contacts with California are through Trailways. Therefore, an analysis of limited jurisdiction focuses on Trailways's two activities on behalf of Southern: California ticket sales and California advertising.

1. Ticket Sales

Ticket sales alone are insufficient to establish limited jurisdiction. *Kenny v. Alaska Airlines, Inc.*, 132 F. Supp. 838, 852 (S.D. Cal. 1955). In *Kenny*, a California resident and stockholder in Alaska Airlines sued to enforce certain corporate proprietary rights. In granting the motion to quash service of summons for lack of personal jurisdiction, the court noted that Alaska Airlines was incorporated in Alaska, maintained its principal offices in Seattle, and flew in Alaska, Washington, Oregon, and Canada. Alaska Airlines had no employees in California. Its only contacts with this forum were ticket sales through various California ticket agents and connecting air carriers. At that time, none of its flights entered California airspace. *Kenny*, 132 F. Supp. at 841–42.

The *Kenny* court stated that such ticket sales were insufficient to find jurisdiction. *Id.* at 852. The court noted that to find otherwise would subject every common carrier involved in national transportation to the jurisdiction of the California courts, a prospect the court found to violate notions of "fair play and substantial justice." *Id.* at 853 (citations omitted).

Other jurisdictions have also confronted this issue. In *Pike v. New England Greyhound Lines, Inc.*, 93 F. Supp. 669 (D. Mass. 1950), the court held similarly on facts nearly identical to those of Southern. Interstate, the defendant bus line in *Pike*, was a member of the Greyhound association. The Greyhound membership services closely parallel those provided here by Trailways. The Boston office of the Greyhound associate sold transcontinental tickets that routed passengers through Interstate's territory. Interstate maintained no offices or employees in the forum. *Pike*, 93 F. Supp. at 670. The *Pike* court held that "[t]he selling of tickets over the lines of a foreign [bus] corporation by agents of other corporations, does not, standing alone, constitute the doing of business by the foreign corporation within the state of sale of the tickets." *Id.* at 671.

The ticket sale activity found insufficient in *Kenny* was more substantial than that here. Unlike Alaska Airlines, neither Southern nor Western sells tickets in California for exclusive travel in Southern's territory. The transcontinental tickets sold in California involve Southern merely as one of many interconnecting carriers. Therefore, if Alaska Airlines's ticket sale activities were insufficient for purposes of jurisdiction, a court is likely to find such sale activities by others indirectly for Southern even less sufficient.

Southern's contacts with California are nearly identical to those deemed inadequate in *Pike*. Just as the forum contacts of the defendants in *Pike* consisted merely of their membership in the Greyhound association and the forum-related benefits that membership provided, Southern's sole contacts with California are through its membership in Trailways and receipt of similar benefits.

As a result of *Kenny* and *Pike*, it is unlikely that the mere sale of tickets in the forum is sufficient for an assertion of limited jurisdiction over Southern.

2. Advertising in the Forum

California case law also establishes that advertising services to promote the sale of those services in the forum state is insufficient for limited jurisdiction. In *Pike*, the court stated: "If the fact of such [ticket] sales is not sufficient to bring [defendant] within the court's jurisdiction, it adds no substantial element that [the association] also advertises that fact, or provides such incidental services as furnishing timetables for use by the purchasers of the tickets." 93 F. Supp. at 671.

Circus Circus Hotels, Inc. v. Superior Court, 120 Cal. App. 3d 546, 174 Cal. Rptr. 885 (1981) [*Circus Circus Hotels, Inc. v. Super. Ct. of Cal.*, 120 Cal. App. 3d 546, 174 Cal. Rptr. 885 (4th Dist. 1981)], further illustrates that promotion of ticket sales through advertising in the forum is insufficient for jurisdiction. In *Circus Circus*, a California citizen sued Circus Circus Hotels, a Nevada corporation, for a theft of property while plaintiff was a guest in defendant's Nevada hotel. Circus Circus moved to quash service of process based on an alleged lack of personal jurisdiction. The hotel's only contacts with California were the advertising of its Nevada services in California and the maintenance of an "800" telephone number for hotel reservations. *Circus Circus*, 120 Cal. App. 3d at 551, 174 Cal. Rptr. at 887. [*Circus Circus*, 120 Cal. App. 3d at 551.] The *Circus Circus* court found that these activities could not support an assertion of jurisdiction. *Id.* at 567, 174 Cal. Rptr. at 897. [*Id.* at 567.]

Trailways advertised in California on behalf of Southern to promote ticket sales in the forum. Unlike the defendant in *Circus Circus*, Southern did not directly advertise its service in California; it did so indirectly through Trailways. Since the direct advertising activities in *Circus Circus* were insufficient to support an exercise of jurisdiction, Southern's indirect advertising through Trailways is likely to be even more inadequate.

Southern's ticket sales and advertising activities do not satisfy the first prong of the *Cornelison* test.

B. Nexus Between the Cause of Action and the Forum Contacts

The second prong of the *Cornelison* test requires a nexus or substantial connection between plaintiff's cause of action and defendant's forum-related activity. *Cornelison*, 16 Cal. 3d at 148, 545 P.2d at 267, 127 Cal. Rptr. at 354–55. [*Cornelison*, 16 Cal. 3d at 148.] The *Kenny* court focused on whether the court could assert jurisdiction where there was no relationship between the stockholder's fraud cause of action concerning proprietary rights in Alaska Airlines and the airline's in-state ticket sales through agents and connecting carriers. The court held that the necessary nexus between the cause of action and those contacts was missing. *Kenny*, 132 F. Supp. at 852–54.

Based on *Kenny*, there is no nexus between a bus accident on a Louisiana highway and Southern's membership in an association that advertises and sells tickets in California and elsewhere. The only conceivable connection between the alleged negligent acts of Southern in Louisiana and Southern's contacts with California is that plaintiff started her journey in California and allegedly heard grinding noises while in the state. Under *Kenny*, such a relationship is too weak to establish jurisdiction under the second prong of the *Cornelison* test because plaintiff's injuries, which arose in Louisiana, are too attenuated from Southern's indirect advertisement and sale of tickets in California through Trailways.

C. Balancing of Parties' Convenience and Interests of the State

The third prong of the *Cornelison* test is the balance between the convenience of the parties in litigating in the forum and the interests of the state in asserting jurisdiction. *Cornelison*, 16 Cal. 3d at 148, 545 P.2d at 267, 127 Cal. Rptr. at 354–55. [*Cornelison*, 16 Cal. 3d at 148.] California would be an extremely inconvenient forum for all parties except for Clark. Clark is an 80-year-old California resident who would find it inconvenient to litigate her action in Louisiana. Except for Clark, however, no other party resides in California. All relevant evidence is in Louisiana and Mississippi: the bus and its maintenance records, emergency and hospital personnel and records, and eyewitnesses to the accident. Although California may have a minimal interest in maintaining the action in California because the plaintiff is a California resident, the relative inconvenience of the parties as to appearing in California weighs against the exercise of jurisdiction in the forum. When combined with the indirect presence of Southern in the forum and the lack of a nexus between the accident and Southern's California activities, the court is likely to decline to exercise limited jurisdiction over Southern.

CONCLUSION [OPTIONAL]

____

Research Associate

Chapter Fourteen: Writing a Memorandum of Points and Authorities or Brief

CONTENTS

A. A Persuasive Piece

1. Memorandum of Points and Authorities or Brief [§254]

A memorandum of points and authorities (also known as a brief in support of a motion), a trial brief, and an appellate brief are persuasive adversary documents. They are designed to convince a judge (or hearing officer in an administrative hearing) to decide the law in your favor. Emphasis is on your strong points. Little mention is made of your weak points. Your opponent's strengths must be neutralized if not entirely undermined. Yet you do not want to appear overzealous. The impression you give should be one of fairness and reasonableness. The reader wants to be persuaded, but she will not be if you appear unreasonable and arrogant.

2. Format [§255]

A memorandum of points and authorities, brief in support of a motion, trial brief, or appellate brief is more formal than a memorandum of law. Courts sometimes require that such documents be written in certain formats. Generally, a format for these documents would appear similar to the following:

a. Table of contents

b. Table of authorities

Separate lists are made for statutes, constitutional provisions, regulations, cases, and texts, with references to pages on which these authorities appear.

Note: A table of contents and a table of authorities are often not included in a memorandum of points and authorities unless the memorandum is over a certain page length. Trial briefs are more likely to include these tables. Appellate briefs usually include them.

c. Jurisdiction

(This usually appears in federal cases.)

d. Questions presented or issues

These questions are not presented in the same way as they would appear in a memorandum of law. Since the purpose of an adversary piece is to persuade, you should phrase your questions in a way that engenders sympathy toward your client and guides the reader to the result you want. But, just as in a memo of law, your issues should be stated in terms of the facts.

e. Statement of the case

A statement of the case provides the reader with the legal basis for the suit, the remedies requested, and a review of the important court proceedings up to the present.

f. **Statement of facts**

Many judges say that the most important part of a persuasive document is the facts. They feel that they often know the law, but need to understand the situation. Thus, your statement of facts should keep the reader's interest and place your client in the best light. It should "tell a story." Although the facts must be ***complete*** and ***accurate***, they need not be neutral. The same facts can be presented in different ways so as to make a party appear sympathetic or disagreeable.

Since this is a persuasive writing, you should present the facts most favorable to you, while other facts should be de-emphasized. Talk up the positives and play down the negatives. Show justice is on your side. Thus, along with your ***legally significant*** facts (the facts on which the issues turn) and your ***background*** facts, you should also include ***emotional*** facts. Emotional facts can be very effective in persuading the judge to adopt your position. If there is a legally significant fact that goes against you, try to neutralize it by minimizing it, placing it alongside a fact that strongly supports your position, or burying it in the middle of a paragraph. Be sure, however, to include the damaging legally significant fact to show your credibility. Often facts are related chronologically, but if another approach seems more sensible and effective, use it. Always begin your statement of facts with facts that make your client look good.

If you are writing a memorandum of points and authorities or a trial brief, the facts have not yet been established by a court and, therefore, you have more flexibility in choosing which facts to include and emphasize. After you write the argument (*see* below), you will probably revise the statement of facts to emphasize those facts that you used to support your arguments and to de-emphasize those that appear damaging. But be sure that your statement of facts includes all the facts you discuss in your argument section.

g. **Summary of argument or brief answer**

A summary of the argument or brief answer is designed to provide the reader with a quick review of the points and arguments that you will be making. It is usually written in terms of the facts of the problem. It essentially has the same purpose as a brief answer in a memo of law, and like the brief answer, it is prepared after you have written your argument. The summary of the argument or brief answer is sometimes omitted.

h. **Argument heading**

An argument is prefaced by a heading or "point" written in capital letters. The heading should be written as a complete sentence and should be stated in terms of the facts of your case. In effect, it answers your question presented. A point heading is basically a statement of the principle of law that you want the court to adopt for the facts of the situation. It should also include a reason in support of the principle. (Headings to each argument also appear in the table of contents, if you write one.)

CHECKLIST FOR MEMORANDUM OF POINTS AND AUTHORITIES OR BRIEF

gilbert

1. **Issues (Questions Presented)**
   - ☑ Are your issues written in terms of the facts?
   - ☑ Are they framed in your favor?
2. **Statement of the Case (Introduction)**
   - ☑ Do you clearly identify the parties?
   - ☑ Do you explain the legal basis, the important procedural background, and the remedies requested?
3. **Statement of Facts**
   - ☑ Are the facts complete?
   - ☑ Are they accurate?
   - ☑ Do you include legally significant facts, background facts, and emotional facts?
   - ☑ Are you telling a story and making it interesting?
   - ☑ Do you show justice in your client's case?
   - ☑ Do you neutralize or otherwise underplay damaging facts?
4. **Brief Answer (Summary of the Argument)**
   If you include this part:
   - ☑ Does it favorably answer each question presented?
   - ☑ Is it written in terms of the facts?
5. **Argument Headings (Point Headings)**
   - ☑ Are your headings written in terms of the facts?
   - ☑ Do they articulate the rule of law you want the court to apply to the facts of the case?
   - ☑ Do they include a reason for deciding the rule in your favor?
6. **Arguments**
   - ☑ Are you writing in a persuasive tone?
   - ☑ Is your memo organized by argument?
   - ☑ Do you begin with your best argument?
   - ☑ Do you set out your position before distinguishing the opposing party's authorities?
   - ☑ Are you explaining the law accurately?
   - ☑ Are you applying the law ***specifically*** to your facts?
   - ☑ Do you distinguish the opposing party's authorities?
   - ☑ Do you argue policy as appropriate?

i. Argument

The argument in a memorandum of points and authorities or a brief is very different from the discussion in a memorandum of law. You are trying to ***persuade*** the judge to agree with your position. The argument is not an analytical, balanced review of the law, but rather a convincing, well-thought-out, logical demonstration of your position and an attack on your opponent's position.

You should begin with good, sound analysis ***supporting*** your position. Be sure to explain clearly how a case or other authority applies to your fact situation. If it is a case, give a few facts of the case and discuss the rule from the case, the reasoning behind the rule, and whether the facts of your situation fit within the rule. (*See* chapter XI on using the "IRAC" approach.)

Organize your paper by arguments (similar to your organizing a memo of law by issues). Be sure to write an argument for each issue presented. Begin each argument with your best authority. Convince the judge of the correctness of your position early on, and do not dispose of your opponent's arguments until you have made your own argument. And do not overlook important policy arguments.

When you dispose of your opponent's case, do so with grace. For example, recognize the validity of your opponent's position in some situations, but note its inapplicability here. Overcome weak points or authorities favoring your opponent by ***distinguishing*** cases on their facts or by appealing to logic, public policy, and fairness. In making your arguments, do not distort the facts or law—although, of course, people can differ over interpretation.

Also, when writing an appellate brief, do not spend a lot of time criticizing the trial court's opinion. Your opponent is the opposing party, not the trial court.

Finally, when making your argument, get to the point. The reader is eager to move on.

j. Conclusion

In most memoranda of points and authorities and briefs, the conclusion is just a short request for relief. Your actual conclusion has already appeared in the "Brief Answer" or "Summary of the Argument" section.

B. Sample Memoranda of Points and Authorities

The following sample memoranda take opposing positions on the same case. Note how the attorneys use essentially the same facts and law but rework them to favor their positions.

Note also how the formats are slightly different—reflecting the fact that attorneys will differ on formats for memoranda and briefs.

SAMPLE MEMORANDUM OF POINTS AND AUTHORITIES IN SUPPORT OF MOTION

(This memorandum of points and authorities was written and edited by members of the Legal Research, Writing and Analysis Program at the University of San Francisco School of Law. Special thanks to Stuart Sutton, Cristina Morris, Ellyn Moscowitz, and Rochelle Wirshup.)

JENNA SMYTHE, State Bar #345678
PILLSBURY, CROCKER, MILLS & KRAFT
A Professional Corporation
200 Montgomery
San Francisco, California 94118
Telephone: (415) 555-1234

Attorneys for Defendant
CONTINENTAL SOUTHERN

SUPERIOR COURT OF THE STATE OF CALIFORNIA

FOR THE COUNTY OF SAN FRANCISCO

<table>
<tr><td>THORA CLARK,

Plaintiff,

vs.

CONTINENTAL TRAILWAYS,
CONTINENTAL SOUTHERN, WESTERN
TRAILWAYS, and DOES 1 through
40, inclusive,

Defendants.</td><td>)
)
)
)
)
)
)
)
)
)
)
)
)
)
)
)</td><td>
No. 954-234

DEFENDANT CONTINENTAL
SOUTHERN'S MEMORANDUM
OF POINTS AND AUTHORITIES
IN SUPPORT OF MOTION TO
QUASH SERVICE OF SUMMONS

Cal. Civ. Proc. Code §410.10

Date: February 15, 2002
Time: 9:00 a.m.
Dept.: 20 (Judge Jones)</td></tr>
</table>

QUESTIONS PRESENTED

Can plaintiff, Thora Clark, establish that the court may assert either general or limited jurisdiction over defendant Continental Southern in California?

A. Does Continental Southern's membership in Continental Trailways, a national association present in California, fail to represent activity of such a substantial, continuous, and systematic nature that California may decline to assert general jurisdiction over Continental Southern?

B. Is the exercise of limited jurisdiction over Continental Southern improper where the suit is based on an out-of-state bus accident and Continental Southern's only California contact consists of membership in Continental Trailways, a national association present in the forum?

   1. Are Continental Trailways's ticket sales and advertising in California on behalf of Continental Southern insufficient contacts to constitute forum-related activity?

   2. Is there an insufficient nexus between plaintiff's personal injury and breach of contract causes of action and Continental Southern's indirect contacts with California arising from ticket sales and advertising?

   3. Does the balance between the parties' inconvenience in litigating in California and California's minimal interest in hearing the action weigh against asserting limited jurisdiction against Continental Southern?

STATEMENT OF THE CASE

Defendant Continental Southern, Inc. ("Southern"), along with defendants Continental Trailways ("Continental") and Western Trailways ("Western"), was served with a summons and complaint in this action on November 6, 2001, seeking damages for negligence and breach of contract resulting from a Louisiana bus accident. Southern, a Mississippi corporation, does business exclusively in Mississippi and the contiguous states of Louisiana and Alabama. Southern moves to quash service of summons on the ground that California has no basis for personal jurisdiction over Southern.

STATEMENT OF THE FACTS

Plaintiff, Thora Clark ("Clark"), purchased a Trailways bus ticket in San Francisco from Western, a California corporation, for bus passage from San Francisco to Florida. That journey took the bus in which Clark was traveling through Louisiana, part of the territory where Southern conducts its business. On December 27, 2000, while traveling through Louisiana, the left front wheel of the bus malfunctioned, resulting in the bus leaving the road and rolling onto its side.

At the time of this accident, Clark was a passenger on the bus, which was owned by Southern and was being driven by one of its drivers through territory in which it is a licensed carrier. As a result, all of the evidence relating to the accident, including the bus, its driver, eyewitnesses, emergency personnel, and maintenance and medical records are located in Louisiana and Mississippi.

Southern is a Mississippi corporation with its principal offices in Jackson, Mississippi. It is a licensed common carrier and operates bus service throughout Mississippi and in parts of Louisiana and Alabama. It is one of approximately 50 members of Continental, an association whose members share in both the benefits of national advertising under the banner "Trailways" and the coordination of tariffs and schedules for transcontinental travel. Except through this association, Southern has no contacts whatsoever with California. It maintains no offices or employees there and has no designated agent for service of process.

ARGUMENT

PLAINTIFF CANNOT ESTABLISH THAT THE COURT MAY ASSERT GENERAL OR LIMITED JURISDICTION OVER DEFENDANT IN CALIFORNIA.

The notions of "fair play and substantial justice" demand that California decline to assert either general or limited jurisdiction over Southern. California Civil Procedure Code section 410.10 (West 1973) states: "A court of this state may exercise jurisdiction on any basis not inconsistent with the Constitution of this state or of the United States." The California Supreme Court has held that section 410.10 "manifests an intent to exercise the broadest possible jurisdiction, limited only by constitutional considerations." *Sibley v. Superior Court*, 16 Cal. 3d 442, 445, 546 P.2d 322, 324, 128 Cal. Rptr. 34, 36 (1976). [*Sibley v. Super. Ct. of Cal.*, 16 Cal. 3d 442, 445 (1976).]*

In a line of cases commencing with *International Shoe Co. v. Washington*, 326 U.S. 310, 316 (1945), the United States Supreme Court has held that in order to assert jurisdiction, the defendant corporation need only "have certain minimum contacts . . . such that the maintenance of the suit does not offend 'traditional notions of fair play and substantial justice.'" (Citations omitted.) The California Supreme Court applied these principles in *Cornelison v. Chaney*, 16 Cal. 3d 143, 545 P.2d 264, 127 Cal. Rptr. 352 (1976). [*Cornelison v. Chaney*, 16 Cal. 3d 143 (1976).] In *Cornelison*, the court differentiated between two distinct classes of circumstances under which California may assert jurisdiction over a foreign corporation. Where the defendant's in-state activities appear to be extensive, continuous, and systematic, California may assert general jurisdiction over the defendant for any cause of action—even a cause unrelated to the defendant's in-state activity. *Cornelison*, 16 Cal. 3d at 147, 545 P.2d at 266, 127 Cal. Rptr. at 354. [*Cornelison*, 16 Cal. 3d at 147.] Where the defendant's in-state activities are less pervasive, California courts cannot assert general jurisdiction. *Id.*, 545 P.2d at 266, 127 Cal. Rptr. at 354. [*Id.*] However, a court may establish limited jurisdiction over a particular cause of action where there is a direct nexus between that cause of action and the defendant's forum-related activities. *Id.* at 147-48, 545 P.2d at 266, 127 Cal. Rptr. at 354. [*Id.* at 147-48.] "Thus, as the relationship of the defendant with the state seeking to exercise jurisdiction over him grows more tenuous, the scope of jurisdiction also retracts, and fairness is assured by limiting the circumstances under which the plaintiff can compel him to appear and defend." *Id.* at 148, 545 P.2d at 266, 127 Cal. Rptr. at 354 (footnote omitted). [*Id.* at 148 (footnote omitted).]

---

* *In this memorandum, the first citation is in proper Bluebook form; the second one (in brackets) is in proper ALWD form. Note that for some citations, there is no difference between the Bluebook and ALWD forms, and thus only one citation is used.*

A. The State Cannot Justify an Exercise of General Jurisdiction over Southern Because the Forum-Related Contact, Consisting of Mere Membership in an Association Present in the Forum, Is Not Substantial, Continuous, and Systematic.

To establish general jurisdiction under the first of the two jurisdictional standards set out in *Cornelison*, the court must establish that Southern's forum-related activities are "'extensive or wide ranging'" or "'substantial . . . continuous, and systematic.'" 16 Cal. 3d at 147, 545 P.2d at 266, 127 Cal. Rptr. at 354 (quoting *Buckeye Boiler Co. v. Superior Court,* 71 Cal. 2d 893, 898-99, 458 P.2d 57, 62, 80 Cal. Rptr. 113, 118 (1969), and *Perkins v. Benguet Mining Co.,* 342 U.S. 437, 447-48 (1952), respectively). [16 Cal. 3d at 147 (quoting *Buckeye Boiler Co. v. Super. Ct. of Cal.,* 71 Cal. 2d 893, 898-99 (1969), and *Perkins v. Benguet Mining Co.,* 342 U.S. 437, 447-48 (1952), respectively).]

The United States Supreme Court applied this test in *Perkins.* There, the United States Supreme Court found appropriate the exercise of general jurisdiction over a Philippine mining corporation where its president sought refuge in Ohio during the World War II occupation of the Philippines. While in Ohio, the corporate president maintained an office in his home and several corporate accounts in Ohio banks, and performed other acts in the discharge of his duties as general manager. He also held several meetings of the corporate board of directors in Ohio. *Perkins,* 342 U.S. at 447-48.

The *Perkins* Court found these activities to be sufficiently substantial, continuous, and systematic to hold the Philippine corporation subject to Ohio jurisdiction in a matter unrelated to its forum-related activities. *Id.* at 447-49. The basis for this holding rested on the fact that the defendant corporation was actually present in Ohio. *Id.* at 449. The president's residence, the corporate office, and general business operations were present there. *Id.* at 448.

Southern's meager contacts with California fall far short of those considered necessary to the holding in *Perkins.* Southern maintains no office, personnel, or bank accounts in California and, therefore, is not present in the *Perkins* sense. Southern's sole contact with California is through the benefits it derives as a member of the Trailways association—a membership shared with approximately 50 other common carriers.

Even the occasional presence of the defendant in the forum for purposes of conducting business is not sufficient to establish general jurisdiction over all causes of action related or unrelated to the forum contacts. In *Cornelison,* the defendant was a truck driver and a resident of Nebraska. The defendant made approximately 20 trips into California each year to deliver and pick up cargo. The cause of action was the result of a collision in Nevada between a vehicle driven by a California resident and the defendant's truck on its way to California with a delivery. *Cornelison,* 16 Cal. 3d at 146-47, 545 P.2d at 266, 127 Cal. Rptr. at 352-54. [16 Cal. 3d at 146.] The *Cornelison* court found these contacts with California to be insufficient for the assertion of general jurisdiction. *Id.* at 148, 545 P.2d at 267, 127 Cal. Rptr. at 355. [*Id.* at 148.]

Southern's contacts fall short of those in *Cornelison,* where the court did not permit general jurisdiction even though the defendant and equipment under his control entered California as many as 20 times per year. In contrast, Southern has never sent any employee to California to conduct business on behalf of the corporation, and Southern exercises no control over its equipment used in transnational service beyond the territory where it conducts its regular business—Mississippi, Louisiana, and Alabama.

In light of the holdings in *Cornelison* and *Perkins,* Southern's tenuous and indirect contacts with California through its membership in the Trailways association are insufficiently substantial, continuous, and systematic to permit the exercise of general California jurisdiction over Southern. Therefore, limited jurisdiction, the second jurisdictional standard defined by *Cornelison,* is the only alternate basis for the court's exercise of jurisdiction. This ground also must fail.

B. Because the Necessary Nexus Is Missing Between the Out-of-State Bus Accident upon Which this Action Is Based and Southern's Indirect Forum Contacts Through the Trailways Association, California Cannot Exercise Limited Jurisdiction.

Where the relationship between the defendant and the forum is tenuous rather than substantial, and general jurisdiction is therefore unjustified, the court must apply a three-pronged test to determine whether California may exercise limited jurisdiction. *Cornelison,* 16 Cal. 3d at 148, 545 P.2d at 266-67, 127 Cal. Rptr. at 354-55. [*Cornelison,* 16 Cal. 3d at 148.] "The crucial inquiry concerns [1] the character of defendant's activity in the forum, [2] whether the cause of action arises out of or has a substantial connection with that activity, and [3] . . . the balancing of the convenience of the parties and the interests of the state in assuming jurisdiction." *Id.* at 148, 545 P.2d at 266-67, 127 Cal. Rptr. at 355 (citations omitted). [*Id.* at 148 (citations omitted).] Here, the plaintiff cannot satisfy any of the three prongs.

1. Defendant's Ticket Sales and Advertising Do Not Amount to "Forum-Related Activity."

Southern's only contacts with California are through its membership in Continental, which both promotes Trailways as a national bus system and facilitates the sale of Southern's tickets as part of that system. Therefore, any jurisdictional analysis of limited jurisdiction in this matter must be based on Continental's activities in California on behalf of Southern in terms of ticket sales and advertising of passage on Southern's line.

The only court applying California law to a common carrier in a situation similar to the case at bar is *Kenny v. Alaska Airlines Inc.,* 132 F. Supp. 838 (S.D. Cal. 1955). In *Kenny,* a California resident and stockholder in Alaska Airlines filed an action in the Southern District of California to enforce certain corporate proprietary rights. The plaintiff requested both an accounting and the nullification of certain stock issues. *Kenny,* 132 F. Supp. at 840-41.

In granting the motion to quash service of process for lack of personal jurisdiction, the court noted that Alaska Airlines was incorporated in Alaska, maintained its principal offices in Seattle, Washington, and engaged in airline service in Alaska, Washington, Oregon, and Canada. *Id.* at 841. Alaska Airlines had no employees in California. Its only contacts with California were ticket sales through various California ticket agencies and connecting air carriers. None of its flights entered California airspace. *Id.* at 841-42.

The *Kenny* court reasoned that to find jurisdiction under these circumstances "would present a policy problem of such magnitude that we believe the California courts would hold that such ticket sale activities did not constitute doing business." *Id.* at 852. The court noted that if it found jurisdiction, it would subject every common carrier within the vast, interconnected network of national transportation to the jurisdiction of the California courts—a prospect the court found to violate the notions of "fair play and substantial justice." *Id.* at 853.

The ticket sales activities found insufficient in *Kenny* were more substantial than those in the case at bar. Unlike Alaska Airlines, neither Southern nor Western sells tickets in California for exclusive travel in Southern's territory. The transcontinental tickets sold in California that involve Southern treat Southern merely as one of many interconnecting carriers. Therefore, if the *Kenny* court found Alaska Airlines's ticket sale activities in California insufficient for purposes of jurisdiction, this court should find such sales activities in California by others indirectly on behalf of Southern even less sufficient.

While California case law directly on point is scarce, other jurisdictions have confronted this issue. In *Pike v. New England Greyhound Lines, Inc.*, 93 F. Supp. 669 (D. Mass. 1950), the district court dealt with a relationship between the defendant and the forum that was not only close to that facing this court; it was nearly identical. Interstate, the defendant bus line in *Pike*, was a member of the Greyhound association. The membership services of the Greyhound association as described in *Pike* closely parallel those provided by the Trailways association. The office of the Boston Greyhound associate sold transcontinental tickets that routed passengers through Interstate's territory. Interstate maintained no offices or employees in Massachusetts. *Pike,* 93 F. Supp. at 670.

The *Pike* court held that "[t]he 'selling of tickets good over the lines of a foreign [bus] corporation by agents of other corporations, does not, standing alone, constitute the doing of business by the foreign corporation within the state of sale of the tickets.'" *Id.* at 671. In addition, the *Pike* court stated, "If the fact of such [ticket] sales is not sufficient to bring Interstate within the court's jurisdiction, it adds no substantial element that Central also advertises that fact, or provides such incidental services as furnishing timetables for use by the purchasers of the tickets." 93 F. Supp. at 671.

In a fashion similar to that of the Massachusetts court in *Pike*, the New York court in *Napelbaum v. Atlantic Greyhound Corp.*, 171 F. Supp. 547 (S.D.N.Y. 1958), granted Atlantic Greyhound's motion to dismiss for lack of personal jurisdiction. The suit in *Napelbaum* stemmed from a collision in Tennessee between the New York plaintiff's vehicle and a bus operated by the foreign defendant. *Napelbaum,* 171 F. Supp. at 548. The assertion of jurisdiction in *Napelbaum* was based on approximately the same relationship to the forum as had been stated in *Pike*. Again, the sales of defendant's tickets in New York were considered insufficient to justify an exercise of jurisdiction. *Id.* at 549-50.

In the case at bar, the quality of Southern's contacts with California are nearly identical to those deemed inadequate in *Pike* and *Napelbaum*. Just as the forum contacts of the defendants in *Napelbaum* and *Pike* consisted merely of their membership in the Greyhound association and the forum-related benefits that membership provided, Southern's sole contacts with California are through its membership in the Trailways association. As noted earlier, the membership benefits of the Greyhound and Trailways associations are nearly identical in every relevant way. As a result, we urge this court to join the courts in *Pike, Kenny*, and *Napelbaum* in finding the mere sale of tickets insufficient for an assertion of limited jurisdiction.

As to the issue of advertising, Continental advertises in California on behalf of all 50 association members including Southern. This advertising is inextricably wed to the sale of tickets over Southern's line since such sales cannot exist without promotional activity. Just as ticket sales are insufficient to satisfy the first prong of the test for limited jurisdiction, so is the promotion of those sales insufficient.

California has expressly found the mere advertising of one's services in the state insufficient for an assertion of limited jurisdiction. In *Circus Circus Hotels, Inc. v. Superior Court,* 120 Cal. App. 3d 546, 174 Cal. Rptr. 885 (1981) [*Circus Circus Hotels, Inc. v. Super. Ct. of Cal.,* 120 Cal. App. 3d 546 (4th Dist. 1981)], a California citizen brought a negligence action in a California court against Circus Circus Hotels, a Nevada corporation, stemming from a theft of plaintiff's property while plaintiff was a guest in defendant's Nevada hotel. Circus Circus moved to quash service of process based on a lack of personal jurisdiction. Circus Circus's only contacts with California were through the advertising of its Nevada services in various California publications and the maintenance of an "800" telephone number for placing hotel reservations. *Circus Circus,* 120 Cal. App. 3d at 551, 174 Cal. Rptr. at 887. [*Circus Circus,* 120 Cal. App. 3d at 551.] The *Circus Circus* court found that these activities could not support an assertion of jurisdiction. *Id.* at 567, 174 Cal. Rptr. at 897. [*Id.* at 567.]

Just as the defendants in *Circus Circus* and *Pike,* Southern sought to advertise its service in California indirectly through the Trailways association. Unlike Circus Circus: (1) there was no direct advertising of Southern's service in California, and (2) Southern maintained no direct connection between the results of the advertising done on its behalf and the sale of a ticket over an "800" line. Therefore, if the direct advertising activities in *Circus Circus* were insufficient to support an exercise of jurisdiction, then the indirect advertising on behalf of Southern was even less sufficient.

Neither the sale of tickets in California for connecting carriers outside the forum, nor the in-state advertising of those connecting services, represent acts of the quality considered adequate by *Cornelison* to satisfy the first prong of the test for limited jurisdiction. Therefore, the defendant's motion to quash service of summons should be granted.

2. The Nexus Between the Causes of Action and Southern's Forum Contacts Is Insufficient to Establish Jurisdiction.

The *Kenny* court focused sharply on whether California could assert jurisdiction where there was absolutely no relationship between the stockholder's action concerning proprietary rights in Alaska Airlines and the airline's in-state ticket sales through agents and connecting carriers. The court held that the necessary nexus between the cause and those contacts was missing. *Kenny*, 132 F. Supp. at 852-54.

Just as there was no nexus between the cause and defendant's forum-related acts in *Kenny*, there is no nexus between an accident on a Louisiana highway resulting from the alleged negligent maintenance and operation of a bus in Louisiana and Southern's membership in an association that advertises and sells tickets in California and throughout the nation. The only conceivable connection between the alleged negligent acts of Southern in Louisiana and its contacts with California is that Clark happened to be traveling away from California's border. Such a relationship is far too thin a thread upon which to hang jurisdiction.

The analysis of the Ninth Circuit in *Shute v. Carnival Cruise Lines,* 897 F.2d 377, 379 (9th Cir. 1990), *rev'd on other grounds, Carnival Cruise Lines, Inc. v. Shute,* 499 U.S. 585 (1991), is not dispositive of the nexus issue under the circumstances before this court. The *Shute* court stated that a "but for" test applies in the Ninth Circuit in determining whether a cause of action arises out of forum-related activities. *Shute,* 897 F.2d at 381. There, "but for" the advertising of Carnival in the forum, the plaintiffs would not have been on the cruise in international waters, where Ms. Shute was injured. *Id.* at 385.

However, the defendant's forum-related activities in *Shute* far exceeded Southern's mere membership in an association, since it included direct advertising of its services and the holding of periodic travel agent seminars within the forum. Southern's so-called forum-related activities consist of nothing more than its membership in the association—it did no direct advertising of its service in California. The limits of due process are surely exceeded by an assertion that mere membership in an association renders a citizen amenable to suit in every jurisdiction where that association carries out its functions. Therefore, based on *Kenny*, the plaintiff fails to satisfy the second prong of the *Cornelison* test.

3. In the Balancing of Parties' Convenience and the Interest of the State, Limited Jurisdiction Is Not Warranted.

In discussing the third prong of the test for limited jurisdiction, *Cornelison* states some of the factors that may be employed in the analysis: (1) the availability of evidence and the relative burdens of trial in one place rather than another, (2) the state's interest in providing a forum, (3) ease of access to the alternative forum, (4) avoiding a multiplicity of suits with attendant conflicting adjudications, and (5) the extent to which the cause of action arose out of forum-related activities. *Cornelison*, 16 Cal. 3d at 151, 545 P.2d at 268, 127 Cal. Rptr. at 356. [*Cornelison,* 16 Cal. 3d at 151.]

Under the circumstances of this case, the factor weighing most strongly against the assertion of jurisdiction is the relative burden on the defense and prosecution. California would be an extremely inconvenient forum since, with the exception of the plaintiff's testimony, all relevant evidence relating to the cause of action is located in Louisiana and Mississippi. The bus upon which Clark was riding is located in Louisiana. All of the emergency and hospital personnel, as well as the eyewitnesses to the accident, are residents of Louisiana and may be brought to California only at great inconvenience.

The strength of this factor, when combined with the lack of any nexus between the accident and Southern's California activities, throws the balance of the convenience between the parties strongly in favor of a denial of jurisdiction.

Since the plaintiff has failed to meet all three elements of the three-pronged test for limited jurisdiction, the court is justified in refusing to assert limited jurisdiction over Southern.

CONCLUSION

It would offend the notions of fair play and substantial justice to assert either limited or general jurisdiction over Southern based on the tenuous nature of Southern's contacts with California. Southern's forum-related activities were neither substantial, continuous, and systematic nor related to the plaintiff's cause of action.

For the above-stated reasons, the court should grant the defendant's Motion to Quash Service of Summons, and Continental Southern should be dismissed as a defendant in this action.

DATED: ________________________ Respectfully submitted,
Pillsbury, Crocker, Mills & Kraft

By: ____________________________

Jenna Smythe
Attorneys for Defendant

[*Note:* No references are made within this memorandum to supporting declarations or other documents that would establish the factual representations made.]

SAMPLE MEMORANDUM OF POINTS AND AUTHORITIES IN OPPOSITION TO MOTION

This memorandum of points and authorities was written and edited by members of the Legal Research, Writing and Analysis Program at the University of San Francisco School of Law. Special thanks to Stuart Sutton, Cristina Morris, Ellyn Moscowitz, and Rochelle Wirshup.

THELMA HAYDEN, State Bar #789102
HAYDEN, MARKS & PRENTICE
A Professional Corporation
1000 Mercury Street, Suite 200
San Francisco, California 94118
Telephone: (415) 555-6789

Attorneys for Plaintiff
THORA CLARK

SUPERIOR COURT OF THE STATE OF CALIFORNIA

FOR THE COUNTY OF SAN FRANCISCO

THORA CLARK,	)	
	)	No. 954-234
Plaintiff,	)	
	)	PLAINTIFF'S MEMORANDUM OF
vs.	)	POINTS AND AUTHORITIES
	)	IN OPPOSITION TO
	)	DEFENDANT'S
	)	MOTION TO QUASH SERVICE OF
	)	SUMMONS
CONTINENTAL TRAILWAYS,	)	
CONTINENTAL SOUTHERN, WESTERN	)	Cal. Civ. Proc. Code §410.10
TRAILWAYS, and DOES 1 through	)	
40, inclusive,	)	Date: February 15, 2002
	)	Time: 9:00 a.m.
	)	Dept.: 20 (Judge Jones)
Defendants.	)	

INTRODUCTION

Plaintiff, Thora Clark, is suing Continental Southern ("Southern") for damages arising out of a bus accident on December 27, 2000, in Louisiana. Ms. Clark is a California resident and is suing Southern, a Mississippi corporation, in California. Southern has moved to quash service of the summons on the grounds that Thora Clark cannot establish that California has personal jurisdiction over Southern.

Thora Clark opposes Southern's motion to quash service of summons on the grounds that Southern has maintained contacts with California of such a nature that the court may exercise either general or limited personal jurisdiction.

QUESTIONS PRESENTED

I. Does Continental Southern's advertising of its bus service in California, selling its tickets in California, and sending its buses into California represent activities sufficiently substantial, continuous, and systematic to justify California's exercise of general jurisdiction over Continental Southern?

II. Are (1) Continental Southern's contacts with California, (2) the nexus between plaintiff's injuries and the California contract for passage on Continental Southern's bus, and (3) the balance of the parties' convenience against the state's interest sufficient to support California's exercise of limited jurisdiction over Continental Southern?

STATEMENT OF FACTS

Plaintiff Thora Clark, a California resident, is an 80-year-old widow. She suffered a totally debilitating hip injury when a Trailways bus, owned and maintained by Southern, rolled over after its left front wheel collapsed on a Louisiana highway. As a result of the injuries suffered, Thora Clark was hospitalized in Louisiana for four months before being transferred to California for therapy. At this time, Thora Clark manages to walk with great difficulty and pain. She will never fully recover from the hip injury.

In planning a trip from San Francisco to Tampa, Florida, Thora Clark read defendant Continental Trailways's ("Continental") advertisements in *Conde Naste Traveler, Travel & Leisure* (both national publications), and the Travel section of the *San Francisco Examiner.* These ads touted Trailways as the "[n]ational bus system of choice." After confirming that she would ride a single coach throughout the transcontinental journey, Thora Clark purchased a Trailways ticket from Western Continental ("Western") at Western's office in the San Francisco Trans-Bay Terminal. When she purchased her ticket, Thora Clark believed she would be riding on a single coach owned and operated by a single national entity—Trailways. She was unaware that each of the ticket coupons disclaimed responsibility for injuries suffered by Ms. Clark outside the territory of operation of the carrier designated on the coupon.

On December 27, 2000, Thora Clark, along with 13 other California residents, boarded a Trailways bus at the Trans-Bay Terminal—a bus owned by Southern. Within an hour of leaving the terminal and while still in California, Ms. Clark heard a slight but continuous grinding sound coming from the front of the bus. She informed the Western driver of the noise as well as other drivers at the change of shifts. All of these drivers assured Ms. Clark that such noises were normal. About an hour after the coach entered Southern's territory, and a Southern driver took over driving the bus, the left front wheel of the coach collapsed, causing it to swerve off the road and tip over on its side. Every passenger on the bus suffered serious injuries.

In the absence of discovery, Thora Clark tentatively accepts as generally accurate the statement of the relationship among Southern, Continental, Western, and the Trailways "association" as set forth in Southern's Points and Authorities. However, Thora Clark takes issue with Southern's implied assertion that it is not "doing business" in California.

ARGUMENT

I.

SOUTHERN'S "SOLICITATION PLUS" CONTACTS WITH THE FORUM ARE OF SUCH A SUBSTANTIAL, CONTINUOUS, AND SYSTEMATIC NATURE THAT CALIFORNIA SHOULD EXERCISE GENERAL JURISDICTION.

Southern accurately states the general outline of the distinctions to be drawn between circumstances giving rise to a state's power to assert general as opposed to limited jurisdiction. Southern then launches into a litany of cases which, it asserts, hold that advertising taken alone and in-state ticket sales taken alone do not represent acts justifying an exercise of jurisdiction by a California court. However, there are two problems with such an analysis: First, individual classes of contacts with the forum cannot be taken alone; they must be viewed in the aggregate. Second, Southern's contacts extend far beyond mere solicitation and the sale of Southern's tickets. Southern sends equipment onto the highways of California and systematically enters into contracts with California residents to provide common carrier services outside the forum.

In *Circus Circus Hotels, Inc. v. Superior Court,* 120 Cal. App. 3d 546, 174 Cal. Rptr. 885 (1981) [*Circus Circus Hotels, Inc. v. Super. Ct. of Cal.,* 120 Cal. App. 3d 546 (4th Dist. 1981)]*, the court held that advertising in California publications and the maintenance of an "800" telephone number, taken alone, are insufficient for an assertion of jurisdiction. However, the *Circus Circus* court was very careful to distinguish the facts before it from those cases where the "residents of the forum state entered into contractual relationships with the soliciting parties." *Circus Circus,* 120 Cal. App. 3d at 567, 174 Cal. Rptr. at 897. [120 Cal. App. 3d at 567.] In situations where a party is involved in "solicitation plus contracting," a court would find that the party is doing business in the forum. *Id.,* 174 Cal. Rptr. at 897. [*Id.*] Had the California resident in *Circus Circus* entered into a contractual relationship in California with the Nevada defendant, the *Circus Circus* decision would have been markedly different.

**In this memorandum, the first citation is in proper Bluebook form; the second one (in brackets) is in proper ALWD form. Note that for some citations, there is no difference between the Bluebook and ALWD forms, and thus only one citation is used.*

Acts consisting of "solicitation plus" exist in the case at bar. When Thora Clark purchased her ticket at the San Francisco Trans-Bay Terminal, she entered into a binding contract for the services of a group of common carriers—one of which was Southern. Pursuant to that contract, Ms. Clark paid a fee, a portion of which represented Southern's compensation for services it was then bound to provide. While the number of such contracts between Southern and forum residents is as yet unknown, it is reasonable to assume that their number is high, since every California resident traveling on Trailways to Louisiana, Mississippi, Alabama, or Florida must travel on Southern's line. Thus, the substantial, continuous, and systematic solicitation of bus services, when combined with California contracts with Southern for service performed outside the forum, provides the necessary contacts for the assertion of general jurisdiction.

Like *Circus Circus,* other courts have viewed "solicitation plus" adequate for the exercise of jurisdiction. While *Napelbaum v. Atlantic Greyhound Corp.,* 171 F. Supp. 547 (S.D.N.Y. 1958), appears to reach a position contrary to that urged by Thora Clark, such is not the case. In *Napelbaum,* the New York plaintiff's vehicle collided with a bus owned by a Virginia corporation on a road in Tennessee. *Napelbaum,* 171 F. Supp. at 548. While denying jurisdiction, the court stated in dicta: "This Court wishes to point out that its decision would be quite different if plaintiff had been a passenger on defendant's bus through the purchase of a ticket in New York. In such a case, this Court has no doubt that it could properly exercise its jurisdiction." *Id.* at 550 (citation omitted). What the *Napelbaum* court described in dicta is the ***exact*** set of facts at bar. We may conclude from this statement that had it been faced with the facts before this Court, the court in *Napelbaum* would have exercised jurisdiction. Therefore, Southern's reliance on *Napelbaum* is without merit.

In support of its decision, *Napelbaum* relies on *Scholnik v. National Airlines, Inc.*, 219 F.2d 115 (6th Cir. 1955). In *Scholnik*, an Ohio airline passenger commenced an action in Ohio for an injury received in Florida on the defendant's plane. The court held the following factors relevant in the lease agreement: (1) the defendant airline (National) maintained no office in and scheduled no flights into Ohio, (2) a resident airline (Capital) sold tickets in Ohio covering passage over defendant's lines outside of Ohio, (3) the resident airline leased defendant's planes and crews in Ohio, and (4) the two airlines advertised their cooperative service as a through flight between Ohio and Florida. *Scholnik,* 219 F.2d at 116. "[T]he net overall effect of the numerous provisions of the Lease is not to create the relation of lessor and lessee, but rather the relation of participants in a joint enterprise . . . ." *Id.* at 118. As *Scholnik* states, "In such activities, agency clearly exists." *Id.* at 119.

The lease agreement in *Scholnik* is comparable to the association agreement bonding Southern, Western, and the other Trailways members into a single national bus system—all "participants in a joint enterprise." Like the airlines in *Scholnik*, the Trailways members coordinate their interconnecting service, tariffs, and schedules, and advertise their enterprise as a singular service under the banner of Trailways. Like the airlines in *Scholnik*, Western sells tickets incorporating the services of Southern through its territory and collects payment for that service. Like the airlines in *Scholnik*, Western is acting for Southern and with authority from Southern to so act. Therefore, like the court in *Scholnik*, this court should exercise jurisdiction over Southern.

Kenny v. Alaska Airlines Inc., 132 F. Supp. 838 (S.D. Cal. 1955), the only California case involving in personam jurisdiction over a nonresident common carrier, is of no assistance to Southern. *Kenny* is distinguishable from the case at bar since, as Southern notes, none of Alaska Airlines's flights entered California airspace. *Kenny,* 132 F. Supp. at 841. In sharp contrast, Southern sends its equipment into California—equipment that takes advantage of California highways, thus availing itself of the laws intended to govern their use.

As a result of the substantial, continuous, and systematic activity of Southern in California as a member of a joint enterprise with Western and Continental, California may assert general jurisdiction over Southern.

II.

THE TORTIOUS INJURIES SUFFERED BY THORA CLARK ARE DIRECTLY RELATED TO THE CONTRACT FOR SOUTHERN'S SERVICES IN CALIFORNIA, THUS JUSTIFYING THE EXERCISE OF LIMITED JURISDICTION.

Should this court determine that Southern's contacts with California are not sufficiently substantial, continuous, and systematic to justify an exercise of general jurisdiction, the court should exercise limited jurisdiction under the three-pronged test of *Cornelison v. Chaney*, 16 Cal. 3d 143, 148, 545 P.2d 264, 266-67, 127 Cal. Rptr. 352, 354-55 (1976). [*Cornelison v. Chaney,* 16 Cal. 3d 143, 148 (1976).] That test requires (1) an inquiry into the character of defendant's forum-related activity, (2) a determination of whether there is a nexus between the cause of action and those activities, and (3) a "balancing of the convenience of the parties and the interests of the state." *Cornelison*, 16 Cal. 3d at 148, 545 P.2d at 266-67, 127 Cal. Rptr. at 354-55. [*Cornelison,* 16 Cal. 3d at 148.]

In the above discussion, Thora Clark has established the first prong of the test by demonstrating that the quality of Southern's contacts with the forum represent purposeful activities aimed at California consumers. In the remainder of this analysis, Thora Clark will demonstrate that the necessary nexus exists between Southern's forum-related activities and the cause of action, and that a balancing of the convenience of the parties and the interests of the state justify the exercise of jurisdiction.

A. The Second Prong of the *Cornelison* Test Is Satisfied Because There Is a Nexus Between Southern's California Contacts and the Cause of Action.

In *Cornelison*, the Nebraska defendant was a truck driver who made approximately 20 delivery trips into California each year. While near the California-Nevada border on a trip to deliver goods in California, the defendant's vehicle was involved in a collision with a vehicle driven by a California resident. *Cornelison,* 16 Cal. 3d at 146, 545 P.2d at 266, 127 Cal. Rptr. at 353-54. [*Cornelison,* 16 Cal. 3d at 146.] While the *Cornelison* court found these forum-related contacts insufficient to exercise general jurisdiction, it did exercise limited jurisdiction. *Id.* at 149, 545 P.2d at 267, 127 Cal. Rptr. at 355. [*Id.* at 149.] In examining the nexus between the cause of action and the defendant's contacts with California, the court stated:

> He was not only bringing goods into California for a local manufacturer, but he intended to receive merchandise here for delivery elsewhere. The accident arose out of the driving of the truck, the very activity which was the essential basis of defendant's contacts with this state. These factors demonstrate, in our view, a substantial nexus between plaintiff's cause of action and defendant's activities in California.

Id., 545 P.2d at 267-68, 127 Cal. Rptr. at 355-56. [*Id.*] As discussed in Argument I, above, Southern entered into a contract in California with Thora Clark. That contract placed on Southern a common carrier's duty to exercise the utmost care and vigilance in providing the plaintiff with safe transportation. Southern's negligent conduct resulting in the Louisiana accident represents a direct failure to abide by its obligations under the contract. Just as the *Cornelison* court found an appropriate nexus between the careless driving of a truck outside the forum and the defendant's driving activity within the forum, this court should find a similar bond between a contract entered in this state and its breach in Louisiana.

Southern's sole support for its assertion of lack of the necessary nexus between the cause and the forum contacts is *Kenny*, in which a California stockholder brought suit against Alaska Airlines for matters relating to a proprietary interest in the airline. Plaintiff agrees that *Kenny* stands for the proposition that the necessary nexus is missing where jurisdiction is sought over a stockholder's derivative suit and the only forum contacts consist of the advertising and sale of airline tickets. However, the facts of *Kenny* and those of the case at bar are markedly different. As established above, there is a direct relationship between Southern's in-state contracting for bus services and a breach of its obligations under such contracts. Thus, *Kenny* is inapposite and Southern's reliance upon it is misplaced.

The situation addressed by the Ninth Circuit in *Shute v. Carnival Cruise Lines,* 897 F.2d 377 (9th Cir. 1990), *rev'd on other grounds, Carnival Cruise Lines, Inc. v. Shute,* 499 U.S. 585 (1991), is much more in keeping with the facts before this court than those presented by *Kenny.* In *Shute*, the court applied a "but for" test in determining whether a cause of action arises out of forum-related activities. *Shute,* 897 F.2d at 385. The court rejected the rule urged by Carnival that slip-and-fall claims cannot arise out of solicitation activities. *Id.* at 383. In upholding the exercise of limited jurisdiction, the court reasoned that "but for" the forum advertising, the Shutes would not have been on the ship—the parties would not have been "within tortious 'striking distance' of one another." *Id.* at 385. In like fashion, "but for" the advertising of Trailways in forum media, Thora Clark would not have been on that bus in the middle of Louisiana and would not have been injured.

In its points and authorities, defendant attempts to characterize its forum advertising as "indirect" while characterizing that in *Shute* as "direct." Such a subterfuge cannot withstand analysis. The thrust of the *Shute* decision rests firmly on whether solicitation occurred. Nothing in the *Shute* opinion leads to the conclusion that the analysis would have been any different had the advertising at issue been done by some third party under its own name (but for the benefit of Carnival) rather than in Carnival's own name. Whether direct or indirect, Southern engaged in, and profited from, the solicitation of California citizens.

Therefore, Thora Clark has established both the existence of Southern's contacts with California and the direct nexus between those contacts and the injury suffered. All that remains is to affirmatively establish that the balancing of party conveniences and the interests of California demand the exercise of jurisdiction over Southern.

B. The Balancing of Parties' Convenience and the State's Interest Satisfies the Third Prong and Establishes that California Has Jurisdiction.

Southern correctly states that among the factors to be considered in the determination of this prong of the *Cornelison* test are the following: (1) the relative availability of evidence and the burden on defense and prosecution between California and the alternative forum, (2) the state's interest in providing a forum, (3) the ease of access to that alternative forum, (4) the avoidance of a multiplicity of suits and conflicting adjudications, and (5) the extent to which the cause of action arose out of defendant's local activities. *Cornelison*, 16 Cal. 3d at 151, 545 P.2d at 268, 127 Cal. Rptr. at 356. [*Cornelison,* 16 Cal. 3d at 151.]

In its points and authorities, Southern focuses primarily on the first and fifth of these factors. As to the first factor, while it is true that the physical evidence as well as many of the witnesses are in Louisiana, it is equally true that records concerning the plaintiff's ongoing treatment are located in California, as are witnesses—five of the 13 California residents who boarded the bus in San Francisco. And, of course, this court must also consider the plaintiff's advancing age and her poor physical condition. Therefore, the first factor's balancing of party conveniences tips decidedly in Thora Clark's favor.

As to the fifth factor, Thora Clark established in the discussion above that there is a strong connection between the cause and Southern's forum-related activities. Thus, the assertion that a nexus is missing is without merit.

Southern is strangely silent concerning California's interest in providing a forum for its citizens, factor two. Southern sent the bus on which Thora Clark and 13 other California residents were riding onto the highways of this state. While here, that bus enjoyed the protection of the laws of this state in the same manner as all other vehicles on California highways. The grinding sound of the damaged wheel of the bus became apparent while still within California. Because of California's strong interest in the safety of its citizens traveling by common carrier on its highways, California is an appropriate forum for the trial of the issues in this case.

Finally, under factor four, this court may consider whether a failure to exercise jurisdiction will subject Thora Clark to a multiplicity of suits and conflicting adjudications. Thora Clark has joined three defendants in this action—Continental, Western, and Southern. As a California corporation, Western is amenable to suit in California. In like fashion, service of process on Continental has been achieved through service on its designated California agent. Only Southern protests the exercise of California jurisdiction. However, to the extent that Southern denies any connection with this forum, so may Western deny any connection to either Louisiana or Mississippi. As a result, the failure to exercise jurisdiction over Southern will expose Thora Clark to a multiplicity of suits and potentially conflicting adjudications—a suit against Western and Continental in California and another against Southern in Louisiana or Mississippi.

Based on the above analysis of the three-pronged *Cornelison* test, Thora Clark has established the right of this Court to exercise limited jurisdiction over Southern for purposes of adjudicating a cause directly related to its forum-related activities.

CONCLUSION

For the above reasons, the plaintiff, Thora Clark, respectfully requests that this court deny Southern's motion to quash service of summons and exercise either general or limited jurisdiction over it.

DATED: ______________________ Respectfully submitted,
HAYDEN, MARKS & PRENTICE

By: ______________________________
Thelma Hayden, Attorneys for
Plaintiff Thora Clark

[*Note:* No references are made within this memorandum to supporting declarations or other documents which would establish the factual representations made.]

Chapter Fifteen: Writing an Opinion or Client Letter

CONTENTS

A. An Objective Piece

1. An Opinion or Client Letter [§256]

Often, attorneys will provide informal opinions to their clients over the phone, in conference calls, or in person. However, there are times when attorneys will write opinion letters to their clients. The purpose of a client or opinion letter is to inform and advise the client about the case. The letter may respond to a particular concern raised by the client, or it may be a more general assessment of the situation. The letter may offer strategy as well as an opinion on the law.

The client letter is an ***objective*** document. Thus, you need to provide a balanced presentation of both sides of the problem. Then, based on your knowledge of the law, explain what you suppose the likely outcome will be. Be realistic.

2. Format [§257]

The tone of a client letter is very important. Since it is written to a layperson (unless your client is an attorney), your tone will be more informal than it would be if you were writing the same information to a supervising attorney. You do not need to cite any legal authorities in your letter, although sometimes attorneys will cite relevant statutes. If you have an attorney for a client, or perhaps a client who likes to research the law, you may want to refer to cases and other authorities as well.

a. Introduction

You should begin your client letter with a short introduction. The introduction would indicate that you are writing to keep the client abreast of the case, or that you are writing in response to a question or concern raised by the client. You can also set out the issue or issues that you will respond to or analyze in this letter.

b. Statement of facts

You should follow up the introduction with a short statement of the facts of your client's situation. This guarantees that you and the client are on the same wavelength when she reads your letter. It also indicates that it is these facts and no others to which you are responding.

c. Explanation of law and application to facts

You then proceed with an explanation of the relevant law and its application to the particular facts of the client's case. Your analysis should proceed in the same order in which you set out your issues above (*i.e.*, issue by issue). The legal analysis process of applying the law to the facts is the same as that in other objective documents. (*See* chapters XI and XIII.)

d. Conclusion/recommendation

If you are drawing a conclusion about the law, be sure that it is objective. The client can only make an informed decision if she is given a fair assessment of the situation. If an important fact is missing, be sure to point it out and consider alternative conclusions based on the missing fact.

If you are making a recommendation about strategy, be sure to leave room for the client to make the final decision. As an attorney, you may wish to counsel your client on the position you think that she should take, but the ultimate decision on which way to go (for example, whether to settle a case or proceed to trial, or how much money to accept or pay in settlement) is up to the client. Be careful that you do not impose your own judgment on the client.

e. Closing

Your closing should be short and friendly.

B. Sample Client Letter

The following is a mock client letter designed solely to show you what a client letter might look like. It is not intended to be an accurate statement of the law.

Dear Ms. Monroe:

You have asked me to comment on whether the landlord may retain your $600 "cleaning fee" which you paid to him on February 1, 2008, when you moved into apartment number 11 at 30 Norma Rae Lane in San Francisco. My understanding is that he is refusing to return it although you moved out on February 1, 2011, and have left the place in immaculate condition. His argument is that only "deposits" are returned, not "fees."

Under a state statute (Civil Code section 1234), landlords must return cleaning fees as well as cleaning deposits within two weeks after the tenant moves out of the apartment. A landlord cannot refuse to return the money by labeling it as a "fee." A landlord can only keep whatever he can prove he needs to clean the apartment.

From your description, you left the premises in immaculate condition. Thus, you are entitled to receive your $600 back. Since you moved out more than two weeks ago, the landlord should have returned the money by now.

A recent case dealt with a similar situation. In that case, the landlord claimed that he did not need to return a "lease key fee" after the tenant moved out. The court held that the landlord could not show any justification for retaining the lease key fee. The tenant had returned the key and had never made a duplicate of it. Thus, the landlord could not argue that he had to expend money to either replace the key or the lock.

Although the facts are somewhat different in your situation, the rationale behind that case and yours is the same. Landlords cannot retain deposits or fees unless they can prove some justification. From the facts you have given me, it does not appear that the landlord has any justification for withholding your cleaning fee. He does not need to clean the apartment or repair any damage. In fact, it sounds as if you left the apartment in even better condition than when you moved in.

By the way, the statute I mentioned also allows a court to award up to $200 in punitive damages (which are damages designed to punish or use as an example) when the landlord does not return the deposit or fee within the two-week period. So you might even receive more than the return of your fee if you have to go to court on this matter.

Please let me know whether there is anything else I can do for you.

Respectfully,

Attorney

Appendix—Review of Resources

THE BASIC PRIMARY SOURCES

FEDERAL:

Statutes

United States Code
United States Code Annotated ("U.S.C.A.") (West)
United States Code Service ("U.S.C.S.") (Michie/LexisNexis Group)
United States Statutes at Large

Cases

United States Reports (Official)
Supreme Court Reporter (West)
United States Supreme Court Reports, Lawyers' Edition (LexisNexis Group)
Federal Reporter (West)
Federal Supplement (West)

Administrative

Code of Federal Regulations ("C.F.R.")
Federal Register ("Fed. Reg.")

STATE:

Statutes

State codes (*e.g.*, Deering's Annotated California Codes, McKinney's Consolidated Laws of New York Annotated)
State session laws

Cases

Official state reports
West's National Reporter System—Regional reporters (*e.g.*, West's Pacific Reporter) and state reporters (*e.g.*, California Reporter and New York Supplement)

Administrative

State administrative codes

SECONDARY SOURCES

Selected Treatises

Williston, Contracts
Corbin, Contracts
Powell, Real Property
Davis, Administrative Law
Collier, Bankruptcy
Gordon & Mailman, Immigration Law and Procedure
Anderson American Law of Zoning
Hazard & Hodes, Law of Lawyering
Grad, Environmental Law

Selected Hornbooks

Prosser & Keeton, Torts
Calamari & Perillo, Contracts
Farnsworth, Contracts
Davis, Administrative Law
LaFave & Scott, Criminal Law
LaFave, Israel & King, Criminal Procedure
Henn & Alexander, Corporations
Rodgers, Environmental Law
Wright, Federal Courts
McCormick, Evidence
Bogert, Trusts
You will often hear a treatise or hornbook referred to as follows: (the author's name) on (the subject), e.g., Corbin on Contracts.

Encyclopedias

National

Corpus Juris Secundum ("C.J.S.")
American Jurisprudence 2d ("Am. Jur. 2d")

State

Witkin's Summary of California Law 10th
California Jurisprudence 3d
Florida Jurisprudence 2d
Michigan Law and Practice
New York Jurisprudence 2d
Strong's North Carolina Index 4th
Ohio Jurisprudence 3d
Summary of Pennsylvania Jurisprudence 2d
Texas Jurisprudence 3d
and others

Selected Practice and Procedure and Form Books

Federal

Moore's Federal Practice
Federal Practice and Procedure, Wright & Miller
West's Federal Forms
Federal Procedural Forms, Lawyers' Edition
Bender's Forms of Discovery
Bender's Federal Practice Manual

General

Am. Jur. Legal Forms 2d
Am. Jur. Pleading and Practice Forms
West Legal Forms (West)

California

Continuing Education of the Bar ("CEB") publications (http://ceb.com)
California Procedure 5th, Witkin
California Civil Procedure Before Trial (CEB)
California Forms of Pleading and Practice (Matthew Bender & Co., Inc./LexisNexis Group)
West's California Code Forms series
California Legal Forms (Matthew Bender & Co., Inc./LexisNexis Group)
California Civil Actions: Pleading and Practice, Arnold

New York

Carmody-Wait 2d: Cyclopedia of New York Practice with Forms (Lawyers Cooperative)
New York Practice 3d, Siegel (West)
McKinney's New York Civil Practice Law and Rules (West)
West's McKinney's Forms
New York Forms (Lawyers Cooperative)
New York Civil Practice (Matthew Bender & Co., Inc./LexisNexis Group)
Bender's Forms of Pleading, New York
Bender's Forms for the Consolidated Laws of New York

Digests

United States Supreme Court Digest
Digest of United States Supreme Court Reports, Lawyers' Edition
West's Federal Practice Digests 2d, 3d, and 4th
United States Federal Claims Digest
West's Atlantic Digest
West's North Western Digest
West's South Eastern Digest
West's Pacific Digest
American Digest System (Ten Decennials plus General Digests)

Selected Looseleaf Services and Materials

Commerce Clearing House ("CCH")

Labor Law Reports
Employment Safety and Health Guide
Unemployment Insurance Reporter
Medicare and Medicaid Guide
Consumer Product Safety Guide
Consumer Credit Guide
Bankruptcy Law Reporter
Energy Management and Federal Energy Guidelines
Nuclear Regulatory Reports
Standard Federal Tax Reporter
State Tax Reporters
Congressional Index
Trade Regulation Reports

Bureau of National Affairs ("BNA")

ABA/BNA Lawyers' Manual on Professional Conduct
Environment Reporter
Occupational Safety and Health Reporter
Product Safety and Liability Reporter
Labor Relations Reporter
Criminal Law Reporter
Family Law Reporter
Patent, Trademark & Copyright Journal
United States Law Week
Media Law Reporter

Online Sources

LexisNexis (http://www.lexis.com)
Westlaw (http://www.westlaw.com)
WestlawNext (http://next.westlaw.com)
LexisONE (http://www.lexisone.com)
Fastcase (http://www.fastcase.com)
Versus Law (http://www.versuslaw.com)
Loislaw (http://www.loislaw.com)
Bloomberg Law (http://www.bloomberglaw.com)
HeinOnline (http://heinonline.org)
Findlaw (http://www.findlaw.com)
WashLaw Web (http://www.washlaw.edu)
Legal Information Institute (http://www.law.cornell.edu)
THOMAS (http://thomas.loc.gov)
GPO Federal Digital System ("FDsys") (http://www.gpo.gov/fdsys)
Guide to Law Online (http://www.loc.gov/law/guide)
National Conference of Commissioners on Uniform State Laws ("NCCUSL") (http://www.nccusl.org)
Lexis Web (http://www.lexisweb.com)
Google Scholar (http://scholar.google.com)
Public Library of Law (http://www.plol.org)
Social Science Research Network ("SSRN") (http://www.ssrn.com)
Berkeley Electronic Press (http://www.bepress.com)
ABA Journal's Blawg (legal blog) Directory (http://www.abajournal.com/blawgs)
Public Access to Electronic Records ("PACER") (http://www.pacer.gov)
United States Courts (http://www.uscourts.gov)
National Center for State Courts (http://www.ncsc.org)
United States Department of State (http://www.state.gov)
United States Department of Justice (http://www.justice.gov)
USA.gov (http://www.usa.gov)

Other Useful Sources

ALI-ABA publications (http://www.ali-aba.org)
ACLEA publications (http://www.aclea.org)
Practising Law Institute ("PLI") publications (http://www.pli.org)
American Law Reports ("A.L.R.")
Martindale-Hubbell Law Digest (http://www.martindale.com)
Index to Legal Periodicals
Checklist of Basic American Legal Publications
Daily Legal Newspapers
Shepard's Citations
West's Blue and White Books
The Bluebook: A Uniform System of Citation ("The Bluebook")
ALWD Citation Manual: A Professional System of Citation
Black's Law Dictionary
Gilbert Pocket Size Law Dictionary
Words and Phrases
The Gilbert Law Summaries series

CHAPTER 49—DISTRICT COURTS

Cross References

Bankruptcy court officers, appointment, duties and compensation, see section 61 et seq. of Title 11, Bankruptcy.

District Court of Guam, chapter as applicable, see section 1424b of Title 48, Territories and Insular Possessions.

General provisions applicable to court officers and employees, see section 951 et seq. of this title.

§ 751. Clerks

(a) Each district court may appoint a clerk who shall be subject to removal by the court.

(b) The clerk may appoint, with the approval of the court, necessary deputies, clerical assistants and employees in such number as may be approved by the Director of the Administrative Office of the United States Courts. Such deputies, clerical assistants and employees shall be subject to removal by the clerk with the approval of the court.

(c) The clerk of each district court shall reside in the district for which he is appointed, except that the clerk of the district court for the District of Columbia and the Southern District of New York may reside within twenty miles thereof. The district court may designate places within the district for the offices of the clerk and his deputies, and their official stations.

(d) A clerk of a district court or his deputy or assistant shall not receive any compensation or emoluments through any office or position to which he is appointed by the court, other than that received as such clerk, deputy or assistant, whether from the United States or from private litigants.

This subsection shall not apply to clerks or deputy clerks appointed as United States commissioners pursuant to section 631 of this title.

(e) The clerk of each district court shall pay into the Treasury all fees, costs and other moneys collected by him, except naturalization fees listed in section 742 of Title 8 and uncollected fees not required by Act of Congress to be prepaid.

He shall make returns thereof to the Director of the Administrative Office of the United States Courts under regulations prescribed by him.

June 25, 1948, c. 646, 62 Stat. 920.

Historical and Revision Notes

References in Text. Section 742 of Title 8, referred to in the text of subsection (e), was repealed by Act June 27, 1952, c. 477, Title IV, § 403(a) (42), 66 Stat. 280 eff Dec. 24, 1952, and is now covered by section 1455 of Title 8, Aliens and Nationality.

Reviser's Note. Based on Title 28, U.S.C., 1940 ed., §§ 6, 7, 8, 524, 557, 567, 568, and 569, sections 644 and 863 of Title 48, U.S.C., 1940 ed., Territories and Insular Possessions, and section 11-401 of the District of Columbia Code, 1940 ed. (R.S. § 833; June 20, 1874, c. 328, § 2, 18 Stat. 109; May 28, 1896, c. 252, § 8, 29 Stat. 181; Apr. 12, 1900, c. 191, § 34, 31 Stat. 84; Apr. 30, 1900, c. 339, § 86, 31 Stat. 158; Mar. 3, 1901, c. 854, § 174, 31 Stat. 1218; June 28, 1902, c. 1301, § 1, 32 Stat. 475; June 30, 1902, c. 1329, 32 Stat. 527; June 30, 1906, c. 3914, § 1, 34 Stat. 754; Mar. 3, 1909, c. 269, § 1, 35 Stat. 838; Mar. 3, 1911, c. 231, §§ 3, 4, 291, 36 Stat. 1087, 1167 [Derived from R.S. § 558]; Jan. 7, 1913, c. 6, 37 Stat. 648; Mar. 2, 1917, c. 145, § 41, 39 Stat. 965; Feb. 26, 1919, c. 49, §§ 1, 4, 9, 40 Stat. 1182, 1183; Feb. 11, 1921, c. 46, 41 Stat. 1099; Mar. 4, 1921, c. 161, § 1, 41 Stat. 1412, 1413; June 10, 1921, c. 18, §§ 301, 310, 42 Stat. 23, 25; June 16, 1921, c. 23, § 1, 42 Stat. 41; July 9, 1921, c. 42, § 313, 42 Stat. 119; June 1, 1922, c. 204, Title II, 42 Stat. 614, 616; Jan. 3, 1923, c. 21, Title II, 42 Stat. 1084; Feb. 12, 1925, c. 220, 43 Stat. 890; Dec. 13, 1926, c. 6, § 1, 44 Stat. 919; May 17, 1932, c. 190, 47 Stat. 158; June 25, 1936, c. 804, 49 Stat. 1921; Mar. 26, 1938, c. 51, § 2, 52 Stat. 118; June 16, 1938, c. 465, 52 Stat. 752; June 14, 1941, c. 203, §§ 1, 2, 55 Stat. 251).

This section consolidates provisions of section 11-401 of the District of Columbia Code, 1940 ed., sections 644 and 863 of Title 48, Territories and Insular Possessions, and Title 28, U.S.C., 1940 ed., sections 6, 7, 8, 524, 557, 567, 568, and 569 relating to district court clerks. Other provisions of such sections 8 and 524 are incorporated in sections 505, 541, and 954 of this title and other provisions of such section 11-401 of the District of Columbia Code have been retained in such Code.

Words "with the approval of the court" were substituted for "Attorney General." The power to approve appointment of court officers is more properly a judicial one. (See section 711 of this title.)

The provision in section 6 of Title 28, U.S.C., 1940 ed., that the clerk be appointed by the district judge or senior judge where there was more than one member of the court was changed and the power vested in the court.

The provisions of section 644 of Title 48, Territories and Insular Possessions, relating to compensation of clerks and deputy clerks were omitted as covered by section 604 of this title. Other provisions of said section 644 are incorporated in section 753 of this title.

Provision for similar officers in Alaska, Canal Zone, and the Virgin Islands is made by sections 106, 1349, and 1405y, respectively, of Title 48. A part of section 863 of said Title 48, was retained in title 48. For remainder of such section, see Distribution Table.

Words in sections 6 and 7 of Title 28, U.S.C., 1940 ed., "Except as otherwise provided for by law," were omitted as obsolete and superfluous.

References in section 7 that the clerk recommend appointment of deputies and clerical assistants were omitted as unnecessary.

The provision that each clerk shall be subject to removal by the court is new. No tenure was provided for by Title 28, U.S.C., 1940 ed., but said title contained provisions that other clerks should hold office during the pleasure of the courts which appointed them, and that deputies should hold office during the pleasure of the clerks. The Supreme Court held, in 1839, that a judge of a district court could remove the clerk thereof at pleasure in absence of any law fixing the clerk's tenure. In re Hennen, 38 U.S. 230, 13 Pet. 230, 10 L.Ed. 138. (See also, Meyers v. U. S., 47 S.Ct. 21, 272 U.S. 52, 71 L.Ed. 160.)

Words "circuit or" after "Every clerk of the" in section 524 of Title 28, U.S.C., 1940 ed., were omitted because of the abolition of the circuit courts by Act Mar. 3, 1911, ch. 231, § 289, 36 Stat. 1167, Title 28, U.S.C., 1940 ed., § 430.

c. Other Places

§ 63(126). Bars and Taverns

A patron of a bar, tavern, or similar establishment serving intoxicating liquors is an invitee to whom the owner or operator owes the duty to exercise due care for his safety.

Library References

Negligence ⇐32(1, 2.8).

A patron of a bar, tavern, saloon, or similar establishment engaged in the serving of intoxicating liquors,[2] or other person who enters ostensibly for a purpose directly connected with the business,[3] is an invitee or business guest, to whom the owner or operator owes the duty to exercise ordinary or reasonable care for his safety, including the duty to keep the premises in a reasonably safe condition,[4] and to warn him of unknown or hidden hazards or risks.[5]

The standard of care demanded of the owner or operator of an establishment serving intoxicating liquors has variously been described as a high degree of care,[6] or as not a high degree of care,[7] or as the same as that in other places of public resort, but adapted to the character of the business and commensurate with the conditions and circumstances involved in a particular situation.[8] In any

2. Cal.—Shaw v. Colonial Room, 175 C.A.2d 845, 1 Cal.Rptr. 28—Seabert v. Aiello, 289 P.2d 30, 136 C.A.2d 613.
Ga.—Rollestone v. Cassirer, 59 S.E. 442, 3 Ga.App. 161.
Ill.—Cooley v. Makse, 196 N.E.2d 396, 46 Ill.App.2d 25.
Mass.—Denton v. Park Hotel, Inc., 180 N.E.2d 70, 343 Mass. 524—Greco v. Sumner Tavern, Inc., 128 N.E.2d 788, 333 Mass. 144.
45 C.J. p 815 note 76.

Employee remaining after working hours

Where tavern waitress remained at tavern after her work hours and had some drinks with customer, one of which she bought herself, she was an invitee at time she fell on tavern steps when she was leaving to go home.
Ill.—Starns v. Postawko, 106 N.E.2d 145, 347 Ill.App. 77.

3. Ky.—Rojo, Inc. v. Drifmeyer, 357 S.W.2d 33.

To use phone

Man who entered barroom to use telephone was an invitee and was entitled to rights and duties devolving on invitees, and he was also a business visitor.
Ohio.—Hartman v. Di Lello, 157 N.E. 2d 127, 109 Ohio App. 387.

4. Cal.—Shaw v. Colonial Room, 175 C.A.2d 845, 1 Cal.Rptr. 28.
Mass.—Greco v. Sumner Tavern, Inc., 128 N.E.2d 788, 333 Mass. 144.
Mont.—Ganger v. Zook, 377 P.2d 101, 141 Mont. 214.
N.Y.—Bragg v. Smilowitz, 226 N.Y.S. 2d 755, 16 A.D.2d 131, affirmed 186 N.E.2d 566, 12 N.Y.2d 769, 234 N.Y.S.2d 718.
Ohio.—Hartman v. Di Lello, 157 N.E. 2d 127, 109 Ohio App. 387.
Wash.—Miller v. Staton, 354 P.2d 891.
Parking lot see infra § 63(130).
Toilet and restroom see infra § 63 (132).

Restaurant which dispenses intoxicating liquors is within the rule.
Colo.—Cubbage v. Leep, 323 P.2d 1109, 137 Colo. 286.

Delegable duty

Relationship between a bar owner and a customer is not such that the bar owner has a duty to protect the customer that may not be delegated.
Cal.—Monty v. Orlandi, 337 P.2d 861, 169 C.A.2d 620.

Fraternal association's building, which was open to public, except on special occasions or for special events, and in which food and drinks were served to public daily, was a public building, and woman entering it to be served a drink was association's invitee, to whom it owed duty to use reasonable care to keep premises in reasonably safe condition except as to dangerous conditions which were obvious, reasonably apparent, or as well known to her as to association.
Tex.—San Antonio Hermann Sons Home Ass'n v. Harvey, Civ.App., 256 S.W.2d 906, error refused no reversible error.

Patron has right to rely on implied promise of proprietor that patron would be protected from injury while lawfully on premises in so far as proprietor could protect him by the exercise of reasonable care and diligence, which is measured by what a person of ordinary prudence would or would not do under similar circumstances.
Colo.—Cubbage v. Leep, 323 P.2d 1109, 137 Colo. 286.

Ingress and egress

Duty of due care includes corollary duty to get invitees safely on or off tavern premises; and owner and operator of tavern owed duty to invitees to illuminate brick walk, and to give invitees adequate warning of dangerous condition of walk or to repair dangerous condition, even though walk was situated on city easement and dangerous condition was not affirmatively created by owner or operator of tavern.
Ill.—Cooley v. Makse, 196 N.E.2d 396, 46 Ill.App.2d 25.

Depression in dance floor

Depression which was eighteen inches in diameter and one-half to one inch deep near center in concrete dance floor of bar and dance hall was defect not reasonably observable to a dancer exercising ordinary care, and dancer's failure to see depression and likelihood of stumbling in it was reasonably foreseeable, and, therefore, bar-dance hall operator who knew of condition of floor but neglected to repair it or give warning of hazard was negligent.
La.—Huckaby v. Bellow, App., 175 So. 2d 914.

5. Mass.—Smith v. August A. Busch Co. of Massachusetts, 109 N.E.2d 843, 329 Mass. 615.
N.Y.—Bragg v. Smilowitz, 226 N.Y.S. 2d 755, 16 A.D.2d 131, affirmed 186 N.E.2d 566, 12 N.Y.2d 769, 234 N.Y. S.2d 718.

No duty as to obvious conditions

Mo.—Howard v. Johnoff Restaurant Co., 312 S.W.2d 55—Wattels v. Marre, 303 S.W.2d 9, 66 A.L.R.2d 433.
Tex.—Wesson v. Gillespie, 382 S.W.2d 921.

6. Wyo.—Fisher v. Robbins, 319 P.2d 116, 78 Wyo. 50.

Stricter accountability

While the owner and operator of a public tavern and grill is held to a stricter accountability for injuries to patrons than is the owner of private premises generally, the rule is that such owner is not an insurer of the patrons against all accidents which may befall them on the premises, but owes them only what, under the particular circumstances, is ordinary and reasonable care.
Kan.—Huddleston v. Clark, 349 P.2d 888, 186 Kan. 209.

7. Wash.—Miller v. Staton, 354 P.2d 891.

8. Mo.—Gregorc v. Londoff Cocktail Lounge, Inc., 314 S.W.2d 704.

event, the owner or operator of a bar or tavern is not an insurer of the safety of his patrons.[9]

A patron of a tavern may lose his status as invitee or business visitor where he goes, for his own purposes, to a part of the premises to which his invitation does not extend.[10]

Protection of patron from own intoxication. It has been held that the proprietor of a bar or cafe is under no special duty to protect a patron from the results of his own voluntary intoxication,[11] except in so far as the rule may be affected by civil damage statutes, discussed in Intoxicating Liquors § 430 et seq., and particularly § 442.

§ 63(127). —— Acts of Other Persons

The owner or operator of a bar or tavern must exercise reasonable care to protect guests and patrons from disorderly acts of other persons, including other guests and patrons.

Library References

Negligence ⇐32(1, 2.8).

It is the duty of the owner or operator of a bar, tavern, or similar establishment engaged in the serving of intoxicating liquors to exercise reasonable care, vigilance, and prudence to protect his guests and patrons from disorderly acts of other guests and patrons,[12] or other persons,[13] and to warn them of the danger from a third person, where it is known to the tavern keeper and not to the guests.[14]

The owner or operator owes a duty to those who come on his premises to exercise reasonable care to see to it that they are not injured by vicious or drunken individuals whom he permits to come on his premises and whose conduct he might reasonably have anticipated;[15] and to escape liability therefor

9. Cal.—Rose v. Melody Lane of Wilshire, 247 P.2d 335, 39 C.2d 481.
Colo.—Cubbage v. Leep, 323 P.2d 1109, 137 Colo. 286.
Kan.—Huddleston v. Clark, 349 P.2d 888, 186 Kan. 209.
Mont.—Ganger v. Zook, 377 P.2d 101, 141 Mont. 214.
Wash.—Miller v. Staton, 354 P.2d 891.

Operator of cocktail room was not an insurer of the safety of its premises but was liable only for negligence in constructing, maintaining, or inspecting the premises.
Cal.—Rose v. Melody Lane of Wilshire, 247 P.2d 335, 39 C.2d 481.

10. Wis.—Ryan v. O'Hara, 6 N.W.2d 209, 241 Wis. 389.

Customer meddling with electric fan

One whose hand came into contact with blades of electric fan on top of cupboard over seven feet from floor of liquor tavern, which he had entered as customer solely for his own pleasure and convenience, was a trespasser and hence not entitled to recover damages from tavern operator for resulting injuries, although blades were not guarded as required by industrial commission's orders.
Wis.—Ryan v. O'Hara, 6 N.W.2d 209, 241 Wis. 389.

Defense held not available

In action by patron against proprietor of bar for injuries sustained when he fell in a hole at end of porch which had no barricade around it, defense that patron was off that part of premises to which his original invitation applied was not available to proprietor.
N.M.—Mitchell v. Pettigrew, 333 P.2d 879, 65 N.M. 137.

11. N.Y.—Moyer v. Lo Jim Cafe, Inc., 240 N.Y.S.2d 277, 19 A.D.2d 523, affirmed 200 N.E.2d 212, 14 N.Y.2d 792, 251 N.Y.S.2d 30.

Contributory negligence see infra § 143.

12. Ill.—Lipscomb v. Coppage, 197 N.E.2d 48, 44 Ill.App.2d 430.
Mo.—Gregorc v. Londoff Cocktail Lounge, Inc., 314 S.W.2d 704.
N.J.—Reilly v. 180 Club, Inc., 82 A.2d 210, 14 N.J.Super. 420.
Pa.—Hertzler v. Molly Pitcher Hotel Co., Com.Pl., 5 Cumb.L.J. 105.

Civil damage laws see Intoxicating Liquors §§ 430–485.

Sponsorship of convention did not enlarge bar proprietor's responsibilities to patrons on premises beyond those owed by proprietor of any place of amusement to business invitees, and bar proprietor did not have extraordinary duty to prevent injury to patrons on the premises.
Minn.—Evanish v. V. F. W. Post No. 2717, Ely, 130 N.W.2d 331, 269 Minn. 209.

13. Pa.—Hertzler v. Molly Pitcher Hotel Co., Com.Pl., 5 Cumb.L.J. 105.

Armed robber

While in a proper case, the proprietor of a business may have a duty to his customers to take measures to keep armed robbers off his premises for the protection of his customers, under the particular circumstances, proprietor of bowling alley bar which was open late at night in a neighborhood in which there had been some increase in criminality had no duty to his customers to protect his premises against armed robbery.
N.J.—Genovay v. Fox, 143 A.2d 229, 50 N.J.Super. 538, reversed on other grounds 149 A.2d 212, 29 N.J. 436.

14. Mass.—Smith v. August A. Busch Co. of Massachusetts, 109 N.E.2d 843, 329 Mass. 615.

Obvious danger from armed patron

Where patron of cocktail lounge observed another patron holding a gun on a third patron for between fifteen and twenty minutes, patron had as much knowledge as anyone of whatever peril existed in the situation and that conduct of patron with gun was dangerous to safety of others, and he was not entitled to be warned by proprietor of cocktail lounge of danger of which he already had knowledge.
Mo.—Gregorc v. Londoff Cocktail Lounge, Inc., 314 S.W.2d 704.

15. Minn.—Priewe v. Bartz, 83 N.W.2d 116, 249 Minn. 488, 70 A.L.R.2d 621.
Mo.—Durbin v. Cassalo, App., 321 S.W.2d 23.

Circumstances when duty arises

Duty of tavern keeper to protect patron from injury by another arises only when one or more of the following circumstances exist: First, where tavern keeper has allowed on premises person with known propensity for fighting; second, where tavern keeper has allowed to remain on premises person whose conduct has become obstreperous and aggressive to such degree that tavern keeper ought to know that others are in danger; third, where tavern keeper has been warned of danger from obstreperous patron; fourth where he tolerates disorderly conditions on the premises.
Wash.—Miller v. Staton, 354 P.2d 891.

Presence of intoxicated person on the premises immediately exposes the proprietor of a bar to the hazards of liability resulting from the unpredictable conduct of such person.
Minn.—Klingbeil v. Truesdell, 98 N.W.2d 134, 256 Minn. 360.

Statute as to permitting drunkenness

Bar owners were not liable for injuries sustained when male patron, who as he attempted to kiss female patron, was shoved fell off bar stool

SCHOOLS

by

Daniel H. White, J.D.

Scope of Topic: This article discusses the law governing public and private schools of elementary or high school grade, treating also correspondence schools and other private schools of a post-high-school but noncollege level. Discussed are school districts and the officers thereof, school property, taxation by school districts and the expenditure of school funds, teachers and teacher dismissals, pupils and their relationship to the school, student health, the regulation of curricula, the relationship between government and church-related schools, and private schools.

Treated elsewhere are colleges and universities (see 15 Am Jur 2d, COLLEGES AND UNIVERSITIES); the exercise of eminent domain powers relative to schools (see 26 Am Jur 2d, EMINENT DOMAIN); discrimination in public and private schools (see 15 Am Jur 2d, CIVIL RIGHTS §§ 38–50); the tort liability of public schools (see 57 Am Jur 2d, MUNICIPAL, SCHOOL, AND STATE TORT LIABILITY); reformatories for youthful offenders (see 60 Am Jur 2d, PENAL AND CORRECTIONAL INSTITUTIONS); school land grants (see 63 Am Jur 2d, PUBLIC LANDS); charities for educational purposes (see 15 Am Jur 2d, CHARITIES); school bonds, certificates, warrants, orders, and vouchers (see PUBLIC SECURITIES AND OBLIGATIONS); and the education of Indians (see 41 Am Jur 2d, INDIANS § 18).

Federal Aspects: Federal statutes pertaining to such topics as the Office of Education, the Commissioner of Education, and federal aid to elementary and secondary schools, are treated herein. Certain federal matters not within the scope of this article have been mentioned above as treated elsewhere, and specifically, that portion of the civil rights area which pertains to schools and to schoolchildren is discussed in 15 Am Jur 2d, CIVIL RIGHTS §§ 38–50. Also, the education of Indian children is treated at 41 Am Jur 2d, INDIANS § 18.

★ **Table of Parallel References see p vii.** ★

I. INTRODUCTORY

a tenure teacher is dismissed, where the tenure teacher is not qualified to teach the courses to be taught by the nontenure teacher.[79]

Statutes in some jurisdictions provide that no tenure teacher shall be dismissed while a probationary teacher is retained or employed to render a service which the tenure teacher is certificated and competent to render.[80] And subject to various qualifications and conditions, statutes in some jurisdictions have established seniority as the basis for the selection of the tenure teacher or teachers to be dismissed or suspended.[81]

Where seniority is established as the statutory basis for the selection of the particular teacher or teachers to be dismissed or suspended, a question may arise as to whether seniority is meant to be systemwide, for example, and to refer to the length of service in the school system in any capacity, or whether it is meant to be less than systemwide and to refer, for example, to the length of service in a particular position, or specific job, or position or job category, or department, or whatever.[82] The answer to this question must be determined in the light of the applicable statutes, and the cases have reached different results under various statutory provisions and different circumstances.[83] Where seniority is established as the statutory basis for the selection of the particular teacher or teachers to be dismissed or suspended, and where one tenure teacher has greater seniority, within the category contemplated by the statute, than another teacher, the fact that the teacher with the greater seniority is not legally qualified to perform the teaching duties of the teacher with less seniority will not necessarily operate to bar the retention of the teacher with greater seniority, as it has been held that under these circumstances, the school board, in order to effectuate the seniority provision of the statute, must attempt to realign the teaching staff so as to provide for the retention of teachers in accordance with their seniority.[84]

§ 170. Disloyalty.

Public employment, including academic employment, may not be conditioned upon the surrender of constitutional rights which cannot be abridged by direct government action.[85] However, the state has a vital concern in the educational process and has the right not only to screen teachers as to their fitness, but also to be concerned about possible advocacy of overthrow of the government by force and violence.[86] Accordingly, dismissal of a teacher

79. Weider v Board of Education, 112 NJL 289, 170 A 631; Bates v Board of Education, 133 W Va 225, 55 SE2d 777.

Annotation: 100 ALR2d 1141, 1186, § 18.

80. ***Annotation:*** 100 ALR2d 1141, 1191, § 20.

Local statutes should be consulted.

81. Jones v Mt. Carmel Township School Dist. 47 Pa D & C 307, 16 Northum Leg J 34.

Annotation: 100 ALR2d 1141, 1188, § 19.

Practice Aids.—Dismissal of teacher whose services are no longer needed. 22 Am Jur Proof of Facts 563, 585, Dismissal of Teachers for Cause § 16.

—Allegation of violation of tenure rights by continuing employment of teachers with less seniority while dismissing plaintiff. 18 Am Jur Pl & Pr Forms, Schools, Form 18:110.

82. ***Annotation:*** 100 ALR2d 1141, 1188, § 19.

83. Davidson v Board of Education, 26 Ohio Ops 142, 38 Ohio L Abs 6; Walker v School Dist. 338 Pa 104, 12 A2d 46.

Annotation: 100 ALR2d 1141, 1189, § 19.

84. Welsko v School Board of School Dist. 383 Pa 390, 119 A2d 43.

Annotation: 100 ALR2d 1141, 1191, § 19.

85. Keyishian v Board of Regents, 385 US 589, 17 L Ed 2d 629, 87 S Ct 675.

86. Ohlson v Phillips (DC Colo) 304 F Supp 1152, affd 397 US 317, 25 L Ed 2d 337, 90 S Ct 1124, reh den 397 US 1081, 25 L Ed 2d 819, 90 S Ct 1520.

Practice Aids.—Disloyalty of teacher as basis for dismissal. 22 Am Jur Proof of Facts 563, 594, Dismissal of Teachers for Cause § 21.

because of disloyal conduct has been upheld where a statute specifically provided for dismissal for that cause.[87] And the failure on the part of a teacher to deny that she is a Communist, when such an accusation has been made, has been held to warrant dismissal.[88]

Several decisions have upheld the dismissal of teachers who have proclaimed themselves pacifists or conscientious objectors to war.[89]

In a few cases where at least some question of loyalty was involved, the courts have held that the school authorities went beyond the bounds of permissible action, and have reversed dismissals of teachers.[90]

Dismissals of teachers for engaging in subversive activity or for making seditious utterances have been upheld.[91] However, statutes requiring or authorizing the removal of faculty members for seditious utterances have been held unconstitutionally vague where a teacher could not know the extent to which the utterance must transcend mere statements about abstract doctrine, and a statute banning state employment of any person advocating or distributing material which advocates forceful overthrow of the government has been held unconstitutionally vague as prohibiting advocating the doctrine in the abstract, and statutes making Communist Party membership prima facie evidence of disqualification have been held to unconstitutionally abridge freedom of association by not permitting rebuttal by proof of nonactive membership or absence of intent to further unlawful aims.[92]

In several instances, state loyalty oaths required of teachers, with accompanying provisions calling for the dismissal of teachers and prosecution for perjury for falsification or violation of the oath, have been held unconstitutional.[93]

§ 171. —Refusal to answer during loyalty interrogations.

A public employee may not be discharged solely because he invokes or

87. Board of Education v Jewett, 21 Cal App 2d 64, 68 P2d 404.

Annotation: 27 ALR2d 487.

88. Appeal of Albert, 372 Pa 13, 92 A2d 663.

Annotation: 27 ALR2d 487.

89. State ex rel. Schweitzer v Turner, 155 Fla 270, 19 So 2d 832; McDowell v Board of Education, 104 Misc 564, 172 NYS 590; Joyce v Board of Education, 325 Ill App 543, 60 NE2d 431, cert den 327 US 786, 90 L Ed 1013, 66 S Ct 702 (where a teacher was dismissed, following a hearing on charges of conduct unbecoming a schoolteacher, on evidence that she had written a letter to a former student the day following his failure and refusal to register in accordance with the Selective Service Act, congratulating him on his "courageous and idealistic stand," wishing him success, and stating that "you and others who take the same stand are the hope of America").

Annotation: 27 ALR2d 487, 488.

Practice Aids.—Dismissal of teacher for conscientious objection to military service. 22 Am Jur Proof of Facts 563, 608, Dismissal of Teachers for Cause § 25.

90. Hopkins v Bucksport, 119 Me 437, 111 A 734; Board of School Directors of School Dist. v Gillies, 343 Pa 382, 23 A2d 447.

Annotation: 27 ALR2d 487, 491.

91. Board of Education v Jewett, 21 Cal App 2d 64, 68 P2d 404; Re Albert's Appeal, 372 Pa 13, 92 A2d 663.

Annotation: 27 ALR2d 487.

Practice Aids.—Dismissal of teacher for membership in subversive organizations. 22 Am Jur Proof of Facts 563, 606, Dismissal of Teachers for Cause § 24.

—Dismissal of teacher for seditious utterances and acts. 22 Am Jur Proof of Facts 563, 609, Dismissal of Teachers for Cause § 26.

92. Keyishian v Board of Regents, 385 US 589, 17 L Ed 2d 629, 87 S Ct 675.

93. § 130, supra, wherein is discussed the matter of teacher's loyalty oaths generally.

Practice Aids.—Dismissal of teachers; loyalty oaths. 22 Am Jur Proof of Facts 563, 597, Dismissal of Teachers for Cause § 22.

SPERRY RAND CORPORATION, Appt.,
v
WILLIAM R. HILL, Jr.

United States Court of Appeals, First Circuit — January 18, 1966
356 F2d 181, 23 ALR3d 853

Certiorari denied by United States Supreme Court June 6, 1966
384 US 973, 16 L Ed 2d 683, 86 S Ct 1859

SUMMARY OF DECISION

A doctor instituted an action in the United States District Court for the District of Massachusetts, Anthony Julian, J., seeking recovery against the manufacturer of an electric shaver for libel and for the alleged violation of the New York right of privacy statute, on the ground that the defendant, in newspaper and national magazine advertising, had exploited an article published in a national medical magazine that was favorable to its shaver, and had furnished reprints of the article which falsely listed the plaintiff as one of the authors. There was evidence showing that the plaintiff had not notified the defendant that the plaintiff had not approved or participated in writing the article until 5 months after the plaintiff first saw the defendant's advertisements. The trial court entered judgment on a verdict for the plaintiff.

On appeal by the defendant, the United States Court of Appeals for the First Circuit vacated the trial court's judgment, set aside the general verdict, and remanded the action for trial on the issue of compensatory damages for libel. In an opinion by Aldrich, Ch. J., it was held, inter alia, that (1) under the New York statute, no right of privacy attached to a matter of general interest that had been publicly released in a periodical of national, albeit specialized, circulation, such article, together with its author's name, having in effect been dedicated to public use, and (2) the plaintiff in the case at bar was estopped to deny his authorship of the article, since his delay in notifying the defendant allowed the defendant, who had no knowledge that the plaintiff had neither written the article nor consented to his name being attached to it, to reasonably entertain the belief that because the plaintiff's name appeared on the article he had in fact written it.

SUBJECT OF ANNOTATION

Beginning on page 865

Invasion of privacy by use of plaintiff's name or likeness in advertising

Brief of Counsel—Cont'd

Civil complaints in federal district courts are not governed by the rules applicable to criminal indictments but by the Federal Civil Procedures Rules, particularly Rule 8. Under that rule the complaint must set forth a short and plain statement of the claim showing that the pleader is entitled to relief. A generalized summary of the case that affords fair notice is all that is required. Conley v Gibson, 355 US 41; S.E.C. v Timetrust, Inc., 28 F Supp 34.

No conduct of appellee Hill induced defendant to continue its advertising activities, including distribution of reprints. Defendant planned to and did run the campaign to its effective limit with full knowledeg of the dangers and a lack of concern for the consequences. Far from establishing estoppel, these facts clearly show malice.

Lawrence R. Cohen, Joseph W. Lobdell, and **Newton H. Levee,** all of Boston, Massachusetts, for appellant.

Before **Aldrich,** Ch. J., **Hastie*** and **McEntee,** Circuit Judges

OPINION OF THE COURT

Aldrich, Ch. J.

Plaintiff, a citizen of Massachusetts, is a physician specializing in dermatology. Defendant is a Delaware corporation with principal offices in New York and Connecticut. Plaintiff brought this action in the district court for the District of Massachusetts, seeking damages for libel and for violation of New York's so-called right of privacy statute, NY Civil Rights Law, McKinney's Consol Laws, c 6, § 51.[1] Although the publications complained of were made throughout the country, the case was submitted on the basis of damages suffered in Massachusetts and New York, only. At the conclusion of the trial the jury answered a number of special questions. It awarded $50,000 actual damages, based upon libel in Massachusetts and New York and invasion of privacy under the New York statute, combined, and also awarded $200,000 punitive damages for libel and the right of privacy combined, limited to New York.[2] The court refused to direct a judgment n. o. v., or to grant a new trial, and defendant appeals.

The facts must be stated in some detail. Defendant manufactures an electric shaver known as the Remington, which is supposedly unique in having adjustable roller combs. In June 1958 defendant was approached by one Paul Murphy, who operated under the name of Medical Research Association, hereinafter MRA, and specialized in "medical public relations." Murphy reported upon a pilot study which indicated that the Remington was better for the skin than ordinary razors and other electric shavers. He proposed a more elaborate pilot study, and suggested that if it worked out, he would arrange for a medical research project to be financed by the defendant. If the project resulted in a paper published in a recognized medical journal, it would be used as the theme for a national advertising campaign. After an investigation of Murphy and his associates, which showed them to be apparently reliable, defendant agreed. Informed of the successful out-

* By designation.

1. Plaintiff waived any claim for invasion of privacy in Massachusetts.

2. Massachusetts does not allow punitive damages for libel. Mass GL c 231, § 93.

ANNOTATION

INVASION OF PRIVACY BY USE OF PLAINTIFF'S NAME OR LIKENESS IN ADVERTISING

TOTAL CLIENT SERVICE LIBRARY REFERENCES

Am Jur, Privacy (1st ed § 22)

16 Am Jur Pl & Pr Forms, Privacy, Forms 16:161, 16:161.1, 16:165.1, 16:167, 16:170, 16:172, 16:172.1, 16:173, 16:174, 16:176, 16:177.1; 16 Am Jur Pl & Pr Forms, Radio and Television, Form 16:1088

ALR Digests, Privacy §§ 3–5

ALR Quick Index, Privacy

Consult POCKET PART in this volume for later case service

INDEX

TABLE OF JURISDICTIONS REPRESENTED

Consult POCKET PART in this volume for later case service

Jurisdiction	Sections	Jurisdiction	Sections
US	§§ 2[b], 3, 4[a, b], 6, 8, 9[a], 10[a, b], 11[a], 12[a, b], 13, 16, 18, 19, 20[a], 21[a], 22	Mich	§§ 10[b], 12[a], 13, 21[b]
Ala	§ 12[b]	Mo	§ 21[a]
Ark	§ 21[a]	Mont	§ 21[a]
Cal	§§ 6, 8, 12[b], 13, 16, 20[a]	Neb	§ 11[a]
Colo	§ 21[a, b]	NJ	§§ 10[a], 12[b], 14, 15, 20[a], 21[a]
Conn	§ 21[b]	NY	§§ 1[a], 3–8, 9[b], 10–22
DC	§ 4[b]	NC	§§ 6, 8, 13, 18
Ga	§§ 6, 8, 9[a], 10[b], 12[a], 15, 18, 21[b]	Ohio	§§ 12[a], 21[a]
Ill	§§ 4[b], 10[a, b], 13, 21[b, c]	Okla	§§ 4[a], 19
Ind	§ 12[a]	Pa	§§ 4[b], 9[a], 10[b], 21[a]
Kan	§§ 9[a], 10[b], 21[b, c]	RI	§ 3
Ky	§ 13	Tenn	§§ 10[b], 21[b]
La	§§ 4[b], 11[b], 13	Tex	§ 11[a]
Mass	§§ 3, 9[a]	Utah	§ 4[a, b]
		Wis	§§ 3, 14

I. Preliminary matters

§ 1. Introduction

[a] Scope

This annotation[1] collects the cases which have passed on the question of whether the use of plaintiff's name or likeness in advertising constitutes an actionable invasion of privacy.[2]

Included herein are cases arising under statutes which specifically give a person whose name or picture is used for advertising purposes a right of action for invasion of privacy,[3] as well as cases arising in those jurisdictions where the right of privacy is recognized as applying to all unauthorized uses of a person's name or picture.

In this annotation "advertising purposes" is deemed to include the use of a person's name or picture for all types of promotional endeavors, including the boosting of a publication's circulation, and the use of plaintiff's name to promote a product or company by naming it after him.

[b] Related matters

Invasion of right of privacy by merely oral declarations. 19 ALR3d 1318.

1. Earlier general treatment of the right of privacy in 138 ALR 22 at page 50, 168 ALR 446 at page 454, 14 ALR2d 750, need not be further consulted on the questions treated herein.

2. Generally, as to invasion of privacy by a publication dealing with one other than the plaintiff, see 18 ALR3d 873.

3. Statutory law is not represented herein except as it is reflected in reported decisions of the courts, and hence the reader is cautioned to consult the current statutes of his jurisdiction.

Although the annotation is not inherently limited to civil actions, it should be noted that even though a New York statute makes invasion of privacy for purposes of advertising or trade a criminal offense, apparently only two prosecutions have reached courts of record (People ex rel. Maggio v Charles Scribner's Sons (1954) 205 Misc 818, 130 NYS2d 514, and People ex rel. Stern v Robert R. McBride & Co. (1936) 159 Misc 5, 288 NYS 501) and in neither case was a conviction obtained.

the modern approach in states not recognizing a common-law right of privacy has been to adopt statutes securing the rights of individuals against commercial exploitation.

Thus, for example, the New York legislature, after a declaration by the highest court of that state that no right of privacy enforceable at law or in equity existed, even in cases of commercial exploitation,[1] adopted a statute which provides that any person whose name, portrait, or picture is used for advertising purposes or for the purposes of trade may, without the written consent of such person, maintain an equitable action against the one using his name to prevent and restrain the use thereof, and may also sue and recover for damages for any injuries sustained by reason of such use; if the defendant knowingly used such person's name, the jury may, in its discretion, award exemplary damages.[2]

Attention is called, however, to the decision of the United States Supreme Court in Time, Inc. v Hill (1967) 385 US 374, 17 L Ed 2d 456, 87 S Ct 534, holding that the New York statute is precluded by the constitutional protection of free speech and press from being applied to redress false reports of matters of public interest in the absence of proof that the defendant published the report with knowledge of its falsity or in reckless disregard of the truth.

§ 4. What constitutes use of name or likeness for advertising or trade purposes

[a] Held to be for advertising or trade purposes

Under the New York and similar statutes[3] the courts, in order to find an actionable invasion of privacy, must first determine that the publication which plaintiff finds objectionable constitutes a use of his name for "advertising purposes" or for "purposes of trade" within the meaning of the statute.[4]

Since there can be no invasion of privacy in these jurisdictions unless this test is met, the courts have tended to be liberal in their interpretation of what constitutes "advertising purposes" or "purposes of trade." Under the circumstances present in the following cases, the publication was found to be for such purposes.

---

with the words, beneath the picture, "Only $10.50" followed by the words: "The auto coats worn by above autoists are waterproof, made of fine quality silk mohair—$10.50—in four colors," although this publication was made without the knowledge or consent of the plaintiff, tended to and did make plaintiff the object of scorn, ridicule, and public comment, and caused him great mental anguish.

And see Judevine v Benzies-Montanye Fuel & Warehouse Co. (1936) 222 Wis 512, 269 NW 295, 106 ALR 1443 (criticized in Martin v Outboard Marine Corp. 15 Wis 2d 452, 113 NW2d 135), wherein the Wisconsin Supreme Court refused to permit recovery against a defendant who distributed handbills offering plaintiff's account for sale to the highest bidder.

Massachusetts has avoided recognizing any right of privacy. See Lahr v Adell Chemical Co. (1962, CA1 Mass) 300 F2d 256; Brauer v Globe Newspaper Co. (1966) 351 Mass 53, 217 NE2d 736.

1. Roberson v Rochester Folding Box Co. (1902) 171 NY 538, 64 NE 442, 59 LRA 478, infra § 21[a].

2. New York Civil Rights Law § 51. New York Civil Rights Law, § 50, makes such use of a name, picture, or portrait a misdemeanor. However, prosecutions thereunder are rare. See § 1[a], footnote 3.

3. § 3, supra.

4. Under the New York statute, it is necessary to allege that plaintiff's name was used without his consent for the purpose of trade; an allegation that plaintiff was caused injury to his feelings is insufficient to meet the requirements of the statute. Association for Preservation of Freedom of Choice, Inc. v Nation Co. (1962) 35 Misc 2d 42, 228 NYS2d 628.

LIBEL AND SLANDER

Scope-Note.

INCLUDES malicious defamation, by words spoken, written, or printed, or by signs, pictures, etc., injurious to a person in his general reputation, or exposing a living person, or the memory of one deceased, to hatred, contempt, or ridicule, or prejudicial to a person in his profession, trade, occupation, employment, or office, or otherwise causing one special damage, or injurious to one's interest in property, real or personal, or tending to provoke a breach of the peace; justification or excuse for or mitigation of such defamation; nature and extent of liability of those speaking or publishing such defamatory words, etc.; actions for damages therefor; and criminal responsibility for libels in general, and prosecution and punishment thereof as public offenses.

Matters not in this topic, treated elsewhere, see Descriptive-Word Index.

Analysis.

I. WORDS AND ACTS ACTIONABLE, AND LIABILITY THEREFOR, 🔑1–33.

II. PRIVILEGED COMMUNICATIONS, AND MALICE THEREIN, 🔑34–51.

III. JUSTIFICATION AND MITIGATON, 🔑52–67.

IV. ACTIONS, 🔑68–129.

A. Right of Action and Defenses, 🔑68–76.
B. Parties, Preliminary Proceedings, and Pleading, 🔑77–100.
C. Evidence, 🔑101–112.
D. Damages, 🔑113–121.
E. Trial, Judgment, and Review, 🔑122–129.

V. SLANDER OF PROPERTY OR TITLE, 🔑130–140.

VI. CRIMINAL RESPONSIBILITY, 🔑141–162.

A. Offenses, 🔑141–150.
B. Prosecution and Punishment, 🔑151–162.

I. WORDS AND ACTS ACTIONABLE, AND LIABILITY THEREFOR.

🔑1. Nature and elements of defamation in general.
1½. Constitutional and statutory provisions.
2. Intent.
3. Malice.
4. —— In general.
5. —— Implied.
6. Actionable words in general.
(1). In general.
(2). Imputation of falsehood, dishonesty, or fraud.
(3). Imputation of indebtedness or delinquency in paying debts.
(4). Imputation of inebriety or mental derangement.
(5). Imputation of libelous or slanderous acts.
(6). Insults leading to breach of the peace.

I. WORDS AND ACTS ACTIONABLE, AND LIABILITY THEREFOR—Continued.

🔑7. Words imputing crime and immorality.
(1). In general.
(2). Nature of crime and punishment.
(3). Arrest and imprisonment.
(4). Intent or attempt to commit crime.
(5). Abortion.
(6). Assault, burglary, robbery and homicide.
(7). Arson and burning of buildings.
(8). Bigamy.
(9). Conspiracy and blackmail.
(10). Crimes against the government and violation of laws concerning elections and the mail.
(11). Disorderly house, gambling, and intoxicating liquors.
(12). Forgery, false pretenses, and breach of trust.
(13). Larceny.
(14). Perjury and subornation of perjury.
(15). Violation of food laws.
(16). Want of chastity or sexual crimes in general.
(17). Adultery.
(18). Fornication, incest, and rape.
(19). Prostitution.
8. Words imputing contagious or venereal disease.
9. Words tending to injure in profession or business.
(1). In general.
(2). Physicians and dentists.
(3). Attorneys at law.
(4). Clergymen.
(5). Teachers.
(6). Contractors.
(7). Merchants, tradesmen, and manufacturers.
(8). Authors and newspapers.
(9). Brokers and advertising agents.
10. Words imputing unfitness for or misconduct or criminal acts in office or employment.
(1). Public officers in general.
(2). Legislative officers.
(3). Executive officers and employés.
(4). Judicial officers.
(5). Corporation and association officers.
(6). Employés.
11. Words actionable as causing special damage.
12. —— Nature and meaning in general.
13. —— Nature and extent of injury.
14. Words written or printed, signs, pictures, and other representations.
15. —— Libels in general.
16. —— Exposing person to hatred, contempt, or ridicule.
17. —— Causing person to be shunned or avoided.
18. —— Tending to injure in business or occupation.

course of arbitration proceedings. 9 U.S.C.A. § 10.

Commonwealth Coatings Corp. v. Continental Cas. Co., 382 F.2d 1010, rehearing denied 88 S.Ct. 1405, 390 U.S. 1036, 20 L.Ed.2d 297, reversed 89 S.Ct. 337, 393 U.S. 145, 21 L.Ed.2d 301, rehearing denied 89 S.Ct. 848, 393 U.S. 1112, 21 L.Ed.2d 812.

C.C.A.Tex. 1948. Conduct of arbitrators appointed pursuant to agreement to arbitrate contained in contracts for grading of streets and building houses, in appointing one as engineer to ascertain true facts with respect to quantities and costs of disputed items and in receiving his testimony in absence of parties, constituted such misconduct as would nullify the final award, notwithstanding that arbitrators were acting in good faith.

Tejas Development Co. v. McGough Bros., 165 F.2d 276, motion granted 167 F.2d 268.

If submission does not provide otherwise, complete decisions made by arbitrators before their misconduct nullifying final award occurred could be permitted to stand.

Tejas Development Co. v. McGough Bros., 165 F.2d 276, motion granted 167 F.2d 268.

D.C.Ky. 1959. In action by gas transmission corporation to set aside an ex parte arbitration hearing with respect to awards of damages for pipeline easements to property owners, mere fact that counsel for property owners was also counsel for bank of which the arbitrator was an officer and employee did not establish "evident partiality" by the arbitrator within meaning of the statute so as to justify setting aside the awards, since something more than a vague and rather remote business relationship is needed, if the losing party seeks to vacate an award on the ground of evident partiality. 9 U.S.C.A. § 10(b).

Texas Eastern Transmission Corp. v. Barnard, 177 F.Supp. 123, reversed 285 F.2d 536.

In action by gas transmission corporation to set aside an ex parte arbitration hearing with respect to awards of damages for pipeline easements to property owners, size of the awards could not be taken as proof of partiality of an arbitrator where there was no proof in the record impeaching the reasonableness of such awards. 9 U.S.C.A. § 10(b).

Texas Eastern Transmission Corp. v. Barnard, 177 F.Supp. 123, reversed 285 F.2d 536.

D.C.N.Y. 1968. When claim is made under Federal Arbitration Act that award of arbitrators should be vacated because of alleged partiality of arbitrators, federal district court must ascertain from such record as is available whether arbitrators' conduct was so biased and prejudiced as to destroy fundamental fairness. 9 U.S.C.A. §§ 4, 9, 10, 13.

Catz Am. Co. v. Pearl Grange Fruit Exchange, Inc., 292 F.Supp. 549.

When claim is made under Federal Arbitration Act that award of arbitrators should be vacated because of alleged partiality of arbitrators, something more than mere error in the law or failure on the part of the arbitrators to understand or apply the law must be shown by party making claim of partiality. 9 U.S.C.A. §§ 4, 9, 10, 13.

Catz Am. Co. v. Pearl Grange Fruit Exchange, Inc., 292 F.Supp. 549.

Comment of one of the arbitrators at beginning of arbitration proceedings that he did not approve of attempts to stay arbitration by recourse to the courts did not show such partiality of arbitrators as to justify vacating the award by federal district court in proceedings under Federal Arbitration Act. 9 U.S.C.A. §§ 4, 9, 10, 13.

Catz Am. Co. v. Pearl Grange Fruit Exchange, Inc., 292 F.Supp. 549.

When arbitrator is not appointed by method provided in arbitration agreement and is found to have a business relationship with one of the parties, vacation of award of arbitrators as being inherently partial is justified. 9 U.S.C.A. §§ 4, 9, 10, 13.

Catz Am. Co. v. Pearl Grange Fruit Exchange, Inc., 292 F.Supp. 549.

Where Michigan corporation did not object to method of appointment of substitute arbitrator and at time of arbitration did not challenge substitute arbitrator, even though Michigan corporation knew that New York corporation and arbitrators had close personal relations, federal district court in hearing under Federal Arbitration Act would not vacate award at request of Michigan corporation on ground that arbitrators were partial. 9 U.S.C.A. §§ 4, 9, 10, 13.

Catz Am. Co. v. Pearl Grange Fruit Exchange, Inc., 292 F.Supp. 549.

Award of arbitrators would not be vacated by federal district court under Federal Arbitration Act on motion of Michigan corporation, on ground that arbitrators were guilty of misconduct because they did not permit Michigan corporation's president to complete his testimony, where his testimony was so confusing and unresponsive to his attorney's questions that attorney was permitted to summarize his testimony, and arbitra-

W Va
193WV528
193WV530
457SE465
457SE467
Wis
190Wis2d [394
192Wis2d [572
194Wis2d [602
526NW829
531NW617
535NW907
542NW205
41CLA365

—183—

Cir. 3
46F3d333

—190—

Litton Business Sys. Inc. v NLRB
1991
(115LE177)
(111SC2215)
Cir. 1
f 775FS32
q 775FS32
d 811FS45
876FS1367
Cir. 2
790FS486
805FS117
807FS951
833FS424
879FS404
890FS112
f 890FS116
901FS149
906FS833
Cir. 3
18F3d1098
26F3d399
26F3d400
28F3d352
f 28F3d363
j 28F3d365
f 805FS315
839FS342
Cir. 4
46F3d343
48F3d1368
f 791FS130
859FS954
Cir. 5
26F3d1321
838FS1158
Cir. 6
17F3d910
17F3d911
23F3d1045
51F3d1261
e 73F3d654
812FS757
827FS1308
894FS308
Cir. 7
f Dk7 [95-2371
e 2F3d236
f 76F3d164
e 767FS946
f 776FS1253
Cir. 8
58F3d1253
61F3d1353
789FS291
e 811FS467
812FS1005
911FS1208
Cir. 9
812FS1036
f 812FS1037
e 816FS1491
Cir. DC
8F3d836
15F3d1108
23F3d521
36F3d1141
j 37F3d1540
39F3d1216
59F3d234
907FS443
19UCR2d [442
Calif
30CA4th653
35CaR2d805
D C
291ADC105
294ADC341
296ADC44
296ADC56
297ADC266
297ADC297
299ADC344
300ADC225
303ADC432
304ADC377
306ADC213
308ADC337
308ADC413
309ADC124
313ADC238
Ind
644NE135
Me
e 651A2d342
655A2d351
j 659A2d847
Mich
505NW218
505NW227
N Y
177NYAD [827
189NYAD [711
150NYM2d [275
575NYS2d [1015
576NYS2d [442
592NYS2d [728
Ohio
95OA3d651
103OA3d [575
643NE563
660NE519
Pa
154PaC348
623A2d924
61ChL400

—221—

Oklahoma v New Mexico
1991
(115LE207)
(111SC2281)
US reh den in 501US1277
s 496US903
s 125LE719
s 126LE306
s 113SC3031
s 114SC341
Cir. 2
793FS422
Cir. 3
783FS884
Conn
234Ct87
662A2d85

—252—

Metropolitan Wash. Airports Authority v Citizens for the Abatement of Aircraft Noise Inc.
1991
(115LE236)
(111SC2298)
s 718FS974
s 286ADC334
cc 845FS902
Cir. 2
f 819FS1245
833FS282
Cir. 5
25F3d241
Cir. 6
47F3d807
61F3d493
Cir. 8
803FS1563
Cir. 9
9F3d750
791FS1429
895FS1328
Cir. 10
818FS1411
Cir. DC
6F3d824
36F3d98
f 36F3d100
56F3d1521
59F3d1258
59F3d1278
807FS813
845FS907
893FS76
Calif
15CA4th872
19CaR2d378
D C
293ADC315
294ADC90
294ADC358
303ADC365
308ADC284
f 308ADC286
312ADC451
313ADC270
313ADC290
Fla
643So2d19
Ill
620NE1055
Va
24VCO337
Wash
76WAp38
882P2d803
61ChL168
80Cor4
87NwL132
88NwL1347
143PaL783
104YLJ94

—294—

Wilson v Seiter
1991
(115LE271)
(111SC2321)
s 125LE22
s 113SC2475
f 503US8
128LE820
128LE826
128LE834
q 128LE836
128LE838
114SC1974
114SC1979
114SC1986
q 114SC1988
114SC1989
114SC1991
Dk5 [93-7192
144FRD169
Cir. 1
794FS66
844FS22
853FS28
874FS466
874FS506
888FS264
893FS3
899FS787
Cir. 2
f Dk2 [95-2589
Dk2 [94-2572
32F3d30
37F3d66
j 37F3d70
43F3d788
62F3d84
f 76F3d480
f 776FS740
784FS43
797FS227
f 797FS235
800FS1155
826FS775
833FS151
860FS973
861FS212
875FS1010
f 877FS93
f 886FS224
887FS401
890FS138
f 894FS746
895FS39
901FS104
901FS762
907FS663
155FRD492
Cir. 3
1F3d187
f 1F3d188
6F3d152
47F3d1318
798FS260
802FS1133
802FS1269
f 823FS301
829FS1495
843FS970
866FS1478
871FS230
876FS1471
f 881FS174
886FS416
f 886FS417
892FS598
896FS1409
910FS220
f 910FS221
910FS1005
912FS815
Cir. 4
Dk4 [94-7122
9F3d1081
25F3d1262
34F3d271
58F3d104
71F3d165
768FS1166
771FS732
f 780FS1075
782FS1096
f 782FS1114

—888—
Cottrill v Russell
1993
(253IlA934)
(192IlD733)
625NE[6]1049
634NE[2]465

—894—
Holloway v Kroger Co.
1993
(253IlA944)
(192IlD739)

—897—
Illinois v Smith
1993
(253IlA948)
(192IlD742)

—902—
Martin v Connell
1993
(254IlA246)
(192IlD747)
Cert Den
in 633NE5
s 602NE453

—905—
Kemp v Bridgestone-Firestone, Inc.
1993
(253IlA858)
(192IlD750)

—911—
Slezak v Lisle Ctr., Inc.
1993
(253IlA876)
(192IlD756)

—913—
Illinois v Belsan
1993
(253IlA1093)
(192IlD758)

—916—
Meyers v Rockford Sys.
1993
(254IlA56)
(192IlD761)
s 614NE913
633NE1007
633NE[5]1008

—923—
Illinois v Doggett
1993
(255IlA180)
(192IlD768)
cc 472NE1246

—930—
In re T.L.
1993
(254IlA230)
(192IlD775)
j 627NE1187

—934—
Binder Plumbing & Heating v Plumbers & Pipefitters Local No. 99
1993
(253IlA972)
(192IlD779)

—940—
Illinois v Rhoden
1993
(253IlA805)
(192IlD785)

—945—
Grames v State Police
1993
(254IlA191)
(192IlD790)

—956—
Leahy Realty Corp. v American Snack Foods Corp.
1993
(253IlA233)
(192IlD801)
Cert Den
in 633NE6

—980—
Illinois v Keith M.
1993
(255IlA1071)
(192IlD825)

—990—
Giammanco v Giammanco
1993
(253IlA750)
(192IlD835)

—1004—
Illinois v Ratzke
1993
(253IlA1054)
(192IlD849)
Cert Den
in 633NE11
632NE1101

—1018—
Illinois v Eiskant
1993
(253IlA773)
(192IlD863)

—1022—
Delvecchio v GMC
1993
(255IlA189)
(192IlD867)
Cert Den
in 633NE4

—1033—
In re Marriage of Diddens
1993
(255IlA850)
(192IlD878)

—1037—
Illinois v Cleveland
1993
(254IlA237)
(192IlD882)

—1044—
Moss v Miller
1993
(254IlA174)
(192IlD889)
Cert Den
in 633NE6

—1056—
Goodwine State Bank v Mullins
1993
(253IlA980)
(192IlD901)
Cert Den
in 633NE4

—1081—
Illinois v Hooker
1993
(253IlA1075)
(192IlD926)
635NE[21]1371

—1095—
Racich v Boone County
1993
(254IlA311)
(192IlD940)
634NE[8]1159
635NE[15]1081

—1101—
Arians v Larkin
1993
(253IlA1037)
(192IlD946)
s 566NE1025

—1108—
In re Marriage of Armstrong
1993
(255IlA844)
(192IlD953)

—1110—
Green Rock v Industrial Comm'n
1993
(255IlA895)
(192IlD955)

—1115—
Illinois v Brasseaux
1993
(254IlA283)
(192IlD960)
630NE[4]1353
635NE[2]822

—1122—
In re Marriage of Richardson
1993
(255IlA1099)
(193IlD1)

—1129—
Cleaver v Marrese
1993
(253IlA778)
(193IlD8)
Cert Den
in 633NE3

—1133—
Illinois v Leggans
1993
(253IlA724)
(193IlD12)
Cert Den
in 633NE11

—1145—
Illinois v Diestelhorst
1993
(253IlA867)
(193IlD24)

—1151—
Illinois v Stein
1993
(255IlA847)
(193IlD30)
Cert Den
in 633NE12

—1154—
Augustine v Regional Bd. of Trustees
1993
(253IlA827)
(193IlD33)
Cert Den
in 633NE1

—1160—
Illinois v Heitland
1993
(253IlA836)
(193IlD39)

—1165—
Carnock v Decatur
1993
(253IlA892)
(193IlD44)
Cert Den
in 633NE2

—1170—
Seiler v Granite City
1993
(255IlA210)
(193IlD49)
631NE[1]367

—1172—
Ficken v Alton & S. Ry.
1993
(255IlA1047)
(193IlD51)
Cert Den
in 633NE4

Vol. 147 ILLINOIS SUPREME COURT REPORTS, 2d SERIES

234IlA[3]237
234IlA[1]239
234IlA[1]507
j 239IlA169
248IlA[1]358
259IlA[3]235

—430—

Illinois v Perry
1992

(590NE454)
(168IlD817)
s 205IlA655
s 230IlA720
f 147Il2d[1]531
f 147Il2d[2]531
d 152Il2d[1]35

—437—

Zannini v
Reliance
Ins. Co.
1992

(590NE457)
(168IlD820)
s 206IlA910
e 238IlA214
242IlA[1]73
247IlA552
250IlA[2]560
f 252IlA[1]474
f 252IlA[2]474
257IlA[1]184
257IlA[2]184
e 257IlA[7]286
e 258IlA[6]595
258IlA[6]595
262IlA[2]609
Cir. 7
d 14F3d[16]1236
827FS1373
f 829FS[3]961

—458—

Hagney v
Lopeman
1992

(590NE466)
(168IlD829)
s 203IlA1108
j 235IlA756
252IlA[2]699
Cir. 7
9F3d1241
e 828FS1300

—467—

Illinois v
Garner
1992

(590NE470)
(168IlD833)
s 205IlA1105

—484—

Chicago v
Department
of Revenue
1992

(590NE478)
(168IlD841)
s 210IlA273
237IlA35
237IlA[1]526
238IlA[4]988
242IlA[1]721
242IlA[13]724

—510—

Illinois v Kidd
1992

(591NE431)
(169IlD258)
cc 129Il2d432
244IlA819
d 255IlA[3]554
d 255IlA[5]554
260IlA[2]795

—548—

Sulser v
Country
Mut. Ins. Co.
1992

(591NE427)
(169IlD254)
s 208IlA15
233IlA[4]67
233IlA[7]363
234IlA[6]106
234IlA[8]107
234IlA[15]107
234IlA[9]113
242IlA[6]154
243IlA[6]688
245IlA[8]409
245IlA[10]409
247IlA[14]482
247IlA[8]483
247IlA[10]484
f 247IlA[10]486
260IlA854
263IlA[15]105
Cir. 7
809FS605
835FS458

—629—

Case 1

Cir. 7
832FS1230

Vol. 148

—1—

Illinois v Reed
1992

(591NE455)
(169IlD282)
f 152Il2d[3]499
f 152Il2d[7]499
152Il2d[8]500
152Il2d[9]500
f 152Il2d[11]502
157Il2d[2]124
157Il2d[9]125
157Il2d[18]176
158Il2d[18]39
231IlA185
231IlA186
240IlA202
f 246IlA787

—15—

Illinois v
Anderson
1992

(591NE461)
(169IlD288)
US cert den
in 61USLW3260
e 232IlA[10]267
f 234IlA[16]495
f 234IlA[17]495
258IlA[8]512
258IlA[12]512
Cir. 7
801FS[3]95

—32—

Illinois v Keith
1992

(591NE449)
(169IlD276)
s 206IlA414
234IlA[3]505
234IlA[4]507
248IlA357
249IlA531

—45—

Illinois v
Griffin
1992

(592NE930)
(170IlD250)
229IlA456
230IlA[9]276
237IlA[2]122
254IlA[2]620

—70—

Illinois v
Palmer
1992

(592NE940)
(170IlD260)
s 118Il2d90
s 139IlA966
s 188IlA378
s 193IlA745
229IlA[3]835
233IlA[1]137
237IlA[7]93
238IlA424
j 238IlA749
241IlA[7]469
f 251IlA[13]360
253IlA1062
d 253IlA[13]1063

—96—

Illinois v
Condon
1992

(592NE951)
(170IlD271)
s 195IlA815
cc 246IlA74
155Il2d393
155Il2d[11]396
d 155Il2d[12]400
229IlA[10]550
e 229IlA[12]550
229IlA[11]551
229IlA[2]907
229IlA[3]907
229IlA[4]907
f 232IlA[10]687
f 232IlA[12]687
j 232IlA691
233IlA78
237IlA710
242IlA[10]276
f 258IlA[1]259
f 258IlA[2]259
f 258IlA[3]259
f 258IlA[4]259
258IlA[5]259
258IlA[7]259
262IlA[4]84
d 262IlA88
262IlA[9]88
93CR686

—116—

Illinois v
Maxwell
1992

(592NE960)
(170IlD280)
153Il2d[19]107
154Il2d[11]517
f 155Il2d497
158Il2d318
158Il2d[4]428
229IlA[10]474
f 233IlA[8]1096
f 233IlA[10]1096
236IlA[4]1062
243IlA[10]169
245IlA[4]140
246IlA[4]38
246IlA[14]55
246IlA[16]55
251IlA[4]804
262IlA[5]571
262IlA[4]884
262IlA[5]884

—151—

Currie v Lao
1992

(592NE977)
(170IlD297)
s 198IlA625
230IlA[1]59
230IlA[2]61
230IlA[3]61
230IlA[5]61
230IlA[6]61
230IlA[7]61
230IlA[8]61
f 230IlA[12]62
236IlA152
236IlA[2]526
236IlA[3]526
237IlA945
d 241IlA[3]338
d 241IlA[4]338
d 241IlA[5]338
d 241IlA[6]338
248IlA950
248IlA[11]952
248IlA[12]952
253IlA[2]941
253IlA[3]942
253IlA[4]942
253IlA[5]942
253IlA[6]942
253IlA[7]942
f 253IlA[10]943
254IlA[10]962
255IlA[2]442
255IlA[3]442
255IlA[8]442
f 255IlA[9]442
f 255IlA[10]445
257IlA97
257IlA[3]98
257IlA[4]98
257IlA[5]98
257IlA[6]98
257IlA[8]98
257IlA[10]98
d 257IlA101
262IlA[1]551
d 263IlA562
263IlA[5]562
Cir. 7
832FS[2]1160

—168—

Illinois v Perez
1992

(592NE984)
(170IlD304)
s 474US1110
s 88LE931
s 106SC898
cc 108Il2d70
h 230IlA[3]956
245IlA[1]955
245IlA[2]955
f 246IlA[1]403
d 246IlA404
20ALR5184n

—196—

Illinois v
Burrows
1992

(592NE997)
(170IlD317)
157Il2d114
f 158Il2d498
228IlA[23]937
233IlA[1]349
233IlA[8]368
233IlA[15]510
234IlA[15]413
236IlA[8]926
236IlA[15]929
237IlA[23]122
238IlA[19]428
238IlA[20]428
241IlA[15]213
241IlA[8]216

—260—

Illinois v
Brockman
1992

(592NE1026)
(170IlD346)
s 143Il2d351
s 192IlA680
242IlA140

—272—

Hoglund v
State Farm
Mut. Auto.
Ins. Co.
1992

(592NE1031)
(170IlD351)
s 210IlA543

150

—985—
Ohio v McDermott
1995
(72OS3d570)
s 598NE147
s 600NE675
s 607NE1164

—989—
Ohio ex rel Bell v Industrial Commission
1995
(72OS3d575)

—993—
Ohio ex rel Carpenter v Jones
1995
(72OS3d579)
cc 639NE1199
662NE [1]338
666NE1134
673NE1370

—995—
Ohio ex rel Herman v Klopfleisch
1995
(72OS3d581)
s 646NE180
660NE [6]465
661NE [10]698
661NE [10]701
662NE [5]19
665NE [7]206
673NE [6]1353
673NE [12]1357
674NE [6]1200

—1001—
Ohio ex rel Huebner v West Jefferson Village Council
1995
(72OS3d589)
s 662NE339
655NE177
655NE178
j 655NE1298

—1006—
Ohio ex rel Jennings v Nurre
1995
(72OS3d596)
659NE [4]1278
659NE [5]1278
659NE [5]1280
667NE [6]391

—1008—
Ohio ex rel Logan v Industrial Commission of Ohio
1995
(72OS3d599)

—1012—
Ohio ex rel Police Officers for Equal Rights v Lashutka
1995
(72OS3d1219)
s 648NE808

—1015—
Globe American Casualty Co. v Cleveland
1994
(99OA3d674)
s 649NE280
670NE [2]1092

—1018—
Howell v Euclid & Wickliffe Services
1994
(99OA3d680)

—1024—
Ohio v Endicott
1994
(99OA3d688)

—1028—
Curran v Walsh Jesuit High School
1995
(99OA3d696)
s 649NE839

—1031—
Houts v Houts
1995
(99OA3d701)
s 649NE838

—1037—
Ohio Department of Human Services v Crespo
1995
(99OA3d709)

—1039—
Ohio Department of Human Services v Kozar
1995
(99OA3d713)

—1041—
Ohio v Baker
1995
(99OA3d718)
s 647NE1388

—1044—
Ohio v Nathan
1995
(99OA3d722)

—1048—
Federal Land Bank Association of Fostoria v Walton
1995
(99OA3d729)
s 647NE1387

—1052—
Stocker v Castle Inspections Inc.
1995
(99OA3d735)
674NE397

—1055—
Illinois v Mahaffey
1995
(209IlD607)
s 539NE1172
660NE [3]928
661NE [17]300
e 661NE [3]376
f 662NE1199
665NE1243
f 665NE [22]1318
668NE583
670NE594
670NE [8]596
f 670NE [22]737
671NE [2]376
671NE [8]722
673NE328
673NE [1]331
673NE [8]1183
674NE [2]851

—1071—
Sanders v Dow Chem. Co.
1995
(209IlD623)
s 624NE1255
655NE [3]36
656NE1106
e 663NE757
663NE [8]757
663NE [9]757

—1083—
Illinois v Rice
1995
(209IlD635)
s 617NE360
f 650NE238
f 655NE914
656NE [2]241
664NE82
668NE640
668NE [5]642
668NE1057

—1089—
Citizens Util. Bd. v Illinois Commerce Comm'n
1995
(209IlD641)
s 626NE728
e 665NE [1]556
665NE [2]557
665NE [3]557
666NE [12]1219
e 666NE [17]1219
666NE [20]1220
d 669NE632
669NE929

—1105—
First of Am. Bank v Netsch
1995
(209IlD657)
655NE [11]1119
j 657NE704
658NE [11]859
660NE [11]216
660NE285
661NE [2]490
664NE339
664NE [11]1086
f 667NE [12]113
668NE592
674NE [11]501
Cir. 7
f 913FS [13]1152
913FS [11]1153

—1115—
Vaughn v West Frankfort
1995
(209IlD667)
s 630NE526
e 651NE [7]693
f 655NE462
657NE [1]905
657NE [2]905
657NE [4]905
657NE [5]905
f 659NE [5]43
e 662NE [5]465
e 665NE [2]436
665NE [4]436
665NE [5]436
667NE505
669NE [5]1191
669NE [6]1191
671NE [2]1132
672NE314

—1120—
Wagner v Chicago
1995
(209IlD672)
s 626NE1227
652NE813
654NE1103
656NE204
657NE [2]891
f 662NE [2]465
f 662NE [3]465
d 665NE [3]438
665NE566
668NE222
669NE1191
671NE1145
e 674NE107
f 674NE112

—1125—
Estate of French
1995
(209IlD677)
655NE [1]1040

—1132—
Hermitage Corp. v Contractors Adjustment Co.
1995
(209IlD684)
s 637NE1201
652NE823
653NE1278
657NE [1]898
657NE [3]899
659NE59
663NE18
668NE85
f 671NE [3]799
f 671NE [4]799
Cir. 7
895FS [3]1077
f 895FS [6]1079
f 909FS [3]1133

—1143—
Illinois v Evans
1995
(209IlD695)
Cert den
657NE629
f 664NE [3]162
664NE [6]162

—1148—
Trammel v Harrisburg Medical Ctr.
1995
(209IlD700)

—1151—
Isom v Indiana
1995
cc 501NE1074
671NE463

—1153—
Professional Laminate & Millwork Inc. v B & R Enterprises
1995
668NE [3]268
668NE [14]269

—1158—
Burbach v Burbach
1995

—1163—
Motz v Johnson
1995
666NE [3]1264

—1171—
Fuehrer v Fuehrer
1995

—1176—
Mumford v Indiana
1995

—1180—
Joseph v Laporte County
1995
659NE [2]1125
659NE [14]1127

§ 5/3-101
A 1993PA88-1
256IlA144
628NE723
195IlD259
202IlD75

§ 5/3-102
A 1993PA88-1
244IlA489
263IlA877
612NE1011
184IlD135
201IlD655
202IlD247

§ 5/3-103
A 1993PA88-1
A 1993PA88-110
253IlA1015
625NE881
192IlD726
202IlD247
202IlD768

§ 5/3-104
A 1993PA88-1
202IlD247

§ 5/3-105
A 1993PA88-1

§ 5/3-106
A 1993PA88-1

§ 5/3-107
A 1993PA88-1
A 1994PA88-655
253IlA382
623NE1061
191IlD471
Cir. 7
835FS1076

§ 5/3-108
A 1993PA88-1
Subd. b
260IlA767
632NE1082
198IlD471

§ 5/3-109
A 1993PA88-1

§ 5/3-110
A 1993PA88-1
158Il2d214
244IlA235
257IlA941
261IlA358
262IlA315
263IlA211
614NE198
629NE719
632NE1037
633NE184
634NE1217
635NE599
185IlD64
196IlD174
198IlD426
198IlD722
199IlD863
200IlD260

§ 5/3-111
A 1993PA88-1
A 1993PA88-184
Subd. a
¶ 1
263IlA446
635NE147
200IlD46
¶ 5
263IlA446
635NE147
200IlD46
¶ 7
262IlA317
263IlA446
634NE1218
635NE147
199IlD864
200IlD46
Subd. b
251IlA993
622NE1262
190IlD945

§ 5/3-112
A 1993PA88-1
202IlD247

§ 5/3-113
Ad 1993PA88-1

§ 5/4-101
et seq.
258IlA849
631NE890
197IlD668

§ 5/4-101
A 1993PA88-378
254IlA1091
627NE269
194IlD153
Cir. 7
8F3d604

§ 5/4-104
254IlA1091
627NE268
194IlD152

§ 5/4-107
254IlA1091
627NE268
194IlD152

§ 5/4-108
254IlA1097
627NE273
194IlD156

§ 5/4-120
254IlA1098
627NE273
194IlD157

§ 5/4-140
258IlA850
631NE890
197IlD668

§ 5/5-105.5
Ad 1993PA88-41

§ 5/5-108
261IlA550
263IlA206
633NE808
635NE1018
199IlD12
200IlD679

§ 5/5-109
263IlA206
635NE1018
200IlD679

§ 5/5-118
255IlA932
627NE1275
194IlD633

§ 5/6-101
et seq.
260IlA252
632NE625
198IlD295

§ 5/6-109
252IlA128
625NE31
192IlD71

§ 5/7-101
et seq.
201IlD755

§ 5/7-101
201IlD759
Cir. 7
837FS937

§ 5/7-103
A 1993PA88-486
A 1993PA88-526
245IlA253
259IlA603
614NE486
633NE20
185IlD352
198IlD558
201IlD774

§ 5/7-104
245IlA254
614NE486
185IlD352

§ 5/7-119
259IlA603
633NE20
198IlD558

§ 5/7-121
245IlA257
251IlA917
614NE489
623NE400
185IlD355
191IlD155
201IlD776

§ 5/7-124
254IlA824
627NE191
194IlD75

§ 5/7-127
201IlD776

§ 5/8-201
255IlA236
258IlA159
259IlA929
262IlA65
626NE388
630NE195
631NE1361
633NE1355
193IlD355
196IlD498
197IlD902
199IlD364
Subd. a
259IlA946
631NE1372

§ 5/8-401
A 1994PA88-609
202IlD691

§ 5/8-802
246IlA585
616NE1326
186IlD694

§ 5/8-802.1
A 1993PA88-33
262IlA9
634NE372
199IlD533

§ 5/8-901
et seq.
259IlA161
630NE1199
197IlD75

§ 5/8-901
259IlA162
630NE1200
197IlD76

§ 5/8-902
Subd. a
259IlA162
630NE1200
197IlD76
Subd. b
259IlA162
630NE1200
197IlD76
Subd. c
259IlA163
630NE1200
197IlD76

§ 5/8-903
259IlA164
630NE1201
197IlD77

§ 5/8-904
259IlA164
630NE1201
197IlD77

§ 5/8-906
259IlA165
630NE1202
197IlD78

§ 5/8-907
259IlA165
630NE1202
197IlD78
Subd. 2
259IlA161
630NE1199
197IlD75

§ 5/8-2101
et seq.
259IlA161
630NE1199
197IlD75

§ 5/8-2101
157Il2d32
257IlA974
259IlA162
260IlA44
623NE247
629NE173
630NE1200
633NE99
191IlD2
195IlD864
197IlD76
198IlD637

§ 5/8-2102
157Il2d32
623NE247
191IlD2

§ 5/8-2201
258IlA242
630NE1324
197IlD200

§ 5/9-101
et seq.
Cir. 7
839FS544

§ 5/9-102
A 1993PA88-47

§ 5/9-106
258IlA788
629NE1194
196IlD350

§ 5/9-111
A 1993PA88-417

§ 5/9-111.1
Ad
[1993PA88-417

§ 5/9-118
A 1994PA88-587

§ 5/9-209
Cir. 7
159BRW233

§ 5/9-211
Cir. 7
159BRW235

§ 5/9-213.1
252IlA31
623NE378
191IlD133

§ 5/10-135
249IlA927
619NE874
189IlD173
202IlD835

§ 5/11-101
et seq.
246IlA437
260IlA427
616NE707
632NE232
186IlD517
198IlD173

§ 5/11-101
201IlD766

§ 5/11-103
255IlA995
627NE699
194IlD362

§ 5/11-110
243IlA892
246IlA436
248IlA660
257IlA1068
612NE1051
616NE707
618NE1272
630NE121
184IlD175
186IlD517
188IlD702
196IlD424
201IlD765

§ 5/12-111
Cir. 7
158BRW118

§ 5/12-183
257IlA780
629NE223
195IlD915

Index

D

E

F

M

T

Legal Research, Writing & Analysis

Peter Jan Honigsberg & Edith Ho

No matter what kind of help you need, you'll get it from Gilbert!

Walk Into Class Prepared!
More Importantly, Understand the Material and Get a Head Start on the Day's Discussion:

- **Comprehensive Outline of the Law ("We Make It Simple")**
  Forget the Socratic method. For a simple explanation of any rule of law or legal concept, use Gilbert's concise, easy-to-read summary. Because Gilbert authors are experts in their field, you know you can rely on Gilbert.
- **Concise Capsule Summary**
  For a quick review before class (or as a final review before exams), turn to this great mini-outline.
- **Charts, Charts, and More Charts (Of Every Kind)**
  Nail down your understanding of the law and how to show it on exams.
- **Text Correlation Chart**
  Match your specific reading assignment to the relevant pages in the Gilbert outline. Every major casebook is included.
- **Index & Table of Cases**
  Find a discussion of a case or rule of law—fast.

Ace Your Final Exams!
When Exam Week Arrives, No One Helps You More Than Gilbert!

- **Approach to Exams**
  Use a step-by-step approach to attack your exam. Exam-oriented approaches for the different topics areas emphasize the issues most likely to be tested—and how to deal with them.
- **Exam Tips**
  Meet the commonly tested topics (and common traps for the unwary) before they show up on your exam.
- **Capsule Summary**
  Base your own outline on this mini-outline or use it for last minute review before your exam.
- **Multiple Choice, True/False Questions**
  Test your understanding of a topic, then refer to the outline to learn from your mistakes.
- **Essay Questions**
  Fine tune your exam skills with real law school essay questions, all with complete explanatory answers.

Gilbert Law Summaries
1 North Dearborn Street, Suite 650
Chicago, IL 60602

Questions?
Local (312) 894-1688
Toll Free (800) 782-1272

Mat. #41163501

ISBN-13: 978-0-314-27618-